The Power of the Feminine

JUNE 2010

DEAR SNOWY,

INSPIRE,

MOTIVATE,

DO.

XX

CHARLIE-P.

The Power
of the Feminine

*Using Feminine Energy to Heal the
World's Spiritual Problems*

by Hua-Ching Ni and Maoshing Ni, Ph.D.

SEVEN STAR
COMMUNICATIONS
www.sevenstarcom.com

The authors wish to express their appreciation to Barbara Wolff, Phoenicia Vuong, Mary Achenbach, Barbara Smith, Pieter Watson, Jono Howard, Alicia Siegall, Cindy Lu, Donna Morton, and the other students and friends who devoted their time and efforts to the transcribing, editing, proofreading, typesetting, and designing of this book. Publication of this work was made possible by the generosity of an anonymous donor.

Calligraphy by Maoshing Ni, Ph.D.

Published by:
SevenStar Communications
13315 Washington Blvd., Suite 200
Los Angeles, CA 90066

© 2004 by Hua-Ching Ni & Maoshing Ni, Ph.D.

Library of Congress Cataloging-In-Publication Data

Ni, Hua-Ching.
The power of the feminine: using feminine energy to heal the world's spiritual problems / Hua-Ching Ni, Maoshing Ni.—1st ed.—Los Angeles, CA : SevenStar Communications Group, 2004.

     p. cm.

     Includes index.
     ISBN 1-887575-17-0

  1. Women—Social conditions. 2. Leadership—Religious aspects.
3. Leadership—Moral and ethical aspects. 4. Feminism—Religious aspects.
5. Women and spiritualism. 6. Spiritual life. I. Ni, Maoshing. II. Title.

HQ1236 .N52 2004   2004104164
305.42—dc22   0409

Reprinted October 2008

*This book is dedicated to the great women and men of the world
who choose to refuse the sole exaltation of masculine worship. The spiritual
deformation of humanity's balanced nature has come from the killing, conquering,
and warring which are characteristic of one gender and have been tragically
repeated throughout the past 4000 years.*

*Those great individuals also see that mutual help, cooperation, and
harmony are essential offerings to the bright collective future of human society.
They see that mass killing and suicide bombers take people to total destruction,
which offers no solution for the survival of humanity. A spiritually balanced world
that respects the superiority of the gentle feminine approach in handling
human affairs is now necessary. Personally and socially, this is the
new awakening spiritual salvation.*

To All Readers,

According to the teaching of the Universal Integral Way or Heavenly Heart, male and female are equally important in the natural sphere. This fact can be observed and confirmed in the diagram of the T'ai Chi. Thus, discrimination is not practiced in our tradition. All of our work is dedicated to both genders of the human race.

Wherever possible, sentence constructions using masculine pronouns to represent both sexes are avoided. Where they do occur, we ask your tolerance and spiritual understanding. We hope that you will take the essence of these teachings and overlook the limitations of a language in which gender discrimination is inherent. Ancient Chinese pronouns do not differentiate gender. We hope that all of you will achieve yourselves well above the level of language and gender. Thank you.

Warning—Disclaimer

This book is intended to present beneficial information and techniques that have been used throughout the orient for many centuries. This information and these practices utilize a natural system within the body; however, no claims are made regarding their effectiveness. The information offered is according to the authors' best knowledge and experience and is to be used by the reader at his or her own discretion and liability.

People's lives have different conditions, and their growth has different stages. Because the development of all people cannot be unified, there is no single practice that can be universally applied to everyone. It must be through the discernment of the reader that practices are selected. The adoption and application of the material offered in this book must therefore be the reader's own responsibility.

The authors and publisher of this book are not responsible in any manner for any harm that may occur through following the instructions in this book.

ABOUT THE AUTHORS

Hua-Ching Ni, author, teacher, and healer addresses the essential nature of human life and works to further the personal growth and spiritual development of this and future generations. He was raised in a family tradition of healing and spirituality that is being continued by his two sons, Drs. Daoshing and Maoshing Ni, and by his many friends and supporters throughout the world.

Maoshing Ni, D.O.M., L.Ac., Ph.D., Dipl. C.H., Dipl. ABAAHP, has lectured and taught workshops throughout the country on such diverse subjects as longevity, preventive medicine, Chinese nutrition, herbal medicine, acupuncture, facial diagnosis, *fengshui*, stress management, *I Ching*, meditation, *t'ai chi*, *chi gong*, and the history of medicine.

Dr. Mao has also authored many books and audio/video tapes. These include *Chinese Herbology Made Easy, The Tao of Nutrition, Energy Enhancement Exercises, Self-Healing Chi Gong, Meditations for Stress Release, Pain Management,* and *The Yellow Emperor's Classic of Medicine*. He was also an editorial member for the best selling book, *Alternative Medicine: The Definitive Guide*.

TABLE OF CONTENTS

NOTE TO ALL READERS

The teaching of the Heavenly Way, the normality of nature, is the collective wisdom of our ancient developed ancestors that manifested during the long pre-historical stage of feminine-centered society. The Virgin Messenger from the Yellow River, known as the Lady-in-Blue of the Ninth Heaven, initially taught it to the Yellow Emperor of China when society was entering the male-centered stage over 4700 years ago. Around 2500 years ago, Lao Tzu developed the Heavenly Way in his work to offer guidance to people during China's Warring States Period (403–222 BCE). Since then the world has become even rougher and tougher. The valuable spiritual vision of the feminine approach was not heeded to hold the world together.

In the Jing Dynasty (265–419 CE), after the physical competitions of the Three Kingdoms, Kou Hong, with his spiritual vision, devoted his life to gather the scattered spiritual teachings of the old days. Part of the content of the Heavenly Way was kept in his work. In the Sung Dynasty (960–1279 CE), after a long rivalry among the many militant groups, a newer version of the Heavenly Way was formed and completed as the basis of the present Chinese work. As a spiritual contribution to the health of the world, I (Hua-Ching Ni or OmNi) translated and published that work in English in the 1970s.[1] Other English translations have appeared, but they were not written as a public spiritual teaching.

As one male teacher, my work of devotion is insufficient to help the world. In the 1980s, I reached a few individuals and began to transfer tasks to those students and friends of the Heavenly Way. I bid them to fulfill the Way's spiritual mission as their social connection and activity. The Universal Society of the Integral Way (now known as the Integral Way Society or IWS) was formed to face the spiritually declining situation of the world.

---

1. Refer to Hua-Ching Ni's *Heavenly Way* booklet.

Heaven is an open society, the spiritual choice of the high life; it has never been a kingdom in the sky. God is the power of Nature in its positive expression. When the natural spiritual faith of the Way began, the name Lady-in-Blue hinted at the sky—the Mother of the Universe, and the sun was seen as one of her sons and as the Heavenly Father of humankind. The Seven Lady Stars that form the Northern Star system were understood to protect the good souls of the earthlings and keep the path to Heaven open. Light inside and outside is good. Darkness inside and outside is bad. The doctrine of Nature is this simple.

Yet during the past 4000 years, people have made doctrines of their emotions, imaginations, and concepts to compete with the spiritual reality that exists in them and in Nature. As societies grew, people sought a kingdom for protection and a just ruler since they were unable to rule themselves. They forsook the natural spiritual faith and separated themselves from the simple truth. Their minds projected the images of Heaven and God and thus created religions.

The dilemma for society is that without religions, people become spiritually scattered, whilst with religions they become competitive within and among the different groups. Religions, like tools, can be serviceable if used well or harmful if not used well as, for example, when they are used to draw people into meaningless rivalry; it all depends in whose hands they lie. You need to understand that spiritual reality is not a matter of unification, as individuals and societies have different levels of growth. The only truthful way to grow is to accept people's various spiritual styles and different levels of spiritual growth, while seeking the true spiritual unity that exists beyond this. With these realities in mind, and with your good understanding, I will show you how you can reshape the destiny of humankind. The later spiritual educational shape of religion, the congregational form, may be adapted to redeliver the simple truth and present the early natural spiritual teachings. This will help rekindle a healthy community spirit and service for all people's peace and growth.

I encourage women to accept the role of spiritual leadership and spread the teachings of the Heavenly Way, and I encourage men to work on the physical problems of life and support women in this leadership.

Finally, I have channeled and simplified my 30 years of teaching in the West into five books to promote the Teachings of the Heavenly Heart: The Path of a Constructive Life (PCL) to the world. The foundation of the PCL is the Universal Integral Way and its initial form is the teaching of the Heavenly Way. The core of the teaching upholds responding to evil with virtue as demonstrated by the life of Jesus. The Christian church, however, deviated from the simple truth of Jesus and his source of the Way. The correction should be made and groups like the newly organized Sisters of the Universal Heavenly Way (SUHW)—a group that adopts women leadership and has a female majority—can mobilize this effort.

The current divine Master of the Integral Way (an unpaid position), Dr. Maoshing Ni, a father of three children and a professor of Yo San University, has ordained and continues to ordain women and men to be voluntary spiritual coaches as the new form of spiritual guide for the PCL. The women of the SUHW also realize the work of the PCL. All share the same purpose of world peace and cooperation.

At the turn of this new millennium, feminine spiritual leadership and constructive work is expected to guide the world away from the conjoint trend of total destruction.

This book is our support to the wise and gentle women and men as they move toward a better world with balanced women in spiritual leadership. They are the hope for a spiritually improved world. May humankind turn the first page of its new destiny of lasting peace.

If you are interested in this endeavor, you can contact the Integral Way Society (IWS) at: *info@integralway.org*; or the Sisters of the Universal Heavenly Way (SUHW) at: *suhw@taostar.com*. Thank you.

Love, OmNi

PRELUDE

The House of Humanity has a leak!
Although you do not see a big flood,
there are many people who smell moldy.

People's moral nature is moldy,
their character is moldy,
and they have caused their societies to become moldy
and their governments too.
Unfortunately, the entire world culture has become moldy,
including religions at their deepest core.

Within the leaky house of humanity,
you can meet leaky people everywhere.
They do not want to renew anything—
no conception of their mind nor style of their lives.

Any house, whether old or new, can have a leak.
Although you may not see the leak,
things become very wet and moldy.

You shouldn't tear down the whole house for a mere small leak.
You should fix the leak.
You may be too lazy or too busy,
or you would rather get angry or complain.

Do not tear down the whole house for a mere leak.
Instead, we have some simple suggestions
on how you can fix the leaky house of humanity.

Do not be a leaky life.
Fix the leak, it isn't that hard.
Even though you are capable of tearing down the entire house of humanity,
you're not capable of rebuilding this unique house which
all people jointly own, whether they are leaky or not.

You *can* follow the Constructive Way,
and balance your life with the gentle feminine approach.
Hold onto these upright principles decisively,
and you can shore up the leaks and clean out the mold,
so that all people can share in the Evergreen House of Humanity.

PART I

The Two Types of Life in the World—
The One Ruled Externally and the One Ruled Internally

"Ruled by Objectivity"

Chapter 1

Ordinary People Can Save the World

The Two Worlds of Life

There are two types of human life and two types of worlds on earth. One type of life has to be ruled by external force, the other is ruled by internal strength.

In the life ruled by the mind, personal interest reigns above all, ensuring constant conflict and confrontation. Society cannot satisfy everyone's different interests, thus external rules are needed, along with external force.

The other type of life is ruled by a growing spirituality and simplicity of life achieved through a deep improvement of the human mind. That life can enjoy both internal peace and the external orderliness of society.

Human society needs God, but the concept of God has developed two meanings. God can be the common social focus of humankind, or God can be the external power enforcing agreement. In other words, God can be the spiritual unity of all life and many lives. Thus God can be above all: the real spiritual power to rule one's life, and hopefully to rule the world. Or, God can be considered an external force, representing a social agreement reached by some people at some point and for some period in time. As such, it cannot represent permanent justice and is far from the eternal truth of life.

The true sense of God has to be associated with the growth of the rational force within life. With God life rules itself, and when developed, rational people live together in the world; the world expresses order and has no need to rely on external force. But when people rely on external force and a concept of God is used to rule the world, physical force is used to kill those with conflicting interests and different beliefs.

The majority of people with historical religious beliefs have misdirected the warmth of their life energy to conquer one another. This mistake should end. All people can be ruled by their own internal growth.

Let there be no more killing for ideological and religious differences, and may people forego their willingness for martyrdom. Paradise is the spiritual motivation for people seeking whole and integrated growth in life. To liberate the soul we have no need to harm ourselves or nail our body to a board, but with growing rationality and balance such great devotion can uplift our sense of life's value.

Now is the time of the Common Era. Although the world has made great material improvements, everyone can see that life's internal spiritual quality is weak and needs a great deal of improvement. If we put effort into the correct and clear spiritual direction, our internal spiritual life can be improved to match the progress in our external, material life. The Universal Integral Way, also known as the Teachings of the Heavenly Heart, promotes this much needed effort in the world. Once the balance of the two sides—the material and the spiritual—is reached, the world will no longer be bloodthirsty and sick.

As people of spiritual responsibility, we can recreate the culture of the world with the goal of Heavenly Paradise on earth. To realize the Heavenly Way is to uphold Universal Morality through our own efforts of spiritual self-cultivation. No life need be negatively sacrificed, but all people can live happily in the bright world.

Chapter 2

Can the World Move Beyond Spiritual Confusion?

Human life is as active on the surface of the earth as ants on the kitchen floor of a farmhouse, and whether human or ant, each is pushed by the natural force to search for life. In this aspect we are similar, but unlike ants, human life is also driven by emotions. People do the strangest things to one another for the sake of emotional needs.

Ants do not question who or what is behind their lives, but people do. Do people really know who or what is behind their lives? No. Most people believe what others tell them, and as a result of their different belief systems they divide into groups that fight and conflict with each other. Living at this level, people pay the price of feeding their lives to the monster of spiritual ignorance.

It is like the fellow who while walking along a crowded street, points at the moon in the sky to someone and everyone looks up at his finger. Everyone believes they should pay attention to the man's finger and ignore the moon in the distant sky. All different religions of human spiritual culture with their various styles of worship, rituals, and wordy presentations are merely the finger pointing in the direction of the moon. The pointing finger is no different from the crowd's fingers, but the crowd interprets its message too seriously, believing that the styles of worship, the rituals, and the design of the houses of worship are the reality of the universal divinity. These old creations are mere customs and traditions that have existed throughout generations, and people have mistakenly accepted them as the real form of God. No one questions them any more.

Now here comes a man and his son from a different part of the world, and they write books about this big mistake of humanity. However, most people don't read them. People would rather lose their lives to someone's nonsense or to the shadow of the pointing finger that they see as a miracle. People mistake the pointing finger and even its shadow as the truth of life. They cheapen their lives by allowing themselves to be managed by religious personnel, priests, and clergy. People are fed nonsense and are brainwashed. This happens to people even today. Though modern people are the new life that has developed from ancestors who had lived on the earth a million years, they have made little or no progress in understanding their lives. We suggest that people go to a quiet place where they can work on rediscovering the true nature of their lives.

All life comes from the subtle origin where there is no gender, no color, no rank, and no conceptual sense of anything but the simple essence of nature. All life has something to do with the sun, the moon, and the planets, and all life is the offspring of the Mother Universe. What does the Mother Universe look like? Does she have weight or size? Does she possess a figure and so forth?

The universe develops from the subtle essence. It is neither big nor small. It is neither far nor near. Life is sustained by holding close to the healthy being of the universe. Life can be lost by not caring about healthy living and by straying away. If we appreciate that the world is as small in the universe as the pointed tip of a snail's shell, and that life is as fleeting as a flash of lightning in a storm, what then is there to be crazy about as a cause for war?

Be honest and look inward for the truth of life; there is a spiritual world within us. We need to grow the light inside. To find our life's real strength, we need to apply the light's truthful and brightening leadership to our internal spiritual world. It is the same for all people and it is the first step that all people should make. When darkness prevails inside, we cannot expect there to be light outside. When we find internal improvement through seeing the light inside, then there is hope for lighting up the world outside.

PART II

The Trouble with External Rule and
Suggestions for a New Integrated Direction

"Overcome the
External Hardness"

Chapter 3

The Old Faith in the Sky for Open People
(Our Relationship with Heaven)

What is the most advanced can look like the most backward.
What is the most backward can appear to be the most progressive.
This is what can happen with the Way of Natural Truth.

Lao Tzu made the above remark around 2500 years ago. He was the spokesperson for the old culture known as the Way, which developed long ago when humanity was in its infancy. His teachings developed from the wisdom of the Way's more famous early ancestors of Fu Shi,[1] Shen Nung (reign 3218–2078 BCE), and the Yellow Emperor (reign 2698–2598 BCE) long before written history. These individuals were the early leaders of humanity.

Today Maoshing and I are the ones who carry and continue the old culture, just as Lao Tzu did back then. We are by far the latecomers, born from the remote descendants of the Yellow Emperor. We are the children of a declined and scattered family.

The teachings of the Way reflect the ancient developed ones' direct experience and keen observations of the deep laws of nature and the universe. They realized that the sky or heaven was the common source of all lives and they recognized that its energies help to cleanse, nourish, and support human energies. The sky constantly provides light for people's growth, both at the deep and superficial levels, without ever asking for anything in return. Without the sky's spiritual support, humans could do very little.

---

1. Fu Shi is said by some to have lived between 6000 and 30000 years ago and by others to have lived between 3852–2738 BCE. Please note that BCE stands for Before the Common Era and CE stands for Common Era. The distinction is the same as between BC and AD.

The old culture of the Way and its social worship of Heaven is the oldest spiritual faith of humanity forming naturally in prehistorical China. Fu Shi's era may have been the time that the social worship of Heaven began. In worshipping Heaven, the ancient developed ones respected the natural facts that the sun, moon, and other celestial bodies hold a subtle influence over all life. They looked to the orderliness of the cyclical nature of the skies as a model for their early communities. More than this, they sought Heaven's protection and Heaven's blessing, both of which come when one establishes a faithful relationship with divine energy and attunes oneself to it. By making offerings to the heavenly energy, blessings and protection naturally came to the ancients in the form of peaceful communities and healthy, vital, and enduring lives.

An emperor's duty reflected the natural functioning of the sky: to protect and maintain the harmony and order of life and to help people's growth without asking for anything in return. The emperors were publicly recognized as the eldest sons of Heaven, the public leaders who served the offerings to the sky. These offerings expressed the ancient people's harmonious relationship with the spiritual realm and their deep gratitude for the good life they enjoyed together. The ordinary civilians were called the children of Heaven. Together, all people belonged to the Heavenly family on earth. The ancient families and communities all performed ancestral worship. The old faith and its customs are still alive today, but most modern Chinese people do not take it as seriously as the people did back then.

The early emperors of society were more spiritual figures than political figures. They were the elders of the tribes, carrying out a great heavenly duty for the public. These elders were accepted as the natural leaders among people without objection or suspicion. That was a good time for people. Up to the time of our ancestor the Yellow Emperor, there was no government or extra social burden.

At this time, worshipping Heaven and loving and caring for their people had become the sacred and Heavenly duty of the emperor. It was a custom inherited from the earlier social leaders. As the emperor, one could not consider personal preference above one's Heavenly spiritual duty of following and practicing the virtue of Heaven toward all people. Spiritual duty was fulfilled that way; there were no separate religions to assist the emperor's function. While other people could have the freedom to enjoy life's pleasures, the emperor could not. He had to uphold his duty and become the model for all other people. It was a hard job.

During the Yellow Emperor's time, Chinese society came to a brand new epoch. After 19 years on the throne of political responsibility, the Yellow Emperor started to dream of a Kingdom of "Flowery Abundance" where the emperor has nothing to do and the people live greatly and without contention. He dreamed of a great society ruled only by the Heavenly Way of Nature, where no other ruler's name need be presented.

Also at this time the Yellow Emperor had to perform religious rituals in the spring and autumn. Many cows were killed as an offering in the worship of Heaven. He and his ministers cut the roasted beef and shared it among all the families. People began to feel glorified or disgraced by the size of the meat they received from the royal feast of the Emperor. The size of meat, however, was merely an accidental matter through the hands of the officials. There was no favoritism practiced.

From the Yellow Emperor (reign 2698–2598 BCE) to his son Shau Haw to his grandson Chuan Hsu (our direct remote ancestor) the meaning and worship of Heaven was passed down as an oral tradition. It continued through the reigns of Emperor Gao (accession 2436 BCE), Emperor Chih (accession 2366 BCE), Emperor Niao (accession 2357 BCE), and Emperor Shun (accession 2257 BCE). Gradually it came to be recorded. It is presented later in this work as the Spiritual Faith of the Yellow Emperor: an elucidation derived from the spiritual training of my (OmNi) early years.

In the first five generations above, the sons continued the royal duties of their fathers. Emperor Niao, as an exception, was chosen to be emperor because he was dutiful. He was the emperor who kept looking for someone wiser to replace him and to take over his duty. He finally found Shun, a young voluntary teacher who taught the five relationships of people.

Earlier, only three big spiritual relationships were considered—those of the Sky, Earth, and Humanity. Around Niao's time, other relationships came to be recognized. Shun, before becoming emperor, developed the teaching of the five inter-relationships among humans. It elucidated the moral duty in every type of relationship as follows.

(1) In the relationship of kings and the general public, there should be loyalty in fulfilling duties.

(2) Among spouses, there should be love and mutual support.

(3) Among parents and their children, there should be love and care.

(4) Among siblings, there should be respect and mutual help.

(5) Among friends there should be trust and help.

Each person has a spiritual duty to fulfill their mutual obligations.

Throughout these times, the worship of Heaven continued. After the earlier emperors came the Hsia (also spelled as Shah) Dynasty (2207–1766 BCE), which was started by the Great Yu who succeeded in overcoming the floods of the ancient Middle Land of China. Yu's descendants continued in the position of emperor until the last emperor of Hsia, Emperor Jey. During his time the quality of the emperor changed. Yu was respected for his virtue of enlightened leadership and he fulfilled the Heavenly assignment to save the people from natural disasters. Jey, however, was the first emperor in Chinese written history to put personal interest and physical pleasure above his spiritual duty to protect his people and to unite and maintain harmony among the multiple small kingdoms.

Emperor Jey ignored the public faith in Heaven and failed to serve his people. He did what he liked and was cruel and oppressive. Eventually his activities were restrained by Tang, one of the leaders of the ancient community. At that time there was a mutual recognition of power among the local leaders and the emperor. These local leaders or kings were different from the feudal princes who existed after the Han Dynasty (206 BCE–219 CE). Jey was put under a type of house arrest, thus he could enjoy what he liked in his palace only. Fifty years passed before the people completely lost hope in Jey. Then Tang could begin a new epoch in the Shang Dynasty (1766–1121 BCE). He could not do so before because he did not want to destroy the public faith in Heaven. Human society reflects the heavenly order on earth, thus Tang had to ensure that the public faith supported him, just as it had done with the previous social authorities.

The Shang Dynasty eventually declined too, but not because the descendants of Tang had lost faith in Heaven. They overindulged in divination using cow bones as oracles. The last emperor of Shang, Tang's descendant Emperor Jou (1154–1121 BCE) was just as tyrannical and indulgent as Jey of Hsia.

The Chou Dynasty (1122–249 BCE) with the support of most of the local leaders replaced Jou. They also replaced the divination system with the *I Ching*[2] which had previously been used mostly as a calendar. It was King Wen who further developed the use of the *I Ching* for divination purposes.

During the time of Shang and Chou, the people continued to believe in the will of Heaven, but searched for an interpretation of it, so they performed divination heavily. By the end of the Chou Dynasty, people's minds began to compete with Heaven. They sought things through competition rather than through a deep acceptance of Heaven's will. And so began the big confusion.

When people think that competition is the only means for self-benefit, the value of cooperation is weakened and force predominates. The new competitive stage began to destroy the love between parents and children, brothers and sisters,

---

2. Also known as the *Book of Changes*. Please refer to Hua-Ching Ni's version of the *I Ching, The Book of Changes and the Unchanging Truth.*

and men and women. All human relationships became tense by the sense of competition.

Religions were created to repair people's faith in Heaven, but this artificial effort only added more struggle. Even though the wish was to return people to Eden, it is far better that people return to what they naturally are—the angels of God or Heavenly Nature.

This is the history of the natural faith in Heaven of the early people. As the distant descendants of the Ni family, Maoshing and I have the duty to preserve it. Some of our ancestors also helped to restore the faith and preserve it in written form in the beginning of the Han Dynasty around 2200 years ago. That period was another new epoch in China's history.

Today it is another epoch over 2000 years later. Should we neglect faith in Heaven simply because most people have a different faith now? I admit that when it comes to the decency of human culture I have a lot of stubbornness: maybe this comes from the influence of my ancestors or my training, since I was chosen to learn the things that are of permanent value for humanity.

Our new efforts today through the Teachings of the Heavenly Heart: The Path of Constructive Life (PCL) is to clearly develop a spiritual content with new life experiences for our fellow people. We wish that you do not become arrogant like Jey or Jou, but that you appreciate and restore the Heavenly Nature that lies within you.

The PCL is to help you reach for and restore the normality of life. It is a new direction and goal for the health of life. In situations where you are seriously unhealthy, emotionally twisted, suffering, or too young or inexperienced to be aware of the conventional heavy baggage you carry, you may not yet be able to appreciate it. Thus, one of the existing conventional religions may better help you return to normalcy rather than the PCL, whose function is to provide an education for your deep spiritual health and to support your entire well-being.

But although religions may be useful as medicine for the sick and troubled, they should not be made out to be the general food for all people.

The spiritual triune of Heaven, Earth, and Humanity is a part of the old Chinese culture. From the earliest time, natural societies were formed in harmony with this great Trinity. My parents gave me this training. We still respect the harmony of the three spheres and have made it our goal to make this tradition available to all humanity. The old culture has not changed much, except now, due to competitiveness, people put themselves higher than Heaven and Earth.

Below, I present my early years' training to you for your evaluation. Though the world we face has changed drastically since the early times, we see that the quality of people's lives has made no great progress. Humanity's old problems have not gone away. Nothing much has changed. What people think of as advanced and new can be the same old problems of humanity. This is why we are bringing back the old faith of people from long, long ago to give to you, the new people of the world. We expect to be the bridge linking the old beliefs to the new generation for your review and comment.

Because people lack spiritual growth and because the fundamentals of human life and the universe have not changed much, the old faith can still be helpful. We can work together to save this sinking ship on its uncharted voyage. May the enduring old faith save the lost lives of modern people. For as Lao Tzu expressed:

> *What is the most progressive looks backward.*
> *What is the most backward can be the most progressive.*
> *This is the Way of the Natural Truth.*

The Spiritual Faith of the Yellow Emperor (Preserved by OmNi)

Nature has a will. The Heavenly will cannot be controlled by people, yet if people conduct themselves correctly they can receive Heavenly support.

People should understand that it is Heaven's will that they are born by nature, raised by nature, and grow by nature. It is best for people to live harmoniously with the rhythmic cycles of nature, which are in accordance with the Heavenly will. Heaven wills people to live and live well.

It is the Heavenly duty of people to fully develop their lives and waste nothing of the Heavenly endowment in their lives.

As a person of Heavenly birth, you need to follow the guidance of Heaven and extend your love to all others. Seeing the Heavenly will, you consider your birth to be fortunate; not seeing the Heavenly will, you live in darkness, considering yourself deserted.

Deserted by whom? You may have been deserted by the love of Life, yet it is not too late. The Heavenly fortune inside you is a great opportunity for you to learn to live the Heavenly Way. It is also an opportunity for those who have missed out on life to live all over again.

Be diligent in doing the Heavenly work of nurturing your life and the lives of others as well, for that is your life.

The Heavenly Way is straight, yet people's minds may be crooked. Heavenly grace is always sufficient for all lives that see the Heavenly Way.

Heaven protects the world. Heavenly protection is realized by living the Heavenly Way.

People who learn the Heavenly Way are like Heaven, since they do not invite the foolish worldly way to damage their souls. To be like Heaven is to eliminate the darkness inside and allow the inner light in you and others to lighten up the world that has been darkened by people's narrowness and selfish ignorance.

The Heavenly Way is the practice of Heavenly concern among people. It means to extend the Heavenly Way to all others.

You can reach directly the deep and far truth of your spiritual life. With openness, kindness, and virtuous supportiveness, Heaven grows within you and by you.

Heavenly forgiveness is granted to those people who have the same heart to forgive someone else who has offended or wronged them.

Heavenly help will come at the right time for those who are not lazy or evasive, but ready to offer their helping hand to others in difficulty.

Heaven nurses the spiritual growth of people with Heavenly milk. Heaven constantly gives people time to learn and grow when they are moving in the right direction.

Heaven prevents people from getting into trouble and endangering their lives by revealing new opportunities to them.

The Heavenly award is sufficient to those who follow the Heavenly Way without deviation.

Life is precious to those who value their life and keep away from evil doing. Life is cheap to those who tempt themselves with wrongdoing. No good life dies in vain.

The Heavenly home is always open to those souls who live a worshipful life. When they live in the world, they have the support of Heaven.

The Heavenly granary above them is always full and there is a Heavenly provision for them that is equal to their own moral capacity.

There is still a Heavenly entitlement given to those who do not worry about their lives, but care for their lives.

Heaven cares for all good people that live a dutiful life. It is the due sense of responsibility of life that dignifies life.

Why does Heaven care about people so much? Because it is the Heavenly Nature to do so.

How far is human nature from Heavenly Nature? It was not far before human nature was spoiled and poisoned, but now it is very far as human nature has been twisted and contorted.

What is the human effort that people should be involved in? People live far from Heavenly Nature when their lives remain at the level of their animal nature. But they live close to Heavenly Nature when they can control and refine their animal nature.

Does Heaven hate? Yes, Heaven hates hypocrisy. What is hypocrisy? It is when people use God or Heaven to gamble the blood of others.

Always live within the Heavenly Domain. Then the soul is in control of life.

There is Heavenly enjoyment, which quietly appeals to your healthy emotion and sentiment. It is inexhaustible, but you can easily tire yourself out by having too much worldly fun.

Heaven will support you, if you are able to free your life from the bondage of too many extra desires and grow the wisdom that is above such unneeded desires. This is the strength to broaden, prosper, and grow.

Heaven is proud of you, for your virtue is equal to Heaven.

The Heavenly carriage can carry you far if you can subdue the demon of self-interest, the demon of self-importance, and the demon of self-aggrandizement.

Your freedom will be unlimited if you attain the power of wisdom in life. Your happy life journey will be endless and Heavenly love will move forward with you.

To others your life may appear humble, but you possess a noble heart. To Heaven, it is the quality of your heart that makes your life distinguished.

It is not the Heavenly will that you live low or high. It is the Heavenly will that though you may live low, the value of your life is high because you possess Heaven within. Those who possess Heaven in life are the Heavenly Beings who live in the world.

People may live high, but their value of life is low because they possess a black hole inside of their lives. Those people are devils in human form.

You are provided with Heavenly Blessings. It does not matter that other people do not understand this. It only matters when you do not understand.

Above the sky, there are the clouds. Beneath the sky, there is the water. Clouds can be water. Water can be cloud. Heaven can be earth. Earth can be heaven. Why don't you value all support equally?

It is Heavenly music if your words are spoken cleanly, clearly, and smoothly. It is Heavenly grace if you transform anger and hatred into peace.

Do not be anxious to live all your lifetimes in Heaven: only be watchful that you do not fall.

Life looks like it is decided by Heaven, but people's own effort can make a big difference.

Your human will can be granted if it meets with Heaven's will. Before you project your will, use your Heavenly wisdom and always respect the Heavenly will.

Success can be meaningless if your motivation is unrighteous. Accomplishing a big task can be valueless if the means applied are mischievous.

To thoroughly learn how to succeed or accomplish a task, remember that the process should be equally valued as the end result; it is not decided by your desire alone.

The destructive trend of human society cannot be altered unless the majority sees the danger. Usually they do not.

The negative trend of human nature can be observed, and by taking preventive measures the damage can be reduced.

Heavenly blessings cannot be received by bargaining, but the path of virtuous fulfillment builds the possibility of winning Heaven's favor.

Heaven does not block peoples' way; it is people who block their own way. To remove a blockage that keeps you from Heaven, change from your wrongdoing and find a new, right way. To remove the blockage of negative people, use the virtue of patience and gentle effort to overcome it.

Sometimes the importance of worldly gain is not very meaningful. It is much more meaningful to maintain the moral value of life. This reveals itself when you see that Heavenly blessings are more valuable than worldly blessings.

Making money is not equal to nurturing life. People who are able to see the Heavenly Law operating in life know this.

If you can actualize the Heavenly Way in your life, all your wishes will be approved by the Heavenly will.

If you are able to implement the Heavenly Way in your life, your life will be Heaven. If people are able to implement the Heavenly Way in society, then society will be Heaven.

Although people of the Heavenly Way may live in the dusty world, their hearts are high above its dusty and dirty tricks and their reward is Heaven.

Occasionally you may feel inconvenienced by living in the world or you may tire of the treadmill of life. But do not live for just yourselves, live for the Heavenly Way.

Too much complaining will pull down your spirit. Too many wishes will scatter your essence. Too many desires will make you sink.

To be specially blessed is decided by Heaven. To live a morally undefeated life is your Heavenly duty.

You may expect the Heavenly accomplishment to come at a time when you face difficulties. The Heavenly accomplishment will come when you see the value of difficulties for they serve to accomplish your spiritual refinement.

Watch how the depth of your spiritual learning is accomplished. This is what your life can do for you. Thus maintain your spiritual cultivation, as life is too precious to be lived in vain.

Heaven witnesses all life in every second. What matters is how people fulfill the value of their life.

Heaven is where the Heavenly Way is accomplished. Heavenly Beings are those who fulfill the Heavenly Way.

If you fulfill your Heavenly duty the Heavenly Way will fulfill its blessing to you. Those benefits continue even to your children.

When you decide to continue your life in Heaven, Heaven also decides to continue your life.

Learn the right teaching. Keep to the right path. Be the source of the right teaching and be the path of being and doing what is right. Do not search for shortcuts, as they are the source of troublesome traps.

The love of God is for all people and all lives. God does not support the contention of the world nor engage in secret plots.

When you pray privately, you say "God, please listen to me." But God is not your servant, even though you think God should be. Why should God listen to you? God forbids arrogance in any human being. This is the number one discipline from God. While Heaven provides peace to people, they fight wars among themselves instead. Fighting and wars are reminders of people's ignorance and arrogance. Humans are strange animals: they expect peace on earth, but they cannot enjoy it for long. This pattern has been repeated throughout human history. You ask God to save the world, but the world values fighting!

God blesses the one of perseverance who holds the simple principle of peace in life. God blesses those individuals who fulfill their achievement by bathing their souls in the cold-hearted snow of the world to help themselves and others.

With utmost sincerity, people can develop themselves by having faith in a Heavenly Life.

These truths are an elucidation of the natural faith of people in the prehistorical stage of human life. This Universal Moral Principle was prescribed by the Yellow Emperor, and the original is what Lao Tzu based his *Tao Teh Ching* on.

I base many of my English and Chinese writings on a version of the Yellow Emperor's work edited in the early Han Dynasty (206 BCE–219 CE), after the long spiritual confusion that began in the Spring and Autumn Period (720–

484 BCE). This confusion caused a response from the sages: Lao Tzu responding with the *Tao Teh Ching*, his vision of the universal moral principle, and Confucius (551–479 BCE) responding to restore the social order set up by Duke Chou, the son of King Wen of the Chou Dynasty. Duke Chou set up official social rules and customs that became the new standard during the time of Chou.

The sages Lao Tzu, Confucius, and other wise people of the time could inspire little change in the society. Then came a time of even worse social conflict, during the Warring States Period (403–221 BCE), when seven states (Chin, Chu, Jie, Hen, Chao, Wei, and Yeng) contended for political control. During this period, cultural efforts were still active and Menfucius (372–298 BCE) continued Confucius's work, traveling among the different states to preach that kindness and righteousness are much more valuable than gain and profit. Chuang Tzu continued Lao Tzu's teaching that contentment can be found in a natural peaceful life. Both these sages also failed in their cultural effort and spiritual downfall continued.

As a result, at the end of this period, Chin Su Huan swallowed all other states and emerged victoriously as the unified ruler, the first Emperor of Chin (reign 246–207 BCE). As a ruler he was unchallenged, but no external power is without some internal corruption. His second son killed his brother and seized the throne to extend the family rule another three years. Then the Han Dynasty arose (206 BCE–219 CE) and adopted the Way of the Universal Moral Principle to replace the tyrannical approach of the Chin Dynasty.

Earlier my family (remote descendants of Emperor Chuan Hsu) had helped King Wen overthrow the tyrannical Jou and establish the Chou Dynasty (1122–249 BCE). This time around, the problem was cultural downfall rather than tyranny, and my ancestors responded differently by helping restore the Yellow Emperor's cultural effort of faith in Heaven, which led the Han Dynasty to prosperity at its beginning. That lasted until Emperor Wu's reign (108–86 BCE) which marked the Han Dynasty's decline.

The spiritual life of the Way is deep, but the new social leaders prefer to make formal shows of piety. In this way they condition people to become shallow and narrow. The rituals, ceremonial styles, and celebrations should come from the people's own interest and natural expressions; they should vary as time goes on. They should not be made rigid and official.

Through the generations, whether in the East or in the West, that which is called "liberation" or the "fight for freedom" is at the level of external institutionalized rituals or ceremonial styles. However, the fundamentals of human culture remain the same and revolutionizing the externals as an expression of the natural growth of people is a better way of allowing the fundamentals to have the proper impact.

Some people might think that if they live the Heavenly Way they will receive less for themselves. These people overestimate their own "wisdom" and use it to compete with their own nature and the nature of humanity. Truthfully, those who appear clumsy in life but who faithfully follow the Heavenly Way get more out of life.

But good people still need to guard themselves from the evil attention of others. Because of worldly competition, good people can unconsciously lose their healthy quality and become the same as bad people. This is the reason the world has continued to decline. And this is why the *Tao Teh Ching* teaches respect for the principle of the left hand of gentleness to go together with the right hand of firmness and decisiveness. More respect should be given to the soft left hand. Although both hands have natural functions, a defensive and yielding approach to life has become necessary, while the offensive approach should stop.

The Way is always with people, directing their lives toward an endless and limitless future.

Chapter 4

The New Direction of the Integral Way
(The Vision for a Spiritual Evergreen Party)

The Motivation for This Vision is the Source of the World's Troubled Condition

When viewing the pathology of the world's problems, we see that throughout generations social rivalry and competition have created trouble and suffering for people. These activities come mostly from the disease we call the "Male Horse Complex." Evidence of this can be found by examining the personalities of the rising leaders in each generation.

Humans come from animals and from the start they lived on the flesh of animals. If we look closely we see that human society is not much different from the horse society. Human nature contains an unresolved and undeveloped animal nature. Competition and fighting is the innate nature of those people who lack spiritual development. Genghis Khan (1162–1227 CE), the Mongolian conqueror, is a typical example.

People have thought too much about conquerors such as Chi Su Huan, the first Emperor of the Chin Dynasty, Alexander the Great, Napoleon, Hitler, and Stalin. All of them proved to be the strongest male horse of their time, and human history is a record of activities of such people.

We hope that we do not offend you by saying that world culture and its conventional religions mostly represent animal culture: the animals that know how to read and write that is. One can find evidence of this in eulogies praising the strongest male horses. The civilization we respect and record in our books is a neutral and balanced civilization. It is different from the civilization that exalts the male horse type above all others in every aspect of life.

In the big land of China, Lao Tzu foresaw problems with the wild horse type and its social competitiveness. He warned people of the coming period of war, which lasted for several hundred years before the first big conqueror of China, the first emperor of Chin.

Lao Tzu, having learned from the wisdom of the early leaders of the Way who had been taught and supported by wise women, was a deep observer of humanity. He encouraged people to learn from the feminine principle with its characteristic benefits of peace, stability, cooperation, and effectiveness in life, without wasteful struggling. Nevertheless, the rivalry and competitiveness of the male horse pattern went on in China and the rest of the world, without any sign of change.

Human civilization is in truth the feminine principle put into practice. However, it always coexists in society with hero worship and a predominance of masculine principle worship. Human culture has suffered as the masculine principle has been exaggerated and the feminine principle suppressed and distorted. This has affected the life of the masses who blindly follow the strongest horse. The aggressive male horse complex is produced from the male sex hormone. Its impulsive force lacks the deep vision that comes from a balanced and developed brain, which is very different from the brain's intellectual energy.

This problem can be helped by guiding and educating people not to produce, encourage or worship the conqueror type. The masculine impulsive energy needs guidance and development. Even in modern democratic societies the race for political office and position are still managed by masculine principles. The momentum of the campaign and the votes of the citizens are based on appearances and the loudest noises, kicks, and bites. It is the modernized version of betting on a horse at the races. People tend to ignore the true character of the candidate and they rarely consider the potential trouble or benefit that the candidate may bring upon them.

Most parents train their young ones to be the fastest running horse, as do most schools. Male and female students are educated to be the best competitors for gain and honor in life, while natural gender functions and important human virtues are ignored. We suggest that to change the destiny of humanity, you do not become or support the fastest running horse in the race of life or in the race of the world. Rather, we encourage you to learn to develop and balance your natural energies for true fulfillment and benefit, both personally and socially.

According to the deep vision of the *I Ching*, nature can sometimes be as wild as a horse, and the nature of human society can be even more so. Instead of expanding the male hormonal effect by being a fast running horse, you can develop and balance yourself to be a good rider of your wild horse nature, of life itself, and of the undeveloped human society in need of spiritual learning.

We direct our effort to correct the cultural conceptions that worship the strong horse type, and support instead ordinary people living a naturally constructive everyday life. The health of society comes from the healthy, balanced behavior of its government, businesses, and people. The problem of world culture is that it glorifies the excitement of social rivalry and ignores the truly productive people that help the normal health of society.

To put it simply: please be a good rider of your life and of the wild horses of the human world. You do not have to prove that you are the strongest horse in school, among your friends, in your workplace, or in the larger society. People with the strongest kicks and bites have difficulty in life and have proved to be big trouble for the world. Value, instead, the normality of your constant and constructive efforts in achieving health and balance in all aspects of your life.

All wisdom in life comes from the reproductive force of life as it is transformed from a coarse substance into a refined essence. The heavenly energies can sharpen this sense of life. Sublimation is the practice of reforming and uplifting your internal situation, which includes your mind and emotions. Respect the strong individuals who constantly improve themselves in life rather than those who use their coarse natures to conquer the world. We encourage you to change your perception of life and be good riders rather than strong horses.

Can You Be a Good Rider of Life?

You cannot be a good ruler of your own life or the life being of a society unless you really understand the nature of life. Look deeply into your life. Life has multiple levels; it goes beyond the mere externals. The internal information of your life is what subtly affects your health and enjoyment. Even so, most people live at the external level.

Today's overly externalized life is caused by the unbalanced dominance of the masculine principle. People don't see the subtle sphere of life, which is the deep sphere of life. In the early days, people called things that they could not see or understand "spiritual." Religions were established upon an insufficient understanding of "spiritual" matters. By putting bits together, certain individuals created the picture of a religion that they could promote to the public. Religion was mostly a way of expressing society's emotions about matters they did not clearly understand.

The deep levels within your life, which manage you less than your apparent thoughts, are subtly affecting you even if you generally don't notice them. There are at least four elements reachable by analysis.

(1) Deep emotions and hidden desires, both of which are strong. They do not however last as long as the other subtle matters in you, such as:

(2) The conscious flow of your mind, which is affected by your real life experiences and the health of your genes. All these things affect your health and good performance in life. As well, there is:

(3) The internal light of life—your conscience and rationality, though these may be weak. These elements can be strengthened through spiritual self-cultivation.[1] Above that you still have:

(4) Numerous spiritual entities within you. Through self-cultivation and spiritual practice, these entities can be developed and unified to enable you to reach the deep, subtle sphere of nature, which is almost the same as the internal subtle elements in your life.

The Mental Frame to Achieve

Generally the term "party" means a group of people who gather together to look for political gain. This is not the meaning we use here to address the party of new spiritual friends and allies we are looking for.

Careful observation of human social life, throughout its long history and even longer prehistory, shows that people form a social force or voice in search of dominance, which does not necessarily bring real progress. Mostly this behavior brings negative results rather than positive contributions. Why then would we adopt the term "party?" Is it a political party, a revolutionary party, or some other new monster we are going to create?

Do not suspect it for one minute! None of those is our interest. Head horses everywhere have played those games among the masses. They are continued as the world's evil competitions that repress the world's health and, at the very least, create a lot of waste in society.

We envisage a party that is revolutionary in nature, but does not engage in the practices of the general parties that tear each other apart to enjoy social and

---

1. You may look into our many other publications that have been written to support your own efforts toward fulfilling your inner potential through spiritual self-cultivation.

political dominance. Such practices are part of the darkness of the world of undeveloped human nature.

The revolutionary direction of our efforts is to support your determination to have a spiritual self-revolution over whatever causes harm to your life's health and to the life of the world. Be proud that the purpose of your strong ambitions and real attempts are not to change the world or any other people, but yourselves. A truly good and healthy world can only be achieved if each individual, like you, works on it. The goodness of the world can be attained by not bothering to change the world and other people, but by valuing the principle that all individuals can work to change themselves.

You can see that unless each member of society works to improve themselves, any conception of paradise in one's life and in the life of the world is mere self-deception. The concept of paradise has been used to lure people to die in vain for unachievable and nonexistent purposes. It is a real tragedy that the trouble of the world has led many to such an end. You do not need high and deep spiritual development to conclude that exclusively external efforts are in vain. You can know this by simply observing the long history of humanity.

We are looking for allies to save the world through individual self-change, and to leave others to make mere external efforts for mere external gains. Social revolutions, political changes, religious salvations, and racial reasons have not uplifted people from their deep darkness. So far, most efforts for world improvement have led to a deepening of worldly trouble, due to the self-deceptive approaches that were taken.

Our personal efforts of lecturing and book writing have not been able to help the majority of people, but they should not be left uncared for. It is time to refocus our work and enlarge our service by adopting a broader vehicle, maybe in the form of a party, to help people out of their wasteful traps. With this intention we wish to reach as many people as possible, and suggest to them that we start a spiritual self-revolution. Do not be fooled by any of the conventional social programs from anywhere or from anytime. Have respect for your own spiritual self-reflection, because deep in your conscious mind there is no one else who is able to inspect you, supervise you, control you, and teach you. Only you can develop your real life.

To start with, real life means to have a true and clear conscious condition and a developed conscience working together to support your life. Then naturally, with all these beams of light, the wider human society will have no need to continue its dark condition.

We have made our spiritual vision concise and clear to earn your precious consent to realize that your own spiritual improvement is just as important as the external aspects of your life, if not more important.

The Direct Meaning of This Movement

Human society tends to be unavoidably self-destructive due to the drastic growth of the human population. People experience their life wearing out quickly, as they bear the burden of both the old and new conditioning from worldly life. The mental condition of a healthy baby before the age of three is therefore chosen as the model of life.

A baby practices indiscrimination toward any well-presenting person. It carries the natural happiness of life before the process of contamination and the possible total loss of life from entering deeply into worldly life. The baby reminds us to keep our spirits evergreen—beyond discrimination and prejudice. This is the salvation for humankind at this stage of life.

The Clear Purpose

Individually, the purpose of an evergreen life is to regain the pure joy of life. We do not need to wait to win the lottery before we become happy. We pay a heavy price by living life quantitatively, while ignoring the fragility of our health. It is understandable though, as we are driven by a strong sense of insecurity or social honor to own more. However, it is better to balance this drive with a real taste for a plain and simple life.

The purpose of this spiritual movement is universal spiritual unity—above and beyond any specific religious expression—for the whole of human society. All religions are at the same level; they are still external. We can think differently, however, through our valuable reflections from our deep consciousness and conscience.

The Support

The pressure of modern life can cause stress to any individual. We can help ourselves through the spiritual learning of the Integral Way, which integrates the essence of natural life in the world.

Socially, we can be supported by the universal spiritual unity that is beyond any specific religious expression. We all need to be aware that this is a critical time for unity.

The Spiritual Light in Life

The Integral Way is the inspired wisdom from taking the entire human life as one life being, and from the external observation of nature and other people, and the deep experience of individual life. It merges the objective and subjective efforts of one's life.

The Way serves as the spiritual guidance and the groundwork for individual and social progress toward reaching universal spiritual unity.

In each individual life and in the life of humankind, the Way stands for the truth that the nature of each individual life and the life of the universe is physically and spiritually united. This unity cannot be split by human conception or belief, though people's emotions and frustrations may create temporary darkness in personal and societal life at some stage or another. Radical thoughts or behaviors do not express the health of universal nature, and thus no hostility or prejudice should be insisted upon or continued.

The Light of Everlasting Life illuminates the path that all human people are one race and all human societies are one big family.

The Moral Pursuits in Life

(1) *Freedom*

The spiritual ambition of this effort is to support you in achieving the authority for self-rebirth into a new life of spiritual freedom in any situation. This means that you will experience an enduring spiritual life. For all individuals pursuing self-cultivation and discipline there are three inescapable goals, whether you accept them or not.

(a) The freedom from physical illness and disease.
(b) The freedom from emotional stress.
(c) The freedom from impulsiveness and the ego's insistence on personal ideas and opinions.

Only those individuals who are able to achieve every one of these freedoms can be the real leaders for world freedom. It seems you have quite a number of things to take care of in your life before you can stand up and proclaim that you can save the world.

(2) *Equality*

    (a) All people should have equal responsibility for the health of society.

    (b) All people should have equal duty to improve the living conditions of worldly life.

    (c) All people should have equal love toward all other people of the world.

(3) *Humanistic Love*

    (a) Offer love to the spiritual effort made by the individuals of the past for the spiritual progress of all people.

    (b) Offer love to the spiritual effort made by the individuals of the present for the spiritual progress of all people.

    (c) Offer love to the spiritual effort made by the individuals in the future for the spiritual progress of all people.

The Spiritual Implementations

There are three basic things that we should always respect.

(1) The right of survival of all races and tribes.

(2) The birthright of each human being, as each possesses equal spiritual potential to develop themselves.

(3) The efforts of all people to make a decent living.

In general life, we have to nurture and strengthen the God within. We need to exercise our conscience to give judgment from within our own inner Supreme Court on the following things.

(1) No personal gain or profit is more important than your effort to keep the world clean and healthy. Therefore, nothing unclean or destructive should come from your industrial or creative activity (such as your writing, moviemaking, and so forth). This is important because the intellectual condition of most people is such that they cannot distinguish the recreational life from the real life and thus they are all too ready to imitate what is not true.

(2) Do not let any public support such as social welfare become your permanent lifestyle.

(3) No law that goes against human nature should be respected.

(4) No judicial system should be placed above human ethics.

(5) No executive powers of government should be placed above humanistic purposes.

(6) No social supervisory system should be valued once it has created trouble.

(7) In current times, people are used to being entertained, but you should keep in mind that the skill of campaigning is not equal to the spiritual quality that public duty requires. Confused influences can come from skillful political campaigns that sell falsity, and people pay a huge price when they wrongly choose a public leader based just on superficial attraction.

(8) There is no examination or qualification system that demonstrates the real capability of a public figure except for the actual service that the particular individual gives.

One who exercises their conscience in the above circumstances is more respectful than one who merely knows and talks about them.

The Historical Models of Humanistic Spiritual Effort

Throughout the life of humanity there have been a few great individuals who led the public toward a new and better direction.

Outside Ancient China

Moses was an outstanding individual who, in 1320 BCE, presented the Ten Commandments to the Jewish tribes. He represents the human effort to break away from the slavery of unruly emotions and improper desires. This effort can extend to all types of slavery resulting from improper emotions and desires. He also raised human spiritual dignity to that determined by God.

Sakyamuni (563–483 BCE) is a great model. He sought a solution to life's troubles and pains and found it in the attainment and constant maintenance of peace of mind.

Jesus (4 BCE–30 CE) is an individual of the highest moral nature. With humanistic love and in a situation of need he was ready to die for the survival of others.

Mohammed (570–632 BCE) is a model of spiritual bravery. He challenged the low spiritual practice of idolatry. He believed that people can live by directly embracing the universal spiritual unity within them, and that there is no form that can be recognized as the final Truth. Unfortunately he is idolized, and idolization hinders the inexpressible unity of the universal life.

Inside Ancient China

Fu Shi is the representative of a whole period of human development during prehistoric life prior to 6000 BCE. Among his other outstanding contributions, he was the first individual to focus on eugenics to ensure the health and survival of the human race.

Shen Nung (reign 3218–2078 BCE) discovered vegetation and herbal medicine as a new survival source for humankind.

The Yellow Emperor (reign 2698–2598 BCE) set the course for humanistic civilization by valuing the Way—the normality of Nature—as the universal standard for individual and social life.

Lao Tzu (active around 571 BCE) shows and teaches us how to conform our individual lives to the normality of Great Nature.

Confucius (551–479 BCE) continued the social efforts of Chou Kung Dan, known as Duke Chou (active 1104 BCE) by promoting the clean blood policy and the orderliness of social, family, and personal life.

Each of these individuals has something to teach. If we only learn from one of them, we would miss the important traits of the others which are useful in different circumstances of life. Our personal recommendation is that while you may respect and learn from them all, a balanced personality and life should be your main goals.

The Toddler Steps of the Giant Infant on the Spiritual Path

Human life developed from small families into large clans. Self-reliance was strongest during the clan stage of life. From clan life, communities were formed and from communities, regional societies were born. It was at this time that some people began to woo social favor for their life's support rather than rely on their own earnest labor. Eventually nations were formed from the big societies and some people became interested in seeking public power. The civilians began to admire those in public office, even though those individuals were interested in living off the public rather than eating the grain gleaned from their own hard work. Some people prefer not to live a self-reliant life.

That new lifestyle gave some individuals special privileges and control over others via the establishment of regimes. The creation of religions and priesthoods did the same. These new social systems of political and religious authority spread everywhere.

Once these public social authorities were established, they wooed people to support them. In some situations the political and religious bodies worked together to ride on the shoulders of the people. The rulers sought the favor and support of the religions out of the need to secure political power. Once religions became part of the ruling political force, social darkness was created. In other situations, the government and the religion became rivals and the government, out of fear of losing political power, persecuted religion. These were the new social situations that evolved after small communities joined together to form bigger societies.

In earlier times, there were some governments that integrated their political force with religious persuasion. Tibetan society is an example. One third of the Tibetan people's income goes to support the religion. Most conventional societies accepted religion as a ruling partner, like the European countries in their early years. The United States, as a new country, was the first country to separate religious and political powers. This new social arrangement differed from the previous convention whereby the social leader and priest worked together in public decision-making.

Independence between government and religion should be supported because the two systems offer different services. Also, due to the intellectual growth of people, governments have no need to rely on religion instilling the fear of God to help their decision-making and ruling processes.

As open people, we should learn from the world's historical lessons to help shape a better future. Below are historical events showing how governments have used religion to mislead people.

In 303 CE, the Roman Empire persecuted the Christians.

In 392 CE, the Roman Empire adopted Christianity as its national belief, and its people fell into the darkness of religious control.

The next type of ruling system was created in China, where society moved from a mostly unenlightened public to the semi-dark control of the ruling dynasties.

During the period of the Three Kingdoms (220–264 CE), a new spiritual movement stirred the public and rivaled the political ruling system. This was unprecedented. The warlords fought it and leveled the military riot begun by the group known as the Yellow Hooded Bandits. Though the new group used the name of Tao or the Way, it was not the same as the great public spirit of the Way carried by Fu Shi, Shen Nung, and the Yellow Emperor. Nor did it come from the teachings of Lao Tzu and Chuang Tzu. After winning the war, the three warlords divided the nation into three.

In the early Han Dynasty, the government and general people sought guidance from Lao Tzu, and through his teachings the Han Dynasty reached a high peak. But later Emperor Wu changed its course to one of more power and expansion by reforming Confucius's teachings to support raising the emperor's power to be above all. As a result, society began to decline. Ambitious people created religion to stir up social turmoil, while the general people began efforts to truly help their society.

During this period, the scholars turned to Chuang Tzu in search of an explanation for the meaning of life. People's warmth toward Chuang Tzu was high. He was recognized as second to Lao Tzu, similar to the way some people understand Paul's relationship to Jesus. Also there were two outstanding scholars, among others, who deeply studied Tao from the books of Lao Tzu and Chuang Tzu. These two active and influential figures were the eloquent Hur Yen, son-in-law of the strongest warlord Tzu Tzau, and his friend, Wong Be, a talented writer.

The cultural fashion created in this time, with its profound research into the attainment of Lao Tzu and Chuang Tzu, paved the way for the reediting of

Buddhism—which led to the creation of Big Vehicle Buddhism (or Mahayana Buddhism) in the later Tang Dynasty (618–906 CE). It also helped in the development of Zhan (or Zen) Buddhism in the Tang Dynasty.

The purpose of integrating cultures into a new big religion was to provide a service that could meet the needs of all people. The effort did not cease with the Tang Dynasty, but has continued through all generations since. It influenced later people to form different sects or new spiritual teachings such as Immortal Taoism, which appeared around the end of the Tang Dynasty, and which adopted Zhan as a part of its conscious training. Neo-Confucianism, also called neo-Taoism, arose during the Sung Dynasty (960–1279 CE). Others appeared during this same period including the Thunder School of Taoism.

These events tell mostly of the efforts of the Chinese people to help their society, but what did the ruling governments of China do?

In 286 CE, Emperor Wu of the Jing Dynasty (265–419 CE) officially sponsored the translation of Buddhist books.

In 405 CE, the short-lived regime of Hau Chin, established by one group of the five border tribes who invaded China from Mongolia, made Buddhism the state religion.

In 505 CE, the northern Wei regime adopted Buddhism as the state religion.

In 527 CE, Emperor Wu of Liang (502–550 CE) became a devotee of Buddhism with the intention of using it to rule. In 546 CE, he preached Buddhism to the kingdom.

During the Tang Dynasty, Emperor Tai Chung (reign 617–650 CE) accepted the advice of his supporters and used Confucianism to rule the country and Buddhism to rule the minds of the people. This policy became the distant cause for China's slow development in scientific research and investigation. Japan was one beneficiary of the new cultural system and it still carries the cultural heritage of the Tang Dynasty today.

In 642 CE, Princess Wen Cheng of the Tang Dynasty married the Tibetan King Chien Tsun Ron Tsiang and together they created Tibetan Buddhism.

In 645 CE, Shuan Chuan returned to China from Hindu (now India), having lived there since 629 CE. With the government's support, he was officially assigned to lead a group of monks and scholars in the translation and creation of the Big Vehicle Chinese Buddhism, which later developed into ten sects.

In 666 CE, Emperor Kao Chung, the son of Tai Chung, retitled Lao Tzu as the Most Superior Emperor in Heaven, not only for his own family honor, but to compensate for the biased policy of his father who had ignored Taoism and its abundant knowledge of health and longevity.

In 684 CE, Queen Wu of the Tang Dynasty enthroned herself as the first and only Empress of China by creating Ta Yon Ching as a Buddhist classic to support a female ruling power. She formed the sect of The Sublime Classic of Buddhism and officially recognized the teaching of Zhan Buddhism and supported the people's spiritual effort to reach the truth.

In 694 CE, Manichaeism reached China where it was reedited to be the sect of Pure Land Buddhism. Manichaeism also helped in the creation of the later Ming Dynasty (1368–1643 CE) that delivered the people from the cruel Mongolian rule of the Yuan Dynasty (1280–1368 CE).

In 794 CE, the Tang Dynasty erected a stone tablet officially recording permission for one branch of Catholicism to be active in China.

In 895 CE, the government of Emperor Wu Chung of the Tang Dynasty suffered from the bitter fruits that had grown from his ancestor's overzealous promotions of Buddhism. Luxurious Buddhist temples were everywhere, land was in short supply, and people became monks and nuns just to enjoy a leisurely life and obtain a lifetime license to enjoy free food from civilians. The number of licenses issued by generations of previous emperors was enormous. The government's revenue was greatly decreased and the country's social strength was weakened. Thus the Emperor decided to abolish the Buddhist temples and order the monks and nuns back to a normal life. Persecution was necessary for the order to be effective.

In 1054 CE, the Greek and Roman Churches separated.

In 1055 CE, the Sung Dynasty made a religion out of Confucius's teaching and titled his descendants with official positions.

In 1119 CE, Emperor Fei Chung of the Sung Dynasty exalted Taoism and rejected Buddhism. His motivation was not racial bias; rather he believed that by promoting Heaven to the northern tribes, who worshipped Heaven in the same way as Taoism, they would be less likely to attack the inland Dynasty.

In 1194 CE, a Confucian scholar, Chu Shi, became head lecturer to the Royal Court and all its ministers in political and social matters. He intended to use Confucianism to strengthen his rule, but the overly philosophical approach only weakened the society more. This sowed the seeds for the later successful invasion by the northern border tribes.

In 1260 CE, Passipa, a Tantric expert from Tibet, became the royal spiritual teacher to the Mongolian ruler of the big empire, which included parts of China. Subsequently the Mongolian emperor indulged in the practice of Tantra and neglected his ruling duties. As a result, he ended up returning to Mongolia in defeat.

Eastern people and their religions are generally more amiable. Their religions mostly teach people to weaken their desires and improper ambitions of life. Western people and those in the Middle regions are harder to rule. Their religions tend to excite people to action. This is exemplified by the military expeditions of the Christian Crusades in the 11th, 12th, and 13th centuries. Rightly or wrongly, this social behavior for religious causes sowed the seeds for the tragic terrorist attacks in New York on September 11, 2001, which involved racial hatred.

In 1295–1336 CE, the Franciscan Order of Catholicism, which was active in China, taught people to remove the tablets used as memorials to their ancestors.

In 1302 CE, France began holding national meetings to deny the authority of the Pope.

In 1366 CE, the British parliament passed the decision to no longer offer taxes to the Pope.

In 1521 CE, the Pope excommunicated Martin Luther (1483–1546 CE) from the Catholic Church. Luther subsequently founded the Protestant movement and completed his translation of the Bible into German in 1534.

In 1534, the British Catholic Church became independent from the Roman Catholic Church.

In 1560 CE, Nicolaus Copernicus's (1473–1543 CE) theories and discoveries of a solar-centered system and moving earth caused the Catholic Church to fear that they may lose control of their business.

From 1563–1598 CE, the French engaged in an internal religious war.

In 1620 CE, the British deported the Quakers to Plymouth, Massachusetts starting its history in America.

In Europe, during the 14th to 16th centuries, the Renaissance Movement occurred. It was the rebirth of art and learning, as human nature revived itself from the extreme social control of the Catholic Church.

In the late 19th and 20th centuries in Russia and China respectively, the communist revolutions adopted and intensified the Catholic Church's total social control —an excellent teacher in the creation of social darkness.

Religions can also be used by leaders to genuinely aid the masses. For example:

In 1622 CE, one of the new branches of Buddhism, the White Lotus Sect, was among the religious groups which rioted against the Ming Dynasty (1368–1643 CE) already weakened by the Manchurian invasions.

In 1717 CE, the Ching Dynasty (1644–1911 CE) had enjoyed ruling China's abundant inland territory for some time. However, it found that outside enemies and vanguards from Western countries were colonizing and making religious conversions deep within the territory. Thus the Ching Dynasty forbade the spread of Catholicism in China, largely because Catholicism denied the validity of ancestors, which were the source of their lives.

In 1805 CE, the Ching Dynasty forbade Western priests and ministers from preaching in inland China.

In 1870 CE, the Christian Churches were burned down in Tientsing.

In 1899, an anti-foreigner uprising was started, which resulted in China being invaded by eight Western countries. The Chinese rioters thought the foreigner's religions were of no value. They found them to be no better than their own popular religions of Confucianism, Chinese Buddhism, and Taoism.

Today, the political situation of society has somewhat improved. As open people we should all update our spiritual condition to move forward into a bright future. We need to remember historical lessons and seemingly meaningless melodramas of the past, because we can use them to refresh our life spirits as ever-new, rather than passively being fed with decayed food from their out-of-date kitchens with their unhealthy materials.

The Universal Integral Way stands for the spiritual learning and wise reflections from the real life experiences of all generations of humanity. People of the Way pursue the Evergreen Spirit of Everlasting Life. This means to undauntedly and bravely live with a developing spiritual vision and use it determinedly to dissolve the darkness inside and outside of one's life. Wayfarers are not defeated by the difficulties and troubles that plagued their ancestors, or by any historical mistakes made by the social leaders or undeveloped masses. They prefer not to float on society's surface by amassing big power or wealth, but embrace the deep strength of life and become the latent supporting root of the everlasting depth of human society.

The Hope: What is Important for Now?

The ethical condition of the world needs to be improved. The aim of the Universal Heavenly Way is to improve the ethical condition of all people and all societies in the world. This is the basic fulfillment of all individuals who accept the spiritual light as a service to their precious life. Socially, men and women have an equal spiritual responsibility for the well-being of their society. In other words, each individual needs to achieve cooperation between the masculine and feminine principles to manage a balanced individual life and balanced human society. This should be the focus for the future of humanity.

Due to the domination by the masculine principle over the past three thousand years, the world has been spoiled. The masculine competitive atmosphere has made it difficult for most people to earn a living. As a result of all the social competitiveness between the different societies with their established religions and strong tendency toward masculine-centered societies, the world teeters on the brink of destruction. It is even the custom of some religious faiths to actually create and support war.

War and aggression began to develop when an interest in slavery arose. In the primitive and barbaric stages of human society, one community might aggressively attack another for the purpose of taking the strong men to increase their male labor force. They would also take women for mating, and the physically weaker men as slaves. In those times communities were self-sufficient. The elder women were the authorities of the younger ones, both male and female, in the community. People did not know their fathers, but they may know their maternal uncles. In most communities the men were simply satisfied by eating and mating. The women guided and held the family and clan together. At that time the main application of the masculine principle was to protect the clan. Naturally social evolution takes place when the means of living changes.

The main feature of a meaningful civilization was to restrain and reform the abuse of the masculine force. This is the simple meaning of civilization.

Today, humanity has not made enough progress. Even the new life of recent generations still cannot enjoy the mellowness of the ripe fruit of a sufficiently developed humanity. Thus, we need to make practical and wise endeavors to encourage further progress in the world. With a real, civilized approach, human relationships can be improved. Knowing that the world suffers from an exaggerated application of the masculine principle, we can see that world salvation will come from applying the feminine principle to correct the imbalance.

The source of the world's trouble lies in the fact that people are born with biological natures and natural impulses. The more physical, masculine principle has been overpracticed in most societies. Thus, spiritually vigilant women need to mobilize their deep life nature, which tends to be more spiritual, to help guide the world to see and turn away from the crisis of competitiveness that is leading us to total destruction. It is women's natural duty to guide people toward social cooperation for spiritual progress.

Both Maoshing and I offer our voluntarily help for this significant effort. We have no interest in being the strongest horse in any society. Maoshing and his male spiritual associates will respond to your requests of help and will support your great interest in such an effort. A safer and better world society can be achieved by women, who for too long have been made to hide behind the world's social screen.

Although the early human societies were matriarchal, the majority of societies and communities entered the masculine-dominated world around three thousand years ago. Inside China, patriarchies grew in the Chou Dynasty, and outside China Judaism rose. Both these events marked the trend of social change. One thousand years later, Catholicism presented the male-centered spiritual concept of social religion. The male soul of the Roman Empire borrowed the feminine form of the newly instituted Christianity, in 392 CE, to extend its male-centered control. And although Jesus's teachings were used, they were not deeply understood.

The source of Jesus's teachings is the Way. Jesus taught humanistic love and tolerance in support of a safer and better life for all. However, it was the self-proclaimed student Paul, a young Jewish scholar, who enhanced the flavor of Jesus's teachings with male-centered views from his own blood and patriarchal cultural background: Judaism was thus created.

The social expansion of Catholicism could not hide its aggressive masculine tendency under its new spiritual intention. This would have stimulated Mohammed, who also faced physical struggling among the Arabic tribes. The masculine instinct did not deter Mohammed's efforts to develop a new spirituality. Like Jesus, he adopted the Way of spiritual unity of all people. This universal spiritual unity cannot be presented by any particular image, name, or ritual, nor is it restrained from being interpreted in different ways. Islam recognizes some of Jesus's teachings, but as the later religion, it was created in a different social environment and one where male-domination was already strong.

Human mentality and deep thought is influenced by gender. Real spiritual achievement is to be above the influence of gender or social discrimination.

New cultures and religions may, in their beginnings, present some social progress. Human social progress cannot happen all at once. No progress is perfect. However, once any social practice becomes rigid and stiff, it hinders any new progress that was developing. If we eliminate the one-gender bias from the cultures and religions outlined above, we can see that all of them have made some degree of social contribution at certain stages of human life.

In the past two thousand years, each of the male ruling systems in the different regions of the world have used or created religions as a means to help reduce rebellious activity. Today, most people choose to rule themselves rather than be controlled by a single ruler. All those old religions have had a strong relationship with the political system of the society. Their purpose was mostly to manipulate the emotions of people to cheat them into accepting the ruling system, rather than serve people directly. We have outlined the major events of the past two thousand years to present the facts of the mixed intentions of masculine rule throughout history, and to show how men used religions to help create a class of social parasites.

It is now time for women to exercise their natural spiritual duty to help the troubled world. Women can reset the course of human society by encouraging the masculine and feminine principles to each fulfill their different natural functions and help each other find balance. Men are the more muscular type: it suits them to conquer the rough challenges of life. Women are gentler: it suits them more to serve the lives of people. Looking at the past, it is obvious that spiritual help and teaching people to be cooperative is more feasible work for women rather than for men.

Now is the right time for meaningful and useful change. To facilitate this change, it is best that all people support spiritually developed women to engage in spiritual leadership to guide their societies to a new and improved stage of life, just like women have previously devotedly done for their families. In this new millennium, feminine spiritual leadership is assigned to prepare a universal society with no discrimination whatsoever; a society where each person can exercise their right to live and grow fully and, at the same time, offer great contributions to society.

The Sisters of the Universal Heavenly Way (SUHW) will work toward realizing this society's content in order to improve personal and social ethical standards. That can be the only real help to improve the world condition. Your support and help for this task is very much appreciated and respected.

The Fulfillment of Health in Life

Spiritual work is your personal and worldly fulfillment. It should not be used to establish any type of social force for suppressing others. Realize that it is for actualizing health in your life and in the life of others and the world. Through the joint efforts of all good people, the spiritual goal of universal unity may be achieved no matter how long the journey takes. This guidance and the following guidance and goals are also the suggested direction of the SUHW.

Outward Goals

(1)   The improvement of the ethical condition of humankind.

(2)   The restoration of the natural joy of a clean and healthy life.

(3)   Finding and following the peaceful solution to all conflicts.

(4)   Starting a worldly cooperative effort for the better life of all people.

The above four points interpret the traditional term of virtuous fulfillment.

Inward Goals

(1)   Attaining the understanding of life that is beyond the narrow presentation of current systems such as anatomy, physiology, biochemistry, genetics, psychology, sociology, and general religions.

(2) Finding a better way of life by engaging in the joint research and study of life and through real life experience.

(3) Finding and enjoying the art of living that is the personal development that comes through finding individual solutions.

The above three points interpret the traditional term of spiritual self-cultivation.

The Green Lights for Modern Life

(1) Do nothing to risk the health of your life.

(2) Do nothing to damage the dignity of your life.

(3) Refuse the world's social and cultural pollution that can affect the well-being of your deep conscious life.

(4) Do nothing to harm the pure joy of your natural life.

(5) Absolutely do nothing to go against the Universal Subtle Law of life.

Your Study

You are welcome to study the publications of the Universal Integral Way, also known as the Teachings of the Heavenly Heart. They aim at universal spiritual integration. There are four recent publications that focus on the new situation we have outlined: *The Centermost Way, Enrich Your Life With Virtue, The Foundation of a Happy Life,* and *The Majestic Domain of the Universal Heart.*

There are also *The Teachings of the Heavenly Heart: The Path of Constructive Life* five-part series of which this book is one.

There are other important publications to suit your personal and group study. Do not expect great English from these books. They are the plain record of generations of spiritual effort—free from any socially confused intentions. These books are for your self-study. You can also join or form a local study group to enrich your life with spiritual healthy growth.

We respect those people who are saving the world by cultivating and disciplining their individual lives and who, at the same time, are not losing interest in helping the public. Individuals of social capability and social conscience may become registered mentors, spiritual coaches, or they may simply exercise the best of themselves and conduct themselves as spiritual leaders to help others move together toward the common direction we have outlined.

The Universal Correspondence

In the traditional version of the *I Ching, Chien* in Hexagram 15 means to be modest. In it there are four lines like these:

(1)   The Way of Heaven diminishes the overextended, but gives to the humble.

(2)   The Way of Earth shifts the plentiful, but flows to the humble.

(3)   The Way of Deities decreases the overexpanded, but blesses the humble.

(4)   The Way of People dislikes the overstretched, but supports the humble.

I present these lines here so you can compare them to Jesus's teachings on the Mount, around one thousand years after King Wen's writing of the *I Ching*. As I see it, Moses, Jesus, Mohammed, and other spiritual models all fulfilled their historical mission in their times. Lu Shiang San, a scholar of the Ming Dynasty, once said:

In the eastern sea there are sages and in the western sea there are
sages, and though they are different people their hearts are the same
and the laws they present are the same.

When most of those spiritual individuals did their teaching they were much younger than I and much poorer than any of the people who listen to me or read my books. If they were alive I would invite them to comment on today's big mess, which by the way none of them were responsible for. It was the later people who used the influence of those spiritual teachers to create new problems for the world.

Your   Support   Can   Make   a   Difference

Anyone who respects that the inexpressible universal spiritual unity is above all, and appreciates that that unity cannot be represented by any one fixed symbol, voice or terminology can be a member of the Spiritual Evergreen Party, which works to refresh your universal spiritual standpoint. You do not need to convert from your personal faith. You may remain faithful to whatever religion and custom you believe in.

People can manipulate the expressible level of spirituality, thus you need to be discerning. Different expressions will naturally arise as people come from different backgrounds; differences are part of nature. But the expression and practice should be decent and without any trace of hostility. What is important is a universal ethical standard as described in the *Heavenly Way* booklet[2] and in the first book of the Teachings of the Heavenly Heart five-part book series called *The New Universal Morality: How to Find God in Modern Times*. A universal ethical standard describes what is most essential about you. Conceptual differences are no reason to make enemies.

---

2. See Chapter 18 for a new elucidation of Hua-Ching Ni's *Heavenly Way*.

We invite you to spiritually support a peaceful and orderly world. All decent spiritual practices are respected. There should be no rivalry in the real spiritual sphere of life or the world. Rivalry expresses an insufficient spiritual reality.

The spiritual sponsors and alliances for this cultural and spiritual promotion are:

The Union of Tao and All People
The Integral Way Society
    (formerly the Universal Society of the Integral Way)
The Taoist Global Mission
The College of Tao
The College of Spiritual Science and Art
The Sisters of the Universal Heavenly Way
Yo San University of Traditional Chinese Medicine
Tao of Wellness Clinic

And the many individual supporters that, hopefully, includes you.

PART III

Feminine Leadership is Natural Leadership

"Accentuate the Gentle Virtue"

Chapter 5

Putting the World Together Is Our Spiritual Effort— and Yours, Too

Dear Friends,

In early times, the world was smaller. Or rather, it was the scope of people's life vision that was smaller. Each community needed to make its own effort to spiritually order itself, based on its stage of growth.

We have taken millions of years to come to this point. Now we need to connect all spiritual efforts under one effort to avoid confusion and offer real help. But first, we have to improve our own less competent spiritual quality. This effort we retitle as the Constructive Human Spiritual Effort or the Path of a Constructive Life.

As descendants of the Yellow Emperor of China, we enjoyed the same euphoric dream that we were the center of the world; we were the masters, until the Tang Dynasty suddenly opened its doors to many far-reaching countries.

People came from all sides of the world to audience with the great Emperor Tai Chung (617–650 CE) of the Tang Dynasty. Along with their national products as gifts, they also brought their religious customs and worships. At that time, each had its own living territory and there was great peace among them all. There was humanistic love and no hatred expressed, at least not to China with her self-sufficient territory. All these different cultures congregated as a great assembly in the one big hall of Tang. For the first time in human history, people could witness many colorful and dazzling cultures gathering in the Central Kingdom.

After absorbing all the cultural efforts of the different human races, Emperor Tai Chung worked with great vision to create a new inclusive spiritual teaching. In his eyes, no religion was perfect enough to meet all spiritual and emotional needs. He decided therefore to take the best from all religions to set up a new big religion to serve all people. Emperor Tai Chung chose to reedit and develop Buddhism, which was already well-known in China and its border countries. Many great spiritual masters from these regions gathered for this work.

The new spiritual effort can be traced back to the time when three influential individuals—Lao Tzu, Sakyamuni, and Confucius—started to shape a great religion to teach the masses. The new effort contained, as its main seam, the spiritual marrow of Lao Tzu's teaching in the *Tao Teh Ching* and, as its promotional tool, it adopted the popular style and mass language of Buddhism; not deeply into its bones, but simply as a framework. The new work broadened and developed original Buddhism, which was the mass language, but old Buddhism was still kept as the Small Vehicle for people who were used to it. The new merged work included the essence from all religions and faiths and was called the Big Vehicle Buddhism. It also retained some early spiritual beliefs from Sakyamuni's heritage. Though Emperor Tai Chung continued the work of those before him, the new integration was definitely his individual effort, a creative synthesis of his time.

Tai Chung's motivation was pure and great. His goal was to develop a service to people of all levels. As spiritual workers and researchers today, we cheer this open spiritual leadership. The new religion was also known as Mahayana Buddhism. It uplifted the spiritual and emotional lives of the Chinese as well as the people in the border countries, such as Korea and Japan. Today, Japan still reflects the cultural model of Tang, while Korea maintains some of the older cultural heritage from the Central Society of the Shang Dynasty.

In the new broader Buddhism the concept of Buddha was improved. No longer was Buddha a single individual known as the spiritually awakened one, but the image of a static sitting figure to illustrate the Way; a spiritual symbol of the Way of non-being or the subtle essence of the universe. The statue represents the highest spiritual principle of The Being of Non-Doing, not in the negative sense but in the sense of denying the vulgar competition that people often strive for. Instead, people are encouraged to live with the normalcy and constancy of universal nature, away from struggling and fighting. The name Buddha now contained and incorporated God from Catholicism, Jehovah from Judaism, Allah from Islam, Ahura Mazda from Zoroastrianism, and the Divinity of Boundless Light from Manichaeism, and many more.

Emperor Tai Chung's vision inspired two female individuals. Princess Wen Cheng was one. She was the Emperor's niece and was arranged to be married to the King of Tibet. Through her spiritual creativity a new spiritual culture was formed in Tibet, to China's west. Through family relation and connection, the Tang Dynasty helped Tibet reedit their old practices to form a new worship for all people: the Buddha of the Multiple Rays. Empress Wu (reign 684–705 CE) was the other: a talented woman who dared to take the lead in a male-dominated society as the first and only Empress. She ruled aggressively and though I do not support or praise her tactics, I recognize her for commanding the cultural integration and for having the vision to officially accept Zhan Buddhism. She allowed individual seekers to have free thought over spiritual matters and toward the royally adopted and established Big Vehicle Buddhism.

This new integration was the effort of China's Central Society, which the Chinese thought to be the center of the world. They realized that spiritual integration was their responsibility. In truth, this has been the direction of Chinese culture since the time of the Yellow Emperor, when it was called the Way.

The Way needs renewal; it is not always the same. New generations come and new effort has to be made. Lazy people insist on the old because they've lost the sense of creativity from a life of ease.

The Tang Dynasty was a creative time in history. It respected the poets. The poems of Tang are great expressions of the genuine feeling of beautiful nature with the spirit of the broad faith of the all-inclusive spiritual style. From the poems of Tang, we learn to appreciate nature with our great lives. Religions are descriptions to represent our great life. They are external depictions with internal meanings.

In human culture, there should be variety to present the abundance of life. And if we nurture our power of spiritual perception, we will be able to enjoy them all without conflict. That is what I am doing and I can take you there.

A humble life, I was brought up in the cultural environment that I described, therefore it's not strange that since my childhood my simple life was meant to continue the constructive spiritual effort of humanity.

As I see it, in early times, people built walls and set doors to exhibit their specific differences with their specific distinctions. Each claims to hold the spiritual secret and to have made the special deal with the high realm. As a naughty boy I tore down all the walls and doors to see the Divine Oneness of all.

I have done that for my life and for the lives of others. I did that in past lifetimes and in this lifetime. Because life carries the permanent essence, that essence, no matter how big or small, whether as big as the cosmos or as small as the tiniest basic particle of the T'ai Chi, carries the same essence of the Universal Divine Oneness.

Now it's your turn to make the spiritual effort to be there, to witness what you are made of and what you are continuing to be. I have my limitation though, and cannot do it for dodo heads, even if you insist. You have to be enlightened. You have to be totally awakened. You have to be absolutely liberated. No matter how long it takes you, then you will see the Divine Oneness of all.

Do not be afraid of hard work, though, whether you prefer to do it by yourself or simply use our books as help. We have made our work the simplest and the most inexpensive vehicle for you, the self-help travelers of the Way.

Our work can help you improve your vision which has been covered over by the dust of your intellectually segmented education and experience of worldly life. Through learning and cultivation you can restore your mind's healthy function, which will then take you further to see the truth that is beyond all verbal communication.

The Integral Truth upholds the life of the universe. At the core there is no more discrimination of God and people, world and us, man and woman, and so on. It is your unimproved vision that keeps you troubled and confused. You have no other choice but to improve your spiritual vision. Until you're able to do that you will not fight, life is too precious for that old game, and you will not cry—for whatever you cry over does not represent any real importance.

All people are spiritual babies. You have to learn to grow. As babies you need adults' care. Now you have to help take care of the world. She is our spiritual baby. We ask you to take on the trouble of the unenlightened world. Although its people have been too noisy, we love them anyway. Let all people grow together and love each other. Follow closely what we say here: The Universe is One Enormous Being. All People Are One Life. There is no you and us, only God's love in all.

The Heavenly Father shines upon us. The Mother Earth raises us. The Divine Light of Universal Divine Oneness keeps us from falling into a self-destructive end by war. Keep away from the stupidity of repeated world wars and do not be misled by your own or anyone else's blind impulse.

We are all one great life being. The happiness of life, the peace of the world, and the destiny of humanity is all tied to our good faith—the great faith in the Universal Divine Oneness.

Love, OmNi

Chapter 6

The World Needs a Goddess
(Kwan Yin, the Aspiration of All Women)

Although Emperor Tai Chung's political and social contributions were well-known and celebrated during his time, few people recognized his spiritual and cultural achievement in creating the new Big Vehicle Buddhism. This is because Shuan Chuan (569–664 CE), as head editor of the new and broader Buddhism, led the general people to believe that all the sutras came from the Kingdom of Buddha (now India). Under his work, the six hundred volumes of *The Sutra of Great Wisdom* were accomplished in one gigantic collection as a Buddhist Canon, obscuring the fact that the work represented a new creation and great cultural integration of the time. This new synthesis, a spiritual achievement, contained new and broader conclusions made by Shuan Chuan and his big team of several hundred teachers and scholars, including representatives from China's bordering regions.

Among the purely new work was the set of sutras called *The Great Sutra of the Big Vehicle* and *The Great Wisdom Enabling One to Cross the Bitter Sea of Life to the Other Shore*. It used the deeper spiritual vision from the *I Ching* and the *Tao Teh Ching* to update the sutras and teachings from India and other regions.

When I was a child, my father's hobby was spiritual work, just as mine is today. Alongside his Chinese medicine practice, he taught those sutras to monks and nuns who devoted their lives to spiritual pursuit.

The *Heart Sutra* was derived from the first chapter of Lao Tzu's *Tao Teh Ching*. Authored by Shuan Chuan, it introduced the key practice of *Kwan* in spiritual life. *Kwan*, in general, means to watch, observe, experience, witness, and reflect. In spiritual terms, it is the spotless spiritual perception as the highest capacity in people.

The direct experience of life means to witness the nature of the world and life itself. Usually it is associated with pain and troubles. Spotless perception is the key power of life. It produces the integral vision of the world we live in and the life we live. That was the main flow of the ancient spiritual culture of the Way. It differs from using intellectual force to explore the small things and produce a segmented and partial view of life and the world. This, though, is the modern fashion among the various branches of human knowledge.

Both Maoshing's and my generations witness a new phase of humankind on the earth, and new spiritual efforts should be made. We have been educated and guided by our family, the descendants of the Yellow Emperor. Our efforts are to link the two best functions of integral vision and intellect together to serve the world and all life. This is why we reintroduce to you the Power of *Kwan*. It is the top function of life, but because most people have not developed it, it is new to them. During the Tang Dynasty the Power of *Kwan* was personalized as *Kwan Yin*.

The Way is the principle of great balance and harmony in both the big society and in each individual life. In the teaching of the Universal Way, *Tao* represents the natural balance, whereas *Teh* is the Humanistic Way to accomplish life in society. *Teh* literally means virtue. From the perspective of *Kwan*, to accomplish is to be considerate, to yield, harmonize, and cooperate. These spiritual qualities derive from the feminine principle, which was worshipped far back in human history. For renewing the teaching of the Way, *Kwan Yin* carries the image and the spiritual vision of the early developed leaders.

Kwan Yin is commonly known as The Goddess of Mercy. She was the new interpretation of Nu Wu, the mother of all human life. In legends, Nu Wu created people on earth. The worship of Nu Wu was even earlier than the time of Fu Shi, and after Fu Shi another Nu Wu continued his reign. I imagine that all earlier female leaders were addressed as Nu Wu.

Kwan Yin is also the new spiritual integration of the inconceivable Lady-in-Blue as worshipped by the early people of the Yellow Emperor's time. *Kwan Yin* was promoted to mend the single gender spiritual practice of religious Taoism and Buddhism. She also absorbed the Holy Mother Worship in Catholicism, since one branch of Catholicism appeared in China during the Tang Dynasty. She is the motherly image of Confucius and Menfucius, both of whom were educated by their mothers. In their time, and even in my time, most people were educated by their mothers. *Kwan Yin* has also been used to promote Mahayana Buddhism.

To people of the Orient with purer mentality, the different ideology is less important than the real service. Mostly, they accepted *Kwan Yin* as the highest spiritual guardian to all life.

Mahayana Buddhism once stood as the newly integrated big religion that was a cultural effort led by the constructive vision of Emperor Tai Chung. He was advised and assisted by the spiritually developed people of the time. Our efforts are no different from the great heart of Tai Chung and Shuan Chuan. Our work, *The Majestic Domain of the Universal Heart*, is derived from the egoless, ageless, and devoted spiritual work of our forerunners. Our personal and family efforts have therefore been devoted in the same direction of humanistic benefit since Fu Shi.

Shuan Chuan was the genuine author of *The Heart Sutra*. He was an eminent individual with a similar birth experience to Moses. He helped Emperor Tai Chung fulfill his great dream of creating a big new religion to contain all the good teachings of humanity. Shuan Chuan was also the first student to travel to other countries beyond the west mountain range of China. His purpose was to attain all spiritual knowledge with Lao Tzu's vision of nature as the foundation. He knew that there were different levels of spiritual teaching in the world.

From his lifetime attainment, Shuan Chuan produced *The Heart Sutra* and introduced the new goddess, *Kwan Yin*, as a popular elucidation of the Power of *Kwan*.

My parents deeply appreciated his work, and it has been the most effective help in teaching people for many generations.

Most people, including the scholars, mistake its source. I am grateful for my parents' direct teachings and their deep knowledge of history. They recommended that I respect and learn the heart of Tai Chung and Shuan Chuan. Thus, in appreciation of their work, Maoshing and I continue this effort to improve people's spiritual condition. From our own development, we wish to serve the current generation of people with all their different spiritual backgrounds.

In conclusion, we would like to invoke the wisdom of Shuan Chuan, the last few lines from his masterpiece, *The Heart Sutra*.

> *Go over to the other shore.*
> *Go over to the other shore.*
> *Make your mind cross the bitter sea.*
>
> *Wisdom is able to help you*
> *go over to the other shore.*
> *That is to develop your vision*
> *to see through all the illusions of life.*
>
> *When you are on the other shore,*
> *there is no more other shore.*
> *But all your troubles are merely your illusions*
> *that you have insisted to be so real.*

Chapter 7

Who is the Goddess in You and in the Universe?
The Goddess of Merciful Life

Goddess of Merciful Life supports life in the subtlest way.
She is at the innermost center of life.
Look inwardly,
She is behind layers of veils to the seeker.
Look outwardly,
She is external too,
with even more layers of veils,
which are invisible to the seeker.

Internally or externally the veils obstruct life,
before such life attains development.
Developed life sees the connection—
Goddess, Mother, Universe—
extending and connecting with the physical.

She has no form,
is beyond imagination.
She can be drawn.
Notice or not,
She is with us.

She is the gentlest.
She is the most merciful.
She is the supporter and giver of life.
Far and near at the same time.
At our right, left, front, and rear.

She can be everywhere, nowhere,
reached at any time of the developed life.

Subtle wave of the inner life,
far behind formed thought and voice.
She is the one that begins the inner life in the outer.
Seen in deep peace beyond the activity
of conscious energy.

Gentle, soft, everlasting vibration
gives forth the form of life,
but remaining formless herself.
Subtle, immeasurable wave of the cosmos
surpassing the wave of light.

She supports whosoever reaches out to her
with similar vibration
they receive healing and revitalization.
She cures all pains, wounds, and
grants all volition with devotion.

She is reachable through the spiritual common sense of the Way.
People with the will find the Way,
not with personal struggle, but with her help.
The seeker in most need is satisfied
as the gentle flow of her subtle wave reaches the life.

She is all-capable.
She is far-reaching.
All physical things are produced
from the flow of this cosmic inner fountain.

Touching the deep heart
whenever and wherever,
giving safety and peace.

From the pores of the skin to the deep marrow
the shallow life starts to change.
In to out—then to the entire life,
and at some special times—a direct audience
with the Goddess's divine light.

Transforming life from
roughness to fineness,
coarseness to subtlety,
the seeker can reach perfection,
but not to stay.

Goddess of Merciful Life is the flow of the cosmic life.
Goddess of Merciful Life is the flow of the natural life.
Goddess of Merciful Life is the flow of the everlasting life.
She is the Goddess of Merciful Life of my life.

She is invisible, inaudible, and untouchable by the physical,
unless seekers know how to develop life itself.
She is the connection to the tremendous, subtlest life of the Mother Universe.
She performs the connection between the small and big life.

She is the prime potency of life of the physical universe.
She is the subtle essence being reached by Lao Tzu.
She is the Invisible *Yi*,
the Inaudible *Shi*, and
the Untouchable *Vi*.

She is the One.
She is the beginning.
She is throughout all time and space.
She is the strength of the evergreen life and
the power of the everspring of life.

People worship what is describable,
but the deep truth is indiscernible.
People worship the highest,
but the deep spiritual truth is unknowable.

In order to be rough and tough,
people create God as rough and tough.
But only they are rough and tough
by not seeing the subtle truth of the universe.
Through self-containment and the gentlest of being,
which is not emotion, a connection is made from my life's depth
to her subtle, gentle, and merciful life.

She is the Way.
Though the Way has various interpretations,
She is what is behind the Way.
No interpretation can reach her.
She is the everlasting power.
She is the source,
the very essence of the Universal Life.

Developed lives can witness her as *Lyn Chi*.
She can thus be nurtured and developed
by spiritual self-cultivation.

Delicate, yet most efficacious spiritual energy

of life and the universe.

She is the root of all wonders.

She is the most wondrous,

above all wonders.

She is in us and outside of us, at the same time.

She is with us in life

as we conduct our lives with healthy normality.

Chapter 8

Which River Runs Deeper, Longer, and Broader— the Euphrates or the Yellow River?

The development of human civilizations is related to those rivers that run through the lands. The Nile River in Egypt, the Ganges in India, the Euphrates in Babylon, and the Yellow River in China, all these big waters have produced different influences, which is why the early Chinese sages made water the symbol of wisdom. Religions are but an expression of how people orient their minds and emotions toward Great Nature. Although different human conceptions of life have been shaped, the reality that supports them continues to run deep in today's human culture.

Looking at the influence of the waterways, one can see that both the social Christianity of Judaism[1] and the later religion of Islam carry the cultural influence of Babylon, which grew around the Euphrates River some 4000 years ago. The Babylonian culture marked the time when paternal-centered society began. God was given the male image of the tribal chieftain, the grandfather and father figure of a family, and the family gradually grew into a whole clan of the same race. As a result of this exaggeration of the masculine principle, the later patriarchal stage of human society has become the arena for beast-like physical competitions. Previously society had long been matriarchal.

In another part of the world, the Yellow River fertilized the land feeding people whose ancestors had produced a vision quite different from the ever-growing male culture on the other side of the world. And this was so even though this society had also entered a paternal stage in the Chou Dynasty around 3000 years ago. To these people, Mother Nature reflected the image of God. From the begin-

---

1. Jesus's real spiritual background is the Way, which exalts the feminine principle rather then the masculine one.

ning, the early people had directly perceived God as feminine-natured. They observed that God bore the responsibility for nature's reproductivity, and thus considered God to be female rather than male, motherly rather than fatherly.

In other words: in the beginning, there was the subtle origin, which was indistinguishable from the reality of nature; there was no need for male and female differentiation. For the purpose of reproduction, however, the Motherly God split herself in two to create a separate male. The male is thus the instrumental creation of Mother Nature and, since the purpose of the universal nature is reproduction, the male is a part of the female and the tool for reproduction. The male's prime natural function is to help fulfill the motherly nature of the female, which is to bear offspring and nurture the young.

Therefore, according to this natural function of the man, their bossy tendencies are simply for aiding the fulfillment of the woman's role. The male brain, however, is limited and not able to see the extent of their life's natural role. Instead many overextend themselves, doing much more than they should by proudly expressing their male machismo just as peacocks do. They amass big money, compete for high social positions, and engage in intellectual exhibitionism, all just to attract women. Truthfully and biologically, there's not much more in it than that, though historically men think they have the main role to play in society. Based on the natural view of reality, all the feverish fighting and war is simply to support this male sense of superiority. Such behavior is utterly foolish.

Generally, the life strength of a woman is much stronger than a man. A young woman is physically capable of taking ten men in one day's cycle. Can a young man take ten women in one day's cycle? If he does, he usually ends up dying very young like most of the emperors in China. Men tend to die much faster than women. From the aspects of longevity and durability, who then is the boss in family and in society? Most men think they are thus causing their own confusion and the confusion of modern women, who imitate their foolish behavior and bring trouble into their lives. But if men lose their vision of natural reality, they are incapable of keeping up with women. Truthfully men are the assistants, and though they can hold bottles of milk, and later, wine, they think they are the bosses in life. Historically, the wise men were students of women.

The young Yellow Emperor was told by the Virgin Messenger, the Lady-in-Blue of the Yellow River that:

> *First, there is Mother Nature.*
> *From Mother Nature, Ti, or God, is formed.*
> *Ti, or God, is female-natured.*
> *She splits herself in two—yin and yang,*
> *as the dual, mutual, and spontaneous functions that*
> *accomplish one another in everything.*
> *There is no superior sense between the male and female.*

The need for propagation made the sexual characters of male and female gradually distinct. Then came the need for the distribution of duties in life. The men take care of the living source, while the women take care of what is internal to life, mainly procreation and the raising of the young.

The proliferation of the human race began with a couple, which gradually developed into a family and then into a clan. From the clan came a race and then societies began. Society is in endless succession. Confusion and disorder are often expressed among the different races even though all human races are one race. In the sense of life, men and women are both the rib bones born of God— the life of the universe.

In any generation, there are few people who see the root of life. They see that their lives are the nature of the universe and they live in harmony with Mother Nature. They live with the open spiritual nature of the sky and the healthy bodily life of the earth. Though their minds and bodies are two, the unity of life is what they pursue. By being and doing so, they do not waste or abuse their lives. Others, however, compete with life and abuse their lives by ignoring the fact that their lives are a part of Mother Nature. Living in union with the subtle depths of Mother Nature is the real spiritual instruction to all advanced human lives.

Chapter 9

Plow to Plant Flowers
(The Universal Family of the Universal Mother)

The teaching of the Way existed long before written history, when the world was still natural and artificial organizations had not yet appeared. Throughout countless generations, some of its ancient conceptions and practices have survived and are still valued today.

The teaching was not artificially contrived like that of the social religions, which appeared much later, when leaders imposed social discipline to secure political rule. The teaching was conducted naturally and openly, as a family and as a sisterhood, to serve people in need. My (OmNi) own mother practiced and continued this universal, spiritual teaching, which is also known publicly as the Path of Pure Light. It has been far too long to remember all the names of this family's spiritual ancestry, but a few I remember well.

Fu Shi was a leader in prehistoric times. Although the Way's spiritual ancestry began long before his time, he was a great model of the Way and became well known for developing the "line system" of the *I Ching*. Nu Wu, a female spiritual leader, continued Fu Shi's rule around 6000 years ago. Then, around 5000 years ago, the Lady-in-Blue educated and assisted the young 17-year-old Yellow Emperor to defeat the aggression of Zhi Yu and his nine-tribe alliance of barbaric cannibals, thereby heralding the beginning of humanistic, civilized societies.

Around 3000 years ago, the mother of Lao Tzu gathered together the entire ancient cultural heritage to teach and transmit it to her son. Around the same time Duke Chou, following his father's (King Wen) vision in establishing the Chou Dynasty, aimed to do away with the insect-like and degenerate lifestyle of the earlier societies where men got what they wanted through physical supremacy. Unfortunately, that sense of masculine supremacy has continued to dominate women throughout generations and has naturally transformed to become the general social and financial supremacy of men in modern times. Confucius continued the positive social effort of Duke Chou. Educated by his mother, Confucius endeavored to update the order of family and social relationships. He became known as the cultural leader of the "clean-blood" principle in family life.

Some early human cultures influenced the later social religions. For example, elements of the Old Testament in the Hebrew Bible were adopted from the cultural heritage of the Babylonians. The story of creation in the *Book of Genesis* was a Babylonian folktale, adopted by later religious leaders who convinced people to believe that the story was actually how the world began. Though the folktale has mythological value, it has no value as the Truth. The myth was adopted to mark the shift from natural societies to male-centered societies in human history. It was less than 3000 years ago that Jewish scribes edited the Hebrew Bible and secured it as their social faith, and less than 2000 years ago that the New Testament (which, in addition to Jesus's teachings, absorbed the Greek cultural heritage) was used to support the establishment of Christianity. Jesus's teachings were misunderstood, however, and the belief in a father-figure God only served to perpetuate the paternal society that had begun with the Old Testament.

In ancient China, the shift from natural societies to patriarchies took place almost simultaneously as it did in other cultures. Yet, unlike the other races, the people of ancient China had a natural spiritual faith in Mother Nature, known as the Way.

Since the time of the Old Testament, western culture has been heavily male-centered and none of the natural influence from the early matriarchal societies has survived. Naturally, whenever an extreme stage reaches its peak a compensating movement appears as a natural adjustment. Thus, as a natural consequence of the extreme religious darkness in the West, when religious faith reigned supreme and humanistic values were denied, the Renaissance was born to bring a sense of humanism back to the West. There came a spiritual liberation from the male-dominated religious culture, and the encouragement of an intellectual perspective of life that sowed the seeds for the development of modern science and art.

But with the growth of science came a divorce between the spiritual and intellectual sides within the Western mind with the West taking an awkward detour in its desire to produce a modern culture. If Western culture presents *the* benefits of a modern culture, we would have to say its society also paid a heavy price of splitting one's life being in half.

Currently in the West, the spiritual side of life is suppressed, while earlier the physical side of life had been restrained. Western culture has swung from one side of life to the other. As a result, a gap exists between the physical and spiritual aspects within each individual. Neither side is able to meet and integrate with the other and fulfill the completeness and balance of individual life and human culture.

Although China's naturally developing culture did not suffer the same disadvantage, it has nevertheless been weakened by the West's strong influence over the last two centuries. After the Industrial Revolution, Western societies found new strength through growing capitalism. China could not resist forsaking its healthy foundation of a natural life for the new Western ideology, despite the fact that it was an untested social creation by people from a totally different cultural background. Though the new ideology found a warm bed in China, it took the Chinese people in an unbalanced direction. The generation of Chinese who pursued the modern fashionable culture and relied on the different economic information to provide a superior cultural service ended up wasting many people's lives. They also lost their natural faith for so-called progress.

The cultural and spiritual mission of the Universal Integral Way is therefore twofold: to help modern Western people find the Way and to help guide a modern China out of its confusion and restore its natural faith. The well-being of China, home to one quarter of the world's population, is significant for the health of the entire world.

The spiritual health of the individual and the society depends on an integral perspective in the direction of life's great balance. No one should value only one part of life and suppress or devalue the other parts. This is what has been done in worldly culture. The world swings back and forth from one aspect of life to another without any correct social or cultural direction from its shortsighted leaders. As a result, the majority of people suffer.

For example, in defining individual health the modern tendency focuses on the physical side and ignores the spiritual side. Under this partial health standard, the perpetrators of the September 11 terrorist attacks in New York, who were quite physically sound, would be considered healthy even though their spiritual and psychological condition would be definitely unhealthy.

In the field of medicine, how can a standard of health that is derived from a partial and one-sided understanding of human life be relied upon to make balanced decisions about people's well-being? How then can we help the world? The world and each individual cannot be helped unless a new standard of health is established and recognized by all. The foundation for such a standard, both for today and the future, should be established above all cultural and religious viewpoints. Only behavior that is conditioned on the new health standard can be considered as the benign behavior of healthy individuals and groups. The world should not be guided by religions, politics, or different ideologies. It should be guided by universal healthy and constructive standards. The universal healthy standard is above all standards and is called the Way by the ancient developed ones. It is the new direction for all individuals and societies.

The Way is common to all people. It does not present any personalized or partial view of life; it presents the universal standard and integral vision of life.

The Way is the health of each individual life and the health of all things, whether big or small, that is above all standards and that comes from an integral focus.

The Way is the standard of health for society.

The Way is presented by healthy political performance.

The Way is not like popular conceptions or ideologies that are only good for a few people and a few things, but damaging to all other people and to all other things.

The Way is not the social policy of any one location or another. The Way applies universally.

The Way is the applicable medicine for all problems. Good medicine uses an integral evaluation, while bad medicine uses a partial evaluation, which may be good for a few people but is bad for all others.

The Way is an ancient natural development that applies in all life and in all societies. Naturally, it is the first principle one uses to value the quality of a culture.

The Way is the nature of life and the nature of the universe. It is different from social religions, which are the social promotion of some society and which are mostly artificial additions to human nature. Some can even be considered cancerous to the organic condition of human life.

The Way is not the highest standard. It is not to be considered as unusual or uncommon or the best. It is the achievable universal standard. It is the common good, the usually good, and the achievable good.

The Way is not the standard of religious saints, some of whom were more subnormal than normal. Religious good is not necessarily humanistic good.

What is unnaturally or unusually good is subnormal and problematic rather than healthy. That which cannot serve or apply universally is untrue. Inhuman good is not beyond the Truth of life.

In the 1950s, I had a conversation with a Southern Baptist friend of mine about the nature of God or Truth. Here is the essence of what we spoke.

God is good. God is the common good. God is not especially good. God is for all people, not just for a special few. God is like the shooting arrow that strikes the bull's eye. God is the center—not left, not right, not too high, and not too low—but just right.

My friend laughed, I laughed, and we all laughed. I respect and love my friend and his family, who devoted their lives to divine work and who, unlike most clergy, had a true attainment in the great faith of the Way. Our friendship came out of sharing the same humanity, not out of any artificial religious style of relationship. Real human life is natural and that is true divinity. Generally, what religionists establish as divinity is not true to life and therefore it is untrue divinity.

I appreciate my father's teaching known as the Subtle Light and my mother's teaching known as the Path of Pure Light. I trust that even though the Mother Universe has multiple expressions and interpretations of the Truth, the Centermost Way[1] that my parents taught strikes the bull's eye of life.

No matter what the time or place, when religious dominance prevails, the human personality becomes unbalanced and spiritual darkness is experienced. It is like a Dark Age. People living in spiritual darkness become unhealthy and suffer. They miss the center of life and become partial to emotional comforts. They lack physical activity and truthful spiritual support. A balanced life needs the healthy integration of all three aspects of life—mental, physical, and spiritual—as well as true related support. No culture should use a partial approach to value things and alternate between one aspect of life and then another, thereby missing the focus of balance.

After many generations, the universal spiritual family of the Integral Way remains to teach normalcy and health in individual and cultural life. The Way is the direction for all individual lives and all societies. Its importance should never be neglected in favor of overly-promoted religions or political ideologies. The

---

1. Refer to Hua-Ching Ni's book *The Centermost Way*.

world should not go the way of some particular person or some artificial belief; it should go the way of universality and humanism. With this spirit we can free ourselves from the games produced and conducted by overly ambitious leaders.

In the West there is a saying that behind every great man there is a great woman. The reference to a woman usually implies a great wife. In China, however, the great women were mostly mothers, not wives. Around 2300 years ago in China, Menfucius (372–289 BCE) traveled among the feudal kingdoms preaching the humanistic love of kindness and righteousness. He was a genuine teacher with no personal social ambition. Menfucius's mother used the influence of the natural, living environment to shape and educate him. He became the most popular teacher of his time.

Jesus was also educated by his mother around 2000 years ago. He was both godly and humanistic. By no means was he an imitator or a hypocrite like the religionists of his own and later times. How powerful a personality Jesus had that he earned respect from at least two artificial religions. In truth, however, they do not respect him. They use him to conduct their social con business. From the Dead Sea Scrolls you can discover that Jesus was a good and normal person. He was a genuine spiritual teacher; not a mob leader as portrayed by some religions. The graves of Jesus and his mother are still in existence in Kashmir, India. This fact cannot be covered up forever by the religious lies that have existed for over 2000 years.

My own mother also devoted her life to the work of the Way and teaching its plain truth to people and society. She was very active during her lifetime up to around fifty years ago. During my childhood she might have had the ambition to become one of the greatest mothers that ever lived. How else could she expect to make a piece of jade out of the piece of tofu that I was? Should this humanistic effort be forgotten?

Up until modern times, mothers were the main educators, spiritual teachers, and moral disciplinarians of their sons and daughters. Now there is a great deal more social interference in the raising of children. This has damaged the deep meaning of life and the spiritual connection between children and their mothers. It has further stripped away women's sacred role and position. Where then do the capable women go? Many of them are busily campaigning for male politicians and are playing the worldly game under masculine principles and for a male agenda. Dear sisters, please campaign for yourselves. You have your own agenda of a safer world, a better life with more humanistic values and less social interference, and a fair relationship among all people, personally, socially, nationally, and internationally.

Human society has become so shallow and its people have become mere tools. Though people may be supported to have an education, modern education mostly turns people into taxpayers rather than educating them to have a sense of their natural spiritual life. As people become old they may become destitute because of this lack of true-life education. The trend of modern life has defeated people's sense of individuality and narrowed and diluted the family foundation. Are people mere robots with identity numbers, or are they human beings who should be allowed to live with and learn about the spiritual depth of their lives?

Young men may need to live like social animals to survive these days, but we hope they don't allow the dignity of their human lives to be degraded to the animal level. If they do, then millions of years of spiritual effort will be wasted. Instead, they may like to preserve the deep, natural sense of family and spiritual life.

Where do we search for the real guidance of life? There are only two books that record and preserve the natural truth that existed before the development of male-centered societies. They are the *Book of Changes* and the *Tao Teh Ching*. Although Lao Tzu wrote the *Tao Teh Ching*, it is mostly a record of the teachings of the earlier women leaders as gathered and transmitted to him by his mother.

The *Tao Teh Ching* means and stands for universal morality. In its latter part, it teaches how to fulfill the Heavenly Way through personal virtue and devotion. Both books serve to teach the way of a centered and balanced life, and were the inspiration and education of all universally kind mothers who lived before written history.

Though both books preserved the truth of achieved females, they have been translated and retranslated, edited and reedited to fit them for use in a male-centered world. What's the use? Most Chinese scholars of the last century thought the teaching was too passive. In reality, the teachings could be applied to help China withstand the international pressure and help guide humankind to safety and natural health. But the scholars had been educated and promoted by male-centered principles and so they only valued teachings that could help competition and winning. They could not see the lasting value of the Way and the deep truth of life as presented by the *Tao Teh Ching*. They believed that to survive personally and nationally, they must fight and win. Although their generation won the revolution in China, in the process many lives were sacrificed and many other lives were reduced to shallowness and superficiality.

How can people save themselves and their societies? Truthfully the only way out of the crisis of self-extinction is to follow the heart of the Universal Mother. The Way always wins; the clever ideas of human leaders always fade. Only that bidding from the heart of the Great, Great, and Great Universal Mother to live well and to do well can be trusted.

Chapter 10

Plow On No Rocks

The social troubles of modern times are like natural growing pains. It is a necessary process that can stimulate better quality leadership and the clarification of society's overall direction. Social leaders should be careful not to overestimate the ethical standard of their people. After all, people are still flesh and blood despite having evolved spiritually over thousands of years. Setting overly high spiritual goals can itself cause problems, as can the setting of no spiritual goals at all.

In human development, ethics should never be neglected. We can't expect to always be trouble free, but with emerging strong ethics we can at least move in this direction. Personal ethics reflect spiritual health and should be given the same priority as physical health. Ethics are the fundamental basis of a healthy life condition.

The neglect of basic ethics in individual lives and in society results in the downfall of humankind's spiritual quality. Spiritual cleanliness, good health, and a balanced life are more realistic and valuable than any of the fanciful holiness and sacredness promoted by the conventional religions. These latter approaches have only heightened people's spiritual fantasies and led them down blind alleys. Most religions are social psychology presented with the intent to influence people toward something other than the truth of life. Yet the truth of life is already complete within each individual, and no social psychology can add to it.

Before 3000 or 4000 years ago, the women, not the men, were the leaders of human society; family life was female-centered. People lived in communities without private property and everyone worked together to benefit the whole. Men and women naturally developed at different rates and with different spiritual qualities. Women developed their mental potential more quickly because they were less involved in men's purely physical pursuits, such as hunting. Because the women's minds generally developed faster than the men's, they provided the wisdom for family guidance, education, and care. As women did not keep husbands, the children usually did not know their fathers. Society was later formed from the expansion of this basic family way of life.

Gradually, as families developed into clans, and clans into races, the status of women as community leaders expanded. They earned the right to lead through their selfless service rather than through any aggressive means. The women did not compete with or conquer the men; both genders naturally coexisted for mutual benefit. Only after society grew and became more competitive did the role of women gradually decline.

Generally the women were more spiritually developed than the men. Some women dedicated their time to spiritual development in seclusion, and among them were those who developed higher wisdom and psychic capabilities. That is to say, they developed a keenness of mind, which results from the ultimate health of the mind. Few people today express such a naturally keen mind. Most express confusion, even the modern day psychics. Naturally, other members of the community began to rely on these early spiritual women for advice and they became the social leaders of their communities. Leadership developed naturally, not as a result of artifice, show, or cunning as we see in today's leadership struggles.

Our current social troubles started to grow only when people placed intellectual knowledge above the plain truth of life. In early times, knowledge was gained through personal, real life experiences, and the collective experiences of the society. Knowledge gained through personal experience is always more valuable and respectable than any gained through mental fantasies—the two usually do not work well together.

When people began to promote mental fantasies above the wisdom gained from their personal experience, they developed emotional preferences and disregarded the simplicity of their own hearts. As knowledge grew, emotional preference grew and internal struggling ensued, defeating the balance of life and inviting danger. The development of religions, a formalization of the mental fantasies and emotional preferences, served only to further disconnect people from simplicity and contentment. Intellectual knowledge and emotional domination overrode the conscience of spirit and, in the struggle, the balance of people and society was lost.

Later in those times, some of the women leaders began to show emotional preference for certain men. These men were given special privileges and became spoiled, living in leisure, while the other men went to work. Subsequently, when men began to dominate society, they continued this practice of emotional favoritism; they did an even better job of creating names and special institutions to clothe their misdeeds. Consequently, society continued to spiral out of balance, becoming more and more extreme and disconnected from its simple roots.

Generally, society is more troubled by its emotional preference-making than by its physical impulsiveness. Even though people are biologically driven with physical and sexual drives, these urges can be refined through spiritual practice; emotional preferences, however, are an unnatural extension of self-importance.

The stubborn adherence to privileges and to preferences for special religions, political parties, and other special groups does not add to the value of life. Rather these preferences generate sadness and discontentment—the basis of all wars, big and small. A little favoritism easily leads to partiality, bias, and social injustice.

Most religions grew out of uncontrolled emotional preference and they have been established in the world at great cost. They promote inequality among people, while supposedly searching for the fairness and impartiality of heaven. It would be more beneficial if people were taught justice, impartiality, and fairness to eliminate religious favoritism. Most religions do not do this. Instead, they tend to promote their belief system as the only way and their followers as the chosen ones.

All people are created equal by nature, but those in authority overlooked this truth when they established the practice of special privileges. Favoritism became the common convention of authority and it was supported by public emotion. When emotion is relied on as the foundation of society, trouble is not far behind.

Both men and women are equally responsible for the world's troubles, which are created by the groundless preferences of whoever happens to be in power. However, in today's society generally the men have led us into imbalance, for those in power still practice favoritism and emotional bias. Although we cannot make men disappear from positions of authority, we can try to decrease the pull of emotional preferences on public policy.

To amend the spiritual direction of the world, feminine principles should be adopted. For instance, we could choose a direction of greater acceptance and move away from the masculine tendency to separate and divide; we could choose more peace and less emotional violence. At this time, it is the softer side of nature that can benefit the world. It is the gentle strength of the conscientious mothers, not the machismo of the fighting sons, that can bring the world back to balance.

Religions would do better to focus on finding universally applicable beliefs and disciplines to contribute real spiritual value. True human spiritual effort is infinitely more valuable than ideology and empty rhetoric, and it is the feminine principle that most naturally adheres to this unassuming spiritual strength. When people abide by the feminine principle, there is peace and happiness. Softer and more malleable, the feminine approach gives the space needed for possible changes in direction. When people learn from the masculine principle, they may easily overextend themselves into contention, competition, and confrontation. Those who abide by the masculine principle often aim toward instant gratification and resolution, even if it causes problems for themselves and their opponents. Thus, although one may have done a great deal of planning over a long period of time, under the pressure of the masculine principle, resolutions must be instantaneous and binding. This approach leaves no room for compromises.

Women should now take the position of spiritual leadership and help men learn from the feminine principle. This is the remedy for our overextended competitive societies. But women should not attempt to emulate the male leaders and their exaggerated masculine approach. If women adopt masculine traits, it can only increase the contention, competition, and confusion—as shown by Empress Wu in the Tang Dynasty.

Empress Wu reigned during the Tang Dynasty. She usurped the throne and became the only woman ever to hold the position of ruling Empress. She was famous for her licentiousness and lavish lifestyle, and she manipulated religion to promote and support her strong ruling leadership as the sole authority.

Wu started out as a young court lady of the Emperor Tai Chung of Tang. In her position she was able to absorb the political skills and strategies of Tai Chung. However, where Tai Chung's policies were open and kind, hers, as Empress, tended to be sharp and cruel.

When Tai Chung died, his eldest son became emperor. Under the new custom of the day, Wu was sent to be a nun. The young emperor, who admired Wu, restored her civilian position and brought her back to the palace as queen. Being more capable, Wu soon gained control of the practical power, which later enabled her to take control of all state affairs and political personnel.

As queen, she took advantage of the former Emperor Tai Chung's new spiritual integration of Mahayana Buddhism to produce a Buddhist sutra called, *The Sutra of the Big Cloud*, to support a female ruling power. In all of Chinese written history, never had a woman been allowed to sit on the throne: it was culturally as well as politically forbidden. Once Wu changed the social precepts, she simply poisoned her husband and took over the throne as Empress. She made it clear that she would punish whoever dared to rebel against her, and many ministers were subsequently killed for doubting her or acting against her wishes. In achieving her ambition, she used the same schemes and tactics that were typically used by her male counterparts in the male-dominated society.

Empress Wu's sexual appetite (her "life strength") was not less, but actually stronger than that of the male emperors. Even in her eighties she still had to have sex, or she suffered from insomnia. Her obsession was unhealthy. From the perspective of a Traditional Chinese Doctor, I would say that there are healthier, nonobsessive ways to help one sleep.

Personally, I would give a different formula to women and to all humankind. The formula would include putting the world in peaceful order through the use of the feminine principle to end war and the effects of the Male Horse Complex forever.

Empress Wu ruled the vast country of China just as aggressively as any male ruler. One reason the Empress was so cruel was because men had taught her. She learned and absorbed all their shortcomings and excessive masculine tendencies. She used both the new Mahayana Buddhism and Tantric Buddhism to support her political and sexual power respectively.

As the product of a man's world, Empress Wu developed the conviction that as a female ruler you have to be crueler than the male rulers to avoid defeat. Was her conviction correct? Basically, yes. If a woman wishes to compete with men in a man's world, she has to be the sharper one. She might actually feel pressure to have no mercy in handling opponents. Whose fault is this? It was the men who gave the Empress the worst examples, and from them she learned well.

Attempting to establish total domination over all people is just one aspect of the Male Horse Complex. Most emperors who ruled before and after the Empress extended the same brutal authoritarian force over their people. They were the violent heads of the "Horse Society." Only a few rulers in Chinese history proved to be exceptions to the masculine, strong-horse ruling style. They were the ancient spiritual leaders of Fu Shi, Shen Nung, and the Yellow Emperor, as well as those emperors around 2500 BCE who ruled with kindness and wisdom rather than force.

Prior to 4000 BCE, human society lived in harmony with nature. After that time, however, society has spiraled away from the natural order. One worst example of social pressure occurred during the Dark Ages, a time of religious control in the West. More recently, the communist societies in Russia and China provided the terrible examples. Even America, with its so-called democratic system and capitalism, has forced people to rely too much on government and society: now people pay extra for goods and yet receive less freedom than people in ancient societies.

Empress Wu effectively used Buddhism to tame the masses of China, at least until the Sung Dynasty. At that time, scholars of deep reflection opened their eyes and realized that an overdose of religion had poisoned the normal health of human nature. To correct this situation, the Sung Dynasty swung back to the teachings of Confucius, but over relying on these teachings in turn stiffened people's natural lives. Then Religious or Folk Taoism became popular, weakening China's national defenses and leaving it vulnerable to invasion from the northern border tribes of Mongolia.

Religion's overly strong effects in Chinese society eventually weakened her scientific progress. We see the result of this trend in modern times as China has fallen far behind most industrialized nations.

The Yuan Dynasty of Mongolian rule followed the Sung Dynasty. There was no cultural leadership under the Mongols and so Tantric Buddhism returned from Tibet to China's Central Society. Sexual indulgence practiced in the name of Buddha weakened the battle strength of the Mongolian soldiers, paving the way for the Ming Dynasty to be established.

During the Ming Dynasty, so many great novels were written that it became known as "The Age of Great Novels." As people lessened their sexual indulgence, they regained the creative energy that they had previously spent.

The Ching Dynasty followed the Ming Dynasty. At that time, the Chinese people were still trapped in the ideological framework of Mahayana Buddhism. Tantric Buddhism continued to present a strong attraction to the Royal Court, as well as the general people. Then, at the end of the Ching Dynasty in 1911, China was thrown into massive cultural confusion due to the strong impact of Western influence.

The human road of spiritual development is a zigzagging path. People often choose to move like a sailboat headed directly against the wind; it is the same for all races and cultures on earth. Where religions dominate, a scientific truth-seeking approach to life is weakened and little or no social progress is made. The same is true for any society that adopts overzealous ideological controls—look at Cuba: what progress has been made there over the past 40 years?

Before World War II, most of the harbors corrupted by Western influence, such as Hong Kong, Singapore, Shanghai, and Havana were much the same. The colonialist input there might have sown the seeds for a constructive revolution if it weren't for the local leaders who ended up taking their people "out of the frying pan and into the fire." In an attempt to avoid the Western colonial extremes, the local leaders overcorrected their societies with communism. Although this approach helped to clean people up a little, it left them very lean and thin.

Our direction is one of balance rather than extremes. What we promote is a balance created by using both sides of the brain. With this approach, overly material and overly spiritual tendencies in personal and social life can be avoided. Though extremes can be interesting, they can also lead to corruption. For example, drinking to extreme or getting drunk at parties because everyone encourages you to is obviously not beneficial. Yet everything has a value if used appropriately. In certain circumstances, even Tantra has value. For example, if it helps return people from overly austere spiritual extremes. Similarly, austerity may be needed occasionally if it leads one back to balance and increased health. Tantra, however, is inappropriate for anyone whose lifeboat is already sinking.

In recent history, both in the East and in the West, women have been mostly responsible for domestic duties. Current social trends, however, lure women away from the home to perform the same duties that men conventionally perform. Most male socialists, as well as the modern feminists of this age, have neglected the differences in the spiritual and biological nature of men and women. Although in some overlapping frontiers of life, women and men can be equally successful and useful, it is unnecessarily stressful for women to try and conduct exactly the same duties as men. To improve the life of the world, we need to be open-minded and intent on observing and learning from our differences to attain the most balanced cooperation between men and women.

The basic differences between men and women should be appreciated and redefined. It is a shortcoming that modern society tries to eradicate rather than respect this difference. Overall, men and women have different individual needs, strengths, and weaknesses. This is why there has been, and always will be, the need to find cooperation between the two. Men need to learn to put aside their aggressive nature and allow women to guide the world with devotion, purity, and the feminine principle to turn people away from their old destructive habits.

The masculine tendency toward personal impulsiveness and aggression, as displayed in the wars of the past, has brought neither harmony nor unification to the human race. The spiritual quality of the masculine principle is not suitable for putting the world back together: a conquering force cannot establish harmony. A new respect for the feminine principle needs to be established to complete this effort. Embracing the feminine principle would bring the hope of creating a new trend in human history for the positive unification of all people. The reestablishment of the feminine virtues of cooperation, kindness, receptivity, reflection, and nurturing can serve all people throughout the world without the obstruction of racial superiority. It can usher in a happy and ethical life from now on, and mark a return to the beginning of history when women taught the Way.

In ancient times, the Lady-in-Blue of the Highest Heaven was the main teacher of the Yellow Emperor, who at 17 years of age followed the guidance of the feminine principle to effectively rule the whole country of China. For us, the Lady-in-Blue is still alive in the form of the beautiful blue sky.

Lao Tzu and Jesus were two other great teachers of the Way who were taught by women. Before Lao Tzu brilliantly elucidated the Way in the *Tao Teh Ching*, he learned it from his mother, an outstanding ancient woman who delivered Lao Tzu underneath a plum tree beneath the star-filled sky. Jesus was also educated and profoundly influenced by his mother.

The Way was the inspiration of ancient people who foresaw difficulty brewing in the future of the human race. The Way could also be considered the collective teachings of the achieved female leaders who bore the burden of human spiritual awakening during the earth's early history.

The early spiritual leaders focused on the balance of the masculine and feminine principles in society. Now the feminine principle is needed more than ever if a balanced international society is to be established. The world should heed the guidance of the Way and utilize the feminine principle to restore harmony to society. It should be the primary function of world politics right now to move toward spiritual harmony and unity for the benefit of the human race as one big family.

Unfortunately, few men so far see the need to shift toward the feminine principle in world leadership. This holds especially true where the shift is most needed: in the religious and spiritual sphere. Despite the ambition of some men to create harmony, the world is still in turmoil. The outstanding women of achievement could help shorten this long period of contention and end the physical struggle in this male-centered world through a spiritual educational approach.

As this mission is the new frontier in spiritual work, we sincerely encourage all wise women to develop a new type of leadership and begin the truthful fulfillment of balance in the world. Men who are wise will lend their support to women and recognize that this work of world peace and cooperation is the frontier of the women around them, their mothers, daughters, sisters, or wives. Some women may choose to live a single life of spiritual devotion, and they too deserve male support to help them serve in accomplishing this task.

Again, our simple request to any potential female leaders is that they do not imitate men. Rather, use your innate nature—the motherly approach that engenders the respect and attention of children. All mothers throughout the generations of human evolution have been most effective when extending their discipline with kindness.

The main theme of our spiritual tradition is set out in the *Heavenly Way* booklet, which is a basic text on personal ethics. As you know, today's main problem is the poor ethical condition and inferior morality of most individuals, businesses, governments, and religions. Social religions, as out-of-date products of the masculine principle, no longer serve this stage of human progress. Whether we are talking about Catholicism or Islam, both are extensions of the male dream of domination.

Catholicism, for example, actually represents the extended dream of the Roman Empire. Catholicism adopted Judaism, which was derived from the male instinct to protect society, while some aspects of Islam present the dream of the Arabic style of ruling the world. By extending the male dream of domination, all of them have created cultural conflicts in the world, and no one can tell when this tension will end.

For the promise of a new open world, we present to you a simple and different message. Instead of establishing a new set of rules or religious dogma, we need to improve the ethical condition of people based on a conscious and healthy way of living as taught by the *Heavenly Way*. The physical, emotional, and mental aspects of a human life will all improve naturally with an emphasis on improving spiritual health.

Our teaching carries the gentle bidding of an old Mother to her young ones. We ask all wise women to stand up at this time and continue this teaching through universal motherly love and help prevent a world crisis. The teaching of the Way is based on the belief that the universe is one life, all humanity is one family, and the earth is our shared home. We also ask that you do not use the names of sages to establish your personal authority or for negative social purposes as has been done in the past.

For example, Emperor Wu in the later Han Dynasty used Confucius's teachings to establish absolute rule. Similarly, Jesus was used by the Catholic Church to establish the divine right of the Roman Empire, the remnants of which you can still see today. Even Lao Tzu's name has been used at various times throughout history to promote various military efforts, including that of the modern religious Taoism. As well, Sakyamuni's examples and teachings have been used by some lazy-boned people to create a different type of Buddhism to escape their responsibilities in life. This type of false spiritual leadership has obviously brought no real social improvement.

My own teaching has been used for other people's material and personal status gratification. Some men have used my name to support themselves by selling "candy and chocolate," calling those things *chi kung*,[1] and using them as a special technique for making a living. They are conning people, and this nonsense is not my intention or personal wish.

The things they teach are merely unimportant exercises and small techniques. No truthful or great achievement can be attained by doing only those things, regardless of whether they are called *chi kung* or some other fanciful name.

We are not sages. We have been taught to accept that a correct personal standard is to be happy with an ordinary, healthy, and constructive life. This should be the standard used as much as possible in all aspects of life.

---

1. Also referred to as *qigong* or *chi gong*.

Our main message is the development of conscious and self-responsible health through the different stages of human life. This is the reason we have written so many books as support for people during the different stages of their great life journey. All the great sages who have lived in this world have had to develop themselves through stages, and so do you. Helping you with this process has been the main focus of our teaching.

Divinity is the true nature of human life, but spiritual development is needed for an individual to reconnect with divinity and enjoy a greater experience of true health. We feel women are better suited for transmitting this path of spiritual growth and for accomplishing the spiritual mission of updating the ethical condition of the world. People should take care that they are not carried away by religions. Rather, they should be very selective in learning from them. Some parts of the old social religions contain unhealthy elements that have been long established as social customs.

The religious promotion of an external God is man's mistaken attempt to instill confidence in life during times of difficulty. But it is wrong to substitute ideology for the confidence that comes from living a normal, healthy, and constructive life. This is like cutting down beautiful roses to replace them with plastic ones.

A clear vision of life is of utmost importance, but the old social religions cannot give us this clarity. With clarity, we regain our faith in the natural endowment of a complete and constructive life. This comes only as a result of our own effort toward ethical spiritual learning.

As men we have taken advantage of women for too long. Both physically and financially, we have overshadowed and held them down. We hope that the Mother of the Universe hears our wish and confession. We are dreaming for a stronger female role in our society.

If, in the future, female spiritual workers can support themselves by their teaching, we would openly support such a reality. As long as they do not abuse the privilege for the accumulation of power or the creation of wealth, like men have done in the past, their efforts should be supported. Men have long made a living out of what they do in the name of religion. It is women who should now be supported by men in their work for a safe life and an improved world. This is the way we men can pay back our mothers and all the women who have served and brought value to our lives.

To proceed, people could give up the goal of monetary gain and offer more to the world. The female ministers should embrace the motherly feminine principle in their work and in general life to foster balance and harmony.

To conclude our summary of masculine domination in society, let us just say that in a crazy world, men are the craziest. They are crazy by nature and are pushed by their sexual drive toward competition and domination of the world, like roosters and bulls in a futile fight for supremacy.

In the pursuit of pleasure and fun, moderation is the best guideline. When moderation is overstepped, real enjoyment is lost. Always look for balance in relationships and adhere closely to the natural joy of life. If we overextend ourselves toward either the material or spiritual realms, we are off-target.

To improve the destiny of humankind, we need to first do away with emotional preferences and save ourselves from personal pain. When this practice reaches the point of decreasing emotional preferences on an international level, conflicts will be resolved naturally. Although we must do the work individually, the benefit will extend to everyone. It is more realistic to do away with our own conceptual obstinacy than to demand justice from some deity in the sky.

Who among us will rescue the world? We might prefer to rule like Empress Wu, who ruled people like untamed horses that needed to be broken. If the horse could not be trained, it was killed. That is the typical psychotic attitude of tyrannical leaders. Rather than admit personal limitation or accept the organic nature of people and society, they have tried to shape the world by forceful means.

Many people have suffered as a result of their efforts and, in the end, these rulers carried nothing to their graves but their own empty dreams.

This kind of trouble has been repeated over and over again in the world. The ambitions of men continue to damage the organic nature of life and the world. We hope that the world is ready now for a different approach based on the gentle feminine principle. We hope our humble and plain advice can help everyone find balance in their lives.

The most important matter in life is the attainment of personal spiritual development. This is the highest contribution we can make to the world. Be a wild horse no more. Do away with all cruelty. Let us be content with our own simple good lives and not try to rule other people.

The strong horses usually like to be kings or queens, but we can follow the group as a gentle horse. Nature is like a horse that is sometimes aggressive and sometimes gentle; it is sometimes male and sometimes female. But as the god of our own lives, we can live beyond the duality of our own horse nature and learn to ride through life safely.

Five thousand years ago, the Yellow Emperor realized that teaching offers far greater value to the world than ruling. As his descendants, we have followed in his footsteps to replace the aggressiveness of our male horse nature with a gentle and balanced emphasis. Likewise, we hope you will also search for health in all aspects of your life. By so doing, we can together assist the health of the world in the most effective way.

PART IV

How to Effect Constructive Change in the World

"Beneficial Change"

Chapter 11

Give Back What Belongs to Women

In the early stages of our male-centered society, the spiritual traditions developed by men merely appropriated what women had originally developed. In prehistoric human society, people survived largely by virtue of their animal instincts. Men were considerably more physically violent than women, but since they needed mates, women also survived. Women, however, made greater use of their intelligence at a time when their life partners were so violently disposed. Their most effective weapon for self-protection was the ability to tell stories, thus spiritual culture came to be developed by women for the purpose of self-preservation. At the stage when there was an inherent choice to evolve and become more spiritual or devolve and become more physical, women managed to develop their spiritual abilities.

You may wonder how the ability to lie could be considered a spiritual development. This surprising statement is based on the fact that the basic nature of life is an integral partnership between semi-spiritual and semi-material particles. A human life is composed of these two apparently incompatible elements. When I (OmNi) was young, I was able to prove the truth of this theory for myself rather than accept what someone told me or what I read in a book. This is because I was a student of the spirit rather than of conventional religion. To truly know something, you must be able to prove it to yourself through your own experience.

You may wonder why we don't simply write down the process of proving the spiritual essence of life. Although spiritual phenomena are completely natural, experiencing such phenomena can cause problems if a person's mind lacks the necessary understanding to assimilate such an experience. An unprepared mind will respond by embellishing the experience with imaginary meaning and significance, based on its own limited awareness. This of course leads to spiritual storytelling and white lies. It can also lead to self-aggrandizement and the establishment of spiritual or religious organizations. Giving an unprepared person access to certain practices would be like giving them a bottle of genies: if you cannot manage them, they will manage you. Although the benefits of such practices would certainly enhance one's health and lengthen one's years, the disadvantages would be serious mental, emotional, and physical imbalance and illness.

When shamanism developed, the white lies of the medicine-women were small and stayed within the local community. As men took control of society, however, and began merely imitating the women, their white lies grew bigger and bigger to match the size of the society they built.

What then is the true spirituality of human life? First and foremost, we would say that it is the personal effort to do one's best to fulfill all of the truly necessary routines of daily life. When these tasks are correctly performed, they constitute a healthy, normal, and constructive life style. Simply put: whatever you are and whatever you do, the dutiful performance of daily life activities is naturally spiritual. You do not have to wear special clothes or be vegetarian or belong to a church or synagogue or congregation of any kind. The earnest and honest fulfillment of life's regular routines is the standard of a real spiritual life.

In the early stages of human development, women performed spiritual exhibitions using feathers and colorful body paint. When men took over, they developed those customs even further to include colorful costumes, flowers for decoration, perfumes, sweet smelling incense, face-painting, and elaborate dances to accentuate specially arranged rituals and ceremonies. Long before our modern commercial culture developed, these things were utilized not to attract the opposite sex, but as part of so-called spiritual performances. Gradually men began to organize social religions and force people to support their fictitious establishments.

Now we have large-scale world religions, just as we have industrial farming. Men have created a world in which they live on spiritual and physical food that they no longer know how to produce for themselves. Although they were originally students and imitators of women's initiatives, they are now little more than helpless victims of the mental and emotional drives that have replaced the physical aggression once necessary to their survival. When human society shifted from matriarchy to patriarchy, it also shifted to a male-centered focus equipped with double survival skill: violence and the ability to lie.

Modern society is founded on this culture, which first appeared as a social pattern among cunning, lazy-boned leaders around 2500 years ago. Lao Tzu recognized the birth of this trend and revived the teachings of the Yellow Emperor, which were already 2500 years old at that time. Lao Tzu foresaw the high price that would be paid for the new cultural trend and urged people to return to an earnest, natural way of life, but no one was able to turn the tide of human interest in fanciful illusions. In keeping with this growing proclivity of human nature, spiritual activities naturally began to reflect people's emotional inability to face unexciting daily routines. They chose to pay a big price for a little fun. This is how our modern hypocritical spiritual culture developed.

After Lao Tzu, Chuang Tzu also recommended turning away from dishonest social fashions and returning to the simple truth of a natural life. Again, no one listened to or truly understood his message. Throughout the 1960s and '70s, young Americans made use of Chuang Tzu's writings to support the hippie movement and resist the draft when their nation spent the lives of its young citizens on the paddy fields of Vietnam. This was not what Chuang Tzu told people to do 2300 years ago, at the end of Chou Dynasty, when everyone was enthralled with the glory of a new ruling force.

Imperial or political dynasties come and go, but the land and life of ordinary people do not change much. Life itself is very basic. Dynasties are the games of men. They represent the wrong spiritual direction of human life, namely, superficiality. The origins of this trend were the prehistoric customs that women created to influence male adults and children to live in a new way that would reflect the hidden fact of spiritual reality, which you could call the spirit of life. People were made to wear costumes to exhibit an indescribable spiritual reality.

The most suitable way, however, to express this hidden reality has always been through simple cleanliness, neatness, honesty, and dutifulness in daily activities. Men then turned this simple "religion" into a profession from which women, ironically, were eventually excluded as priests or officiants.

Women recognized the human need for healthy emotional support at a social and cultural level, and they created a simple, workable support system. The men turned this practical need into a professional and commercial game in which emotions became the sole truth of human spirituality. The result, needless to say, was a spiritual marketplace filled with base competition and rivalry over whose religion were the biggest and the best. Yet wars and disputes have nothing to do with real spirituality. Differences only illustrate the one spiritual truth within each life: nature itself. The more external one's focus becomes, the further one travels from the inexpressible spiritual essence.

We advise this generation to return to the simple style of worship created by women long ago. People need an emotional life that is cleaner and purer than the commercial customs of modern culture, which include the ostentatious *chi kung* styles that are mostly a matter of show to manipulate the minds of others. True healing power and health are contained in life itself. Whatever another person gives you is worthless unless you nurture it within yourself. This is especially true of the many valuable, time-tested *chi* exercises that are so popular in the spiritual marketplace today.

Neither religious nor physical hypnosis is greater than the power of living the honest nature of life. Health and healing are a matter of correctly aligning oneself with nature, which is life itself. Although spiritual phenomena occur in people's lives, it should not be used by cunning peddlers to create cultural confusion. Once their inferior wares become social customs, they are hard to correct and change. If Christians realized that the true Heavenly Father of Jesus was the sun, or that Jesus was created the same way as all other people whose lives are composed of tiny particles of semi-spirits, would they continue to cheat themselves by believing in an all-powerful authority that rules their lives? Would they continue to rob themselves of the potential divinity that is the birthright of all people who develop themselves spiritually and fulfill the virtue of their own being? So far, no one has realized this more than Jesus himself.

By contaminating the truth of life for social gains, human society has become imbalanced, like a ship that is loaded too heavily on one side. It is time to correct the problem, before the ship is lost in a storm it cannot weather. The time for dogmas has passed. As Abraham Lincoln once said: "You can fool some of the people all of the time, and all of the people some of the time, but you cannot fool all of the people all of the time." Men must now give spiritual leadership back to devoted women. Men have spread the dark force for too long. The situation is reaching the point of critical mass. People who wish to unearth the truth of this for themselves should read the book *The Way, the Truth and the Light*.

With new female spiritual leaders, we believe there will be fewer mistakes made in the human realm. Unlike male priests and gurus who act for a living, spiritual teaching and service is the natural function of women's lives. If you are real men, you should give back what belongs to women. You should then give them whatever support they require. Any man who wonders what he should do spiritually can work on returning to the simplicity of a plain life. This is the best preparation for higher development and it is also the best way to be true to the originality of life.

The world can only be truly ruled by the feminine principle. And when the world is once again so ruled, Jesus will say: "I have come back to you. All of you can live happily in my Heavenly Kingdom. All of you can enjoy each other in spiritual friendship."

Chapter 12

Prayers to the Universal Divine Oneness

Mother of the Universe,
guide us to return to you.
You are the only real, true divinity of the entire universe.
Let the conceptual God of human creation
become a mere supplementary elucidation of you.

Mother of the Universe,
let all of us be enlightened with the understanding that
no conceptual expression of God can be true,
unless the heart of our lives becomes true.

Mother of the Universe,
though we create conceptions of God,
we should see how our descriptions of God
exactly express the limitation of our spiritual condition.

Mother of the Universe,
you guide us to achieve harmony,
and to see the True Source.
No man or woman should be carried away by their conceptual creations
and ignore the universal reality.

Mother of the Universe,
may all of us understand that universal harmony
is the appropriate direction of all religions.

Mother of the Universe,

let all of us see that it is foolish to separate people

by religious diversity, because universal unity

is the only essence of human spiritual reality.

Mother of the Universe,

whatever has been achieved by the socially controlling religions

and the power mania of other systems in the human world,

should be transferred toward the real spiritual growth of people,

so that the world may receive the blessings of true spiritual development.

Mother of the Universe,

human society is ordered by your great spiritual unity

whereby men provide the strength of society,

while women transform it into

a good, safe, and supportive life.

Physical strength is only meaningful

when it is spiritually guided by you.

You have extended your nature of kindness, gentleness, and love

to shape our physical strength to be the real happiness of life.

Mother of the Universe,

let each one of us outgrow our conceptual obstacles,

so we may be able to recognize your spirituality

and observe your law that is the harmony within our own life's nature.

Men should be happy as men.

Women should be happy as women.

No one should create any excuse to disrespect

the natural function of their lives.

Mother of the Universe,
may all people practice real spiritual observances in their lives,
without any conceptual bondage
to personally connect and make contact with you daily.

Mother of the Universe,
let the living of a good life be the true prayer to you.
A good life should include the study of and the reaching for
the Universal Integral Truth.
No life should be lived partially
even though the world religions, with their partial presentations of the truth,
have caused conflict and confusion over how to
live a conscious, healthy, and constructive life.

The living of a healthy, normal life is the true prayer to you.
All lives should reach for and live in union just with you,
Mother of the Universe.

Amour.

Chapter 13

The Female Role in the World

The Source of Human Life

Human life did not suddenly appear on earth. It has undergone a long process of evolution to change from something coarse and unrefined to something higher and more developed. This process occurs naturally and does not involve any preexisting design or plan. It has been addressed as the Way since it was first observed by highly developed beings. Through the Way, each life has to take responsibility for its own growth, no matter what the influence of its surroundings happen to be.

There is a conventional belief that human life is the creation of someone who existed prior to formed life: the only thing that can exist before formed life is the unformed natural energy with its innate tendencies or instincts, also recognized as the nature of cosmic existence. Some people, however, insist that what created the world had to be someone like us, a powerful human ancestor. We agree that the world comes from one giant being, but that being is the natural creativity inside and outside of us. People who try to personalize and individualize this natural creativity are destined to fail because, even though similar nonpersonal creativity can be found in some individuals, it is only one small expression of Great Nature.

To be more specific, the Creator of the universe, or God, can be perceived as the spontaneous impetus of Nature that brings about all lives and all things. This positive trend of Nature is suitable to be recognized as God. To follow this trend of Nature is to be that nonpersonal creativity. God never ceases its healthy function of being creative. God is the natural instinct of creativity. God is positive. God is the power to be. God is subtly traceable and subtly knowable. To be

我獨異於
人
而貴得母
— 因為我看
重內心生活，
所以我以得道
為貴。

Alone I am and different
Because I prize and seek
My sustenance from the Mother

—*Tao Teh Ching*

positive and to be balanced is to be God. God is the Way. God is the divine light. God is the power to be truth, beauty, and goodness.

The formed energy of the universe comes from the unformed energy. The universe itself contains the unformed tendencies and instincts of Nature, though it may be too enormous to be observed. These natural tendencies and instincts are also in all lives and all things, and whoever and whatever goes against Nature ends up in a dead end. As the long-standing saying warns:

> *Though the Way is wide open and leads to Heaven, most people cannot see it and do not use it. Though the darkness of Hell is easy to avoid, people who look for short cuts and expect to receive special treatment end up there with no way out.*

The wonderful shape of human life may be at the top of Nature's creations. It carries almost all of Nature's high essence, but human life can never have a separate existence based on race, social status, or anything else one chooses to believe in. Only blind alleys await those who don't see that Nature is integral. Nature is not partial or particular; it doesn't favor one race or one society more than another. In the universe, coexistence and collective existence are the unchanging truth. Learn to live with the broad concern for all people and the world, as this expresses the Godly nature within us all. Please be kind to one another and be careful in choosing the conditions that let you be trouble-free.

Why Was the Development of Early Human Society So Slow?

Human society has taken a long course to reach its present stage. The Universal Integral Way presents the many social efforts of humankind, particularly since the time of the Yellow Emperor, around 5000 years ago.

Long ago, before the Way's more famous human ancestors of Fu Shi, Shen Nung, and the Yellow Emperor, the earliest human societies were female-centered. People knew only their mothers, not their fathers. Female-centered societies represented a very long stage of early human society.

The inspiration for a healthier and stronger human race came much later. In Chinese society, the new idea of not mixing blood within a family or clan came from Fu Shi. His ideas and knowledge about eugenics may have been learned from his observations of early animal husbandry, and he realized they could be transferred to human life. Fu Shi was an outstanding individual whose ideas and efforts influenced a whole epoch. However, Fu Shi lived long before any written history.

Fu Shi developed the basic structure of the *I Ching*. Not only was the *I Ching* used as an ancient calendar, it also had implications for the serious matter of improving human life and the making of appropriate decisions about mating and marriage to avoid mixing blood.

The effort to improve human life was affirmed and continued by most of the social leaders from later generations, though no one can be sure whether the general populace applied this knowledge in their sexual behaviors. However, this matter of improving the human race became a serious social focus, just over 3000 years ago, leading to the establishment of the Chou Dynasty.

The New Epoch of the Chou Dynasty (1122 BCE–249 BCE)

Before the Chou Dynasty, the mother-centered culture of tolerance and receptiveness was abused by the sexual impulsiveness and physical superior power of men.

The matter of clean-blood, or eugenics, within clans began to receive broad social attention and political focus 3000 years ago in the Chou Dynasty. Duke Chou, the son of the wise King Wen, was the first to produce a written set of strict family disciplines focusing on the clean-blood policy. Fathers were assigned as authorities of family discipline and were also responsible for feeding the family, thus the father came to be recognized as the head of the family. These standards laid down the new social pattern of patriarchy. One should consider the clean-blood policy the foundation of the health of the human race in family and social life. It is one of the most important disciplines in human life.

At this point, we need to make clear the meaning of *family* in those times. Three thousand years ago there were no independent individuals. Each person belonged to a clan that lived and worked together. A family was in fact a clan, whose size was very big, close to that of a tribe. It was definitely not like the small-sized family of today, which is much easier to manage. Even during my (OmNi) youth in the early 20th century there were many families that had four or five generations living and working together as a natural community.

Clans were genuine communes, and among their members was the common spiritual understanding that all people lived and worked for you and you lived and worked for all others. Each commune was a different clan or big-sized family. An example of clan life or commune life still exists on the island of Samoa in the southern Pacific Ocean.

Although people in those early stages lived in communes, you shouldn't assume they were controlled by a slave system: mutual help and interdependency were essential in their lives. It was nothing like the political dogma used by the later leaders to promote socialistic communism. Those leaders didn't see that because of social change and development one couldn't return to that early style of naturally developed society with its strong and direct interdependence. Family and social change is an inevitable and naturally evolving process.

The gathering of individuals into a family has been a long-standing social custom and conventional stronghold, and while it may still be an appropriate custom, some healthy adjustment is needed.

A   Merit   or   a   Fault?

In the beginning, Duke Chou's rules were meant to empower the headmen of a family or nation with the responsibility of maintaining family and social discipline, even by means of execution, to ensure the implementation of the clean-blood principle and therefore avoid mixing blood. The new standards emphasized the concept of social morality, which at that time mostly meant being sexually disciplined to avoid producing any disabled life through inbreeding. The clean-blood principle was enforced throughout, meaning that just as a king could punish a minister (who had wronged) with death, the father held sway over the life or death of the young ones.

Not understanding the origins of this spiritual law, one might well decide that it was an unreasonable feature of this new patriarchal society because it led to later dictatorship and abuse of spiritual duty. But that would overlook how serious a matter it was to maintain a clean-blood society in those early days, when sexual freedom was absolute. Sexual promiscuity was a major problem then, much more than it is today. This policy, which became a custom, prevented unhealthy mating activity between men and women of the same clan for many generations, thus ensuring the health of the human race.

However, the simple disciplinary practices that were intended to avoid the mixing of blood ended up being misused in later years, particularly in the Warring States Period (403–221 BCE) at the end of the Chou Dynasty. The rules became overly rigid and were abused by ambitious political leaders. This abuse truly went against the dreams of Duke Chou and later Confucius (who continued the Duke's social efforts): they both wished only for a clean-blood society. Yet it was through their efforts that the typical pattern of patriarchy was reinforced. Although these disciplinary rules eventually changed in China, you can still find them in neighboring countries such as Korea and Japan.

With the introduction of new cultural rules and customs, people's lives began to change. In the earlier stages of life, men and women worked together, hand in hand and shoulder to shoulder to maintain communal life. Starting with the Chou Dynasty, however, a line was drawn in the sand where on one side men became authorities on matters outside of the home as life providers, and women became authorities on matters inside the home such as: cooking, feeding the livestock, weaving, and bringing up children with simple education and discipline.

In the early years, these were acceptable and clear divisions and it was how patriarchy began in China. It remained China's style of family up until the last century, when the country began experiencing massive changes due to the growing influence of the West and strong new international competition.

The implementation of these new rules and the new emphasis on civility can be considered as social progress. However, when rules lose their flexibility, troubles inevitably arise. For example, the new standards included the rule that men or women could not make direct hand contact, unless they were married and in the privacy of their own rooms.

The Drastic Changes of the Last Two Centuries

Early last century, almost 3000 years after the Chou Dynasty, the Western coeducational system was introduced into China. That century's generation of students stirred up strong resentment toward their ancestors, particularly Confucius, as it was he who continued and exalted the cultural and spiritual efforts of Duke Chou's work for society.

This new young generation attacked the long established rules of Duke Chou, among them the rule that no marriage should occur between a man and woman of the same surname. This rule had been a custom for 3000 thousand years. It had been established at a time when clans were relatively small and people were closely related to each other, so in those circumstances it was very reasonable.

Although Duke Chou's social rules were well-intended, they had become overly strict and unreasonable. Confucius, who came to symbolize the old culture, got into further trouble with the women of the new generation by having said "Only women and children are difficult to raise." The new generation thought Confucius was implying that women and children were inferior to men and they were deeply offended. As we understand it, after having had our own families, we think Confucius meant that women and children are delicate by nature and should be well taken care of. Raising a female is different from raising a male.

The new generation of Chinese students was also influenced by, and embraced the new romantic literature from the West. It took hold of their hearts and they used it to replace the suppressive nature of the old culture, with its social and family disciplines. However, they failed to notice that these literary works were born from the Renaissance Movement, itself a reaction to and liberation from the West's religious Dark Age, while China had not had a religious dark age. Granted, Confucius's teachings had become overly rigid after the Sung Dynasty, yet that was due to the scholarly nature of the time and the influence of Folk Taoism and Buddhism. The following Ming Dynasty was the total opposite. During its time, the general people gave up following the strict scholarly nature of the Sung Dynasty in favor of extreme carnal pleasures. The Manchurian rule of the Ching Dynasty may have presented a cultural dark stage of life, but that was partly because of its politics. Despite the different social and cultural backgrounds, China's young over the last two centuries welcomed the West's open and less stringent rules relating to sexual relationships, and readily forsook their old culture.

The new extreme grew rapidly. The natural organic condition of the old society that would have allowed the old and new cultures to coexist and serve the different experiences of people was overlooked. The younger generation used the new political force to destroy the social and moral foundation of the old society, the peak of which occurred in the 1960s and was called the cultural revolution.

The Chinese communist revolution received the support of the new generation in part because of antipathy toward the old family rules and negativity toward the old patriarchal politics, with its absolute rights.

Looking at the social trends of humankind, which race has been more extreme, the East or the West? In the early stages of life, it was the West. Catholic domination imposed many artificial beliefs on people, which caused harm to society's organic nature. More recently, however, it is the Chinese who have been more extreme, when they leapt into the new untested social system of Russia, after Dr. Sun's moderate republican revolution. China's recent big change has uprooted all of the old culture that had grown from the natural environment over countless thousands of years.

We are not saying that the rebellion against the old culture did not have a real cause, as its customs had become overly rigid. Yet, although those customs appeared like social ideologies, they were actually moderated in people's practical lives. The real cause of China's continuing restlessness and its two revolutions was that its leaders lost their vision after many external invasions and strong internal competitions, which have repeatedly depleted the country.

The Possible Remedy

As mentioned previously, the mother-centered culture of tolerance and receptiveness was abused by men in early human life before the Chou Dynasty. That situation reached a point of needful change, leading to the growth of the stern discipline of the father-centered society. The development of patriarchy brought about a new extreme, causing the need for another big change.

In human society, to bring about a balance of masculine and feminine principles each side needs to value the other in life and needs to ensure their principles' correct application. Today, the masculine principle has become the dominant one with its unhealthy trend of male competitiveness taking the world toward total self-destruction. We should all wake up to see that human development has reached a dangerous and critical level of male competitiveness with its "one-wins-the-other-has-to-die" attitude. Extremists on both sides, Islamic and Christian, have sown such trouble.

However, our purpose here is to affirm the contribution made by women in shaping the early human societies with their all-supporting attitude of motherliness. The masculine and feminine strengths of society need rebalancing, and the *I Ching* presents the correct way of interweaving the two different types of life's strengths.

Though Western culture purports to exalt the equality of men and women, it has in reality abused the good advances that some social movements such as feminism brought to society. The freedom to choose one's career regardless of gender has been tempered by the economic need for both parents in most families to work full time. This economic need has in turn given birth to extreme competitiveness in society which has caused women, as well as men, to act and react according to artificial societal norms, rather than honoring and valuing their own as well as each other's natural energies and virtues. As a result, we have a society that is out of balance, where masculine competitiveness is overvalued and feminine virtues of nurturance and receptivity are undervalued.

The early line of family responsibility drawn up in the Chou Dynasty, where families worked together as a team, has been disturbed. Now, both men and women need to fight the same frontiers to lessen the pressures of life. This aggressive attitude has carried over into home life as well, so men and women fight both outside and inside the home. They end up without any real friendship or partnership in life. Which side of the family has any real relaxation and real enjoyment in life? Modern life is very tense both inside and outside the home.

This is why, in weighing up the real balance of the two natural tendencies of men and women, we expect the feminine principle to be revalued and recognized in the development of a better human life. Throughout the entire human society, women should take a more active role in cultural and spiritual activities, and the highest expression and virtue of motherliness in supporting all people would be their spiritual service.

The Spiritual Leadership in the Early Years When Humanity Was Still in its Infancy

Here we make use of the long experience of Chinese society.

Around 5000 years ago, during the time of the Yellow Emperor, people worshipped the Mystical Female of the Highest Heaven, the Lady-in-Blue. By practicing the teachings of the Mystical Gate of Protection, people received help to avoid battles and minimize harm when facing an enemy attack. A whole set of spiritual practices (which are still in existence) that deal with spiritual protection in times of uncertainty and danger have been developed and passed down. They are deeply related to the ancient calendar of the *I Ching*.

During the time of the Three Kingdoms (220–264 CE), at the end of the Han Dynasty, research into these practices was rekindled as a result of society's interest. The practices guided people away from physical fighting and to use strategies which could minimize war to achieve righteous purposes. However, the question then arises, which side and which purpose is more righteous? That is a philosophical question of the highest moral pursuit.

The practices illustrate one application of the gentle feminine approach that even if wars may not be able to be avoided, confrontation is still not the best policy. The practices became the source of the later concepts of the so-called Religious Taoism to fight spiritual harm with soul-strengthening and protection. They were also used as one of the systems of prediction.

To avoid any spiritual confusion, we should clarify that these practices are for a spiritual training that is very different from any worldly style of spiritual training. They have a scientific value in that they offer to train people to become their own spiritual authority. We emphasize that any superstitious expectations about these practices should be avoided.

However, our main focus is in reviewing the feminine principle, which is highly respected by the Way. While the majority of Chinese society entered into patriarchies around 3000 years ago, there were still many tribes in the vast western regions of China that remained matriarchal with their old feminine-centered customs. Tibet still retains certain traces of that old lifestyle, despite the heavy reforming influence of the later religions of Manichaeism and Buddhism.

We hope you can understand that the world has not always been so tense with its continual threats of war. At different stages of human development, the situation of society was made much safer by correct social guidance from feminine-centered cultures.

The Feminine Principle

The feminine principle has always been the true foundation of human civilization in the past, and it should now be reestablished to provide guidance for cultural leadership in today's heavily competitive world. Aggression and competitiveness are attributes of the masculine principle, and while they can be suitably applied in many creative directions, the gentle feminine approach is more appropriate for easing and harmonizing human relationships.

Masculine nature represents the physical side of the life force, while feminine nature represents the spiritual nature of life. The feminine or *yin* nature is reflective, while the masculine or *yang* nature is impulsive. At the present time, the masculine approach has overexpanded itself into most aspects of human life at the expense of the feminine principle. We can remedy this unbalanced situation by extending the feminine principle in exercising and developing life's spiritual nature, and by allowing the masculine principle to find its positive value in other areas of life.

The Tradition of the Integral Way comes from the wisdom expressed in the *I Ching*. Throughout history, most scholars have studied the *I Ching* as a system of divination, neglecting the fact that it is based on harmony and cooperation with the universal subtle law.

The balance and harmony of nature's main forces of *yin* and *yang* is the *I Ching's* great guidance for personal life, family life, and the entire life of human society. If balance and harmony are missing, trouble inevitably ensues.

Yin and *yang* are fundamentally interrelated and interdependent—one side cannot live without the other. This ageless wisdom applies in all aspects of life, including social administration and management, politics and government. In personal and social life, most people tend to be impulsive, aggressive, interfering, and meddlesome. These *yang* tendencies are overly expressed.

Yin and yang are not totally opposing—they also help to accomplish each other. If a confrontational situation is managed by the *yin* or feminine principle, trouble can be avoided. But if the natural order of harmony is violated, trouble will be experienced. The countless ways in which this may be expressed in personal, social, and natural events are described by the abstract symbols of the *I Ching,* which were systemized over 6000 years ago as the eight trigrams and then into the 64 hexagrams.

Of the eight trigrams, sky or heaven, fire, thunder, and mountain are *yang* in nature, while earth, rain or lake, water, and wind are *yin.* The names do not literally refer to the things named, but stand as metaphors symbolizing eight different types of natural energy. When the trigrams are paired with different trigrams the 64 hexagrams are formed, which describe 64 types of energy arrangements as a summary of all the different possible circumstances in life. Among them, heaven and earth, water and fire, wind and thunder, and lake and mountain are seen to be in opposition when *yang* is above *yin.* In these pairings, harmony occurs when *yin* takes the lead and *yang* follows.

Good fortune is expressed in the following situations: when earth energy is above and sky energy is below forming the hexagram of Great Peace; when water energy is above, and fire energy is below, forming the hexagram of Great Accomplishment; when lake energy is above and mountain energy is below forming the hexagram of Attraction; and when wind is above and thunder is below forming the hexagram of Benefit. When these situations are reversed the corresponding hexagrams express trouble and are respectively known as: Misfortune, Incompletion, Erosion, and Lack of Persistence.

Together, the books *I Ching* and *Tao Teh Ching* express the ancients' valuable discoveries from their observations of nature and human society. The books exalt the feminine principle and include information on how to survive, how to have a good life, and how to have a good government. They are of tremendous value for people, no matter what stage of life they may be in.

Our work rediscovers the value of the Way, and awakens all people who have been unable to see the plain truth of a good life and a good government due to the negligence of the past and present generations.

Universal Spirituality Needs an Open, Broad, Healthy, and Complete Life Stand

As a social spiritual service, we revive the Way with the following interpretations and directions.

(1) The Universal Integral Way is a spiritual path that teaches and promotes a healthy, constructive, and complete life in its three main dimensions of body, mind, and spirit.

(2) The Universal Integral Way embraces universal principles and is thus transreligious. It does not favor any particular custom or religion, but recognizes all good works that benefit the normal lives of people. By not insisting on any specific custom or fashion, it rejects narrowness and partial vision.

(3) The Universal Integral Way provides an education for raising people with normal healthy standards. It promotes the ideal of a good human being whose goal is to have a complete constructive life, harmonious relationships with others, and a perfected sense of morality.

(4) For clarity and understanding, the Universal Integral Way is promoted culturally and spiritually as the Path of a Constructive Life (PCL). It does not educate people to be Christian, Islamic, Buddhist, or Taoist, but rather educates them to be pupils of a complete and constructive three-dimensional life.

Woman's High Spiritual Quality is Motherliness

Among all human spiritual qualities, motherliness is placed above all. The female spiritual quality of motherliness should guide the spiritual leadership of the world.

In human life it is recognized that the most truthful love is motherly love. In nature, for example, the weak hen gathers her chicks under her wings to protect them from the attacking hawk. No mother would agree to the suicide of her son or daughter. How could the mothers of the terrorists of the September 11 attack on New York agree to their behavior? Osama Bin Laden's behavior arises from a need to be loved by someone, such as his mother. He is one son in a family of 52 children. Can money or material things fix the health of the mind?

The later patriarchal societies suppressed the position of women. In view of today's overly hostile world and contentious society, it is clear that the feminine principle should be revalued and restored to the social level of life. Women should be appointed as the spiritual leaders of the world so they can render unselfish spiritual service to all people, in the spirit of motherliness.

Men's Greatest Spiritual Attribute is Generosity

It is time for men to assist women and for both men and women of balanced personality to become the new spiritual leaders of the world.

The learning and teaching of the Path of Constructive Life, also known as the Path of the Subtle Light, recognizes that men and women should be equally dutiful in supporting the value of feminine virtue. This Path chooses the image of the mother bird with its loving and protective qualities as the spiritual symbol and model for all people. It is the new setting for the teaching of this ageless tradition.

We dream that women, with men's generous support, will become the spiritual social leaders of the future. Women should now hold the positions of spiritual leadership and oversee the spiritual health of all people. They would be given the following titles: first is the Lady of the Sun, Overseer of Universal Moral Rebirth; next are the Ladies of Virtue, Directresses of Ethical Upliftment, and next to them are the Ladies of Light, Counselors of Spiritual Care. Each position carries the duties that the title designates.

In respect for men's cooperation and support of women's leadership, they would be given the titles of Ministers and Tutors of the pupils of a complete, constructive three-dimensional life. Further titles may be granted to men in recognition and to honor their good lives and generous behaviors, such as: The Knight of Advocating Ethics; The Knight of Devoting Ethics; The Knight of Adequate Ethics; The Knight of Patron Ethics; The Duke of Proficient Ethics; The Duke of Eminent Ethics; The Duke of Outstanding Ethics, and The Duke of Excellent Ethics.

The Universal Family is the Model

This Path is the healer's tradition that originated with Chuan Hsu, grandson of the Yellow Emperor. Since the Han Dynasty over 2000 years ago, it has developed to become a universal spiritual family. In the spirit of a universal family this Path raises its members to have healthy confidence in life and strengthens them through various traditional protective disciplines. All members choose to live in mainstream life and serve other people with natural healing or good advice. This Path takes people to the bright side of society using a spiritually centered life as its model.

In our teachings of Tao, the word "Tao" is an abbreviation for the Truth Above Oneself, the Truth About Oneself, and the Truth Among Ourselves. The later established Religious or Monastic Taoism represents a small branch of people who have lost the vision to see that life is complete.

My (OmNi) teaching was undertaken in the United States in 1976 as a spiritual school in modern society. The real work of this teaching is about parenting the world. It provides a complete and constructive life education and a context for spiritual discoveries. For those people with young and pure souls, the book *The Foundation of a Happy Life* is one of the basic required study texts. The goal of the teaching is to educate all people to learn to love life and to learn how to help themselves and others achieve the complete range of their natural human potential.

The real practice of this universal family is fatherly love, motherly love, brotherly love, sisterly love, and friendly love. Each expression of humanistic love is highly valued and is practiced in this universal family of the Universal Integral Way. This ancient tradition deeply recognizes that love is the best encouragement and cure for the lives of one another in this mixed plane of human life. The elder ones should love the younger ones and the younger ones should love their elders. With love, life is meaningful. With love of life, we teach others and ourselves. With love of life, we learn to live better. With love of life, we serve our own life as well as the lives of others.

The universal spiritual family supports students' learning to live in the wider human society where they may experience cruelty, uncertainty, and insecurity. Each student can learn how to live a complete, constructive human life and enjoy pleasant life relationships among universal family members.

Each pupil of a complete constructive life should work to attain the knowledge and real practice of the truths that love is gentle and yielding; love is straight and firm; and love is sincere and earnest.

People who do not respect their own life or the lives of others, who are overly selfish, or who hold narrow views about races and nations, are not acceptable as participants of this teaching. Such attitudes counteract the duty of the teaching to provide an open social spiritual education with the goal of teaching all people to recognize that the entire universe is one big life, all people are one big clan, and all positive, healthy, spiritual intentions come from one whole family.

Health in All Aspects of Life is
the New Spiritual Work of Society

For individuals and societies alike, balance should be the guiding principle. The balance of the two forces of *yin* and *yang* is the philosophical foundation of Traditional Chinese Medicine and is applicable to both individual and collective life.

The spiritual learning of the Integral Way and the Path of Constructive Life is a complete life education, based on millions of years of accumulated wisdom and human life experience. It is the invaluable attainment of many achieved ones. To pass on this meaningful heritage, a new schooling system should be structured to complement the existing natural medical training programs in schools and universities.

The Self-Directed Study Program

A number of books are recommended for self-study. They will be used as spiritual examples for students of the Universal Integral Way and the PCL to provide spiritual learning and support.

(1) *Eternal Light* will be the spiritual example for male students.

(2) *The Mystical Universal Mother* will be the spiritual example for female students.

(3) *The Centermost Way* will help to cleanse your spiritual confusion.

(4) *Enrich Your Life with Virtue* will serve as a personal spiritual standard and perhaps as a new social code for self-conduct and acceptance of others. It will serve generally as the Way's spiritual definition and as a basis for the

worldwide spiritual promotion of a new, healthy human society. In emphasizing working with one's personality, the book differs from the prevailing religious emphasis on faith. In encouraging the pursuit of success through honest, personal development, it also differs from the modern, nonreligious or intellectual approach, which constantly tries to find shortcuts and ignores morality.

(5) *The Foundation of a Happy Life* will serve as a foundation for building a healthy personality and a happy life.

(6) *The Power of Natural Healing* will assist students in building confidence in their professional and personal lives.

(7) *The Workbook for Spiritual Development of All People* will be useful as a learning resource for spiritual development within the program.

The ageless teachings of the Integral Way consisting of *The Complete Works of Lao Tzu*; the *I Ching*; *The Yellow Emperor's Internal Classic*; *Tao, The Subtle Universal Law and The Integral Way of Life*; Chuang Tzu's *Attaining Unlimited Life*, and others will be included in the advanced study program.

In addition, a number of unpublished books on the subjects of health, healing, and the living of a long, happy life will help in the higher research of the future. Other books will be introduced on other occasions.

Students who use the new program should also learn a form of *chi* movement such as Eight Treasures, Harmony Style T'ai Chi Chuan, and Self-Healing Chi Gong to supplement their own health in the pursuit of longevity.

The true reward of spiritual work is a better world and a more peaceful sleep. Also, by displaying your high spiritual qualities you invite the blessing of receiving teachings from the divine realm of the true immortals. Although I have seen many teachers turn their spiritual work into a commercial service, similar to that of other professions, that is too limited a return for life, and contrary to this spiritual path.

Nurture Your Daily Spiritual Connection With the Subtle Realm Through the Divine Light of the Heavenly Father Sun

For spiritual learning, it is suggested that students make the morning sunlight their shrine, as well as by living a constructive and integral way of life, to affirm their spiritual connection with universal nature.

Students may begin their day by bowing to the sun, which represents the one source of life's Three Essences, known as the Three Purities. By so doing you will establish your life as the "Shrine of the Eternal Breath of Tao."

In this way and as a real benefit, students will improve their spiritual DNA and open themselves to high spiritual genes, which they may lack or which they may have weakened through their previous life circumstances. The practice enables them to use the sun as a shrine to embrace their souls, as a vantage point for attaining a healthy life spirit, and for developing the healing power to serve their own life and the lives of others. All students will be spiritually benefited by advancing in a different, but decent walk of life.

Chapter 14

Plow On No Sand
(A Message to Sisters of the Universal Heavenly Way)

(P r e s e r v e d   b y   O m N i   F r o m   t h e
T e a c h i n g s   o f   H i s   M o t h e r)

(Note: This message of the Universal Mother transmits the historical voice of women. It also reviews the social fact that over the last three to four thousand years, human society has become a harder environment in which to live. The softening power of femininity can help; women can be supported in stepping forward and taking more responsibility for the world. Spiritual work would be the best aspect for their contribution.

When Chinese society shifted from being female-centered to male-centered, the hardening of the social atmosphere and culture caused women to withdraw. This painful pattern occurred throughout the world at different times in history, and although it may not be the social position of women in much of the modern world, the general trend of male-centered thinking and policymaking has not ended yet.

In earlier stages of male-centered societies, women were denied an education and were not allowed to work outside the home. They were also considered intellectually inferior and had no political voice. In effect they were relegated to the status of slaves, along with men who were physically, financially or socially weak. Among children, female babies were not considered as valuable as male babies and in rural farming areas it was not uncommon to kill or give away female babies. Essentially, females were treated like a commodity, and still are in some primitive societies and cultures.

My [OmNi] own mother [Maoshing's grandmother] was given away by her parents to a couple by the name of Zheng. She was educated and cared for by that couple and spiritually assisted by a woman teacher as well as by my father. In this article, I present my mother's gentle voice of encouragement to all women to do more for themselves and society. In past

decades, I was hesitant about giving this article to the public, but people are more edu-
cated now and they have a better opportunity to objectively observe what has happened in
human history without emotionally overreacting.

Generally, my spiritual offering to modern people is the encouragement to engage in
spiritual self-cultivation and development. Up to now I have not really touched upon the
problems of society. In spiritual matters however, everything must be reflected on by people
as a whole.

Spiritually, it is clear that men and women are equal partners in life and should work
together at solving the problems of human society. Today, Maoshing and I hope that we can
encourage men to listen to their conscience and respect their coessential duty to improve the
condition of the world. The direction in which men have taken the world must be reversed
if life on earth is to survive. The subtle spiritual leadership of women is the key to this
necessary transformation. We hope men can realize the value of supporting women as they
make their due spiritual contribution. Just as women have been the keepers of the home,
they should now become the keepers of the world so that all people can live in peace and
happiness.)

The Way of the Universal Mother

Beloved Sisters,
Men and women are different.
You need to appreciate their differences on the physical,
mental, and spiritual levels.
The nature of women is superior at giving and nurturing life
and managing human relationships.
This work requires tenderness, softness, understanding,
patience, and careful detail.
Men are an expression of nature's impulsive and restless characteristics.
On most occasions, they act like immature boys and daredevils,

who fight and wage war out of a lack of love for life.
Their spiritual depth and spiritual vision
are obscured by the strong influence of their hormones.
They will not achieve themselves spiritually until they are able to
balance masculine initiative with feminine fulfillment.
Otherwise, a man is naturally more physical and less spiritual,
while a woman's nature is quiet and less impulsive;
less physical and more spiritual.

Who can be more effective in helping the spiritual growth of life—
the stern father, brother or husband or the kind mother, sister or wife?

Look at the world today.
Since men put themselves at the center of the society,
their competitiveness has turned the world into a battlefield.
Global society is a big battlefield,
nations are mid-sized battlefields,
and most families are small battlefields.
Men have made the world a rough and tough place to live.
As long as the masculine principle controls every corner of life on earth,
human relationships will only get worse and worse,
with no hope for improvement.

Women were the first to develop themselves
and they were the first to create homes.
Before that, men readily took advantage of women and then walked
away once the women had conceived with their inferior seeds.
But as woman's minds developed faster than men,
they were able to choose the men they wished to be with,
and to teach and discipline their offspring more intelligently.

People in those times were sparse yet valuable, as most of them
had been educated with the high ethics of their mothers.
Men, however, are great imitators,
and so they were quick to learn from women,
and then use their ways to control both women and society.

Once in control, men had the power to pick and choose,
forcing women to receive their bad and inferior genes.
As a result, life became cheap.
Men and boys were prepared for sacrifice or became canon fodder.
This was, and still is, painful for all mothers to witness.
Men, with their inferior genes, like to be kings
and invent reasons to wage war, both visible and invisible.

Beloved sisters,
Your wombs are sacred.
They should not be used to unselectively bear inferior seeds.

Where do inferior seeds come from?
As a rule, men have less self-control than women.
In early times and sometimes even today,
men would force themselves upon any woman,
even close relatives, for the sake of their physical satisfaction.
This indiscriminate behavior has produced many troublesome people
with disabled lives and spiritual defects,
which have been passed on from one generation to the next.
Inferior behavior produces inferior results.
In modern times, drug and alcohol abuse
produce similar destructive results in people,
causing the world to worsen year by year.

It is the responsibility of each individual to choose a spouse
with whom he or she can produce good children.
Marriage should be carefully considered through understanding and insight,
not from the material desires of you or your parents.
A woman should carefully examine the spiritual quality of a man
before making her choice.

The Heavenly Way was developed by ancient women leaders
who realized that an ethical education
is more important than social competition.
They brought the real truth of humanity and spirituality to the world.
But as men gained social control
their lack of a humanistic, universal conscience
created a shallow doctrine of competition and bias
that would serve their individual ambitions.
What kind of teaching could they possibly produce,
except one that was spiritually inferior and unfit?
Racial prejudice and social struggle, in the form of war,
is the legacy that men have bestowed upon the world.

Beloved sisters,
According to one early myth about the origin of the human species,
the Universal Mother Nu Wu[1] created you from mud and water[2]
and vitalized you with her own breath.
You are not someone's rib bone.
You are the first born of the best natural energy
resulting from the integration of earth and sky
through the Universal Mother's will.

---

1. Not the same as Nu Wu, the possible sister of Fu Shi, who continued the rule of Fu Shi long before written history. The name Nu Wu suggests "a gentle whirlpool."
2. Mud means flesh and bones; water means blood and secretion.

Spiritually you should assist no one,
but take the leadership back from the spoiled and degenerated world
that is commanded by the will of men.

Beloved sisters,
Don't worry that you aren't as physically
and as intellectually powerful as men are.
It is you who give them life.
They sucked your breasts and your blood to grow,
and yet after attending school they say that women
cannot manage the world,
which is totally outrageous and most unfair.

Women know how to value life.
Their instincts are those of Mother Nature.
In running their families, their societies, or the world
they are guided by Mother Universe.
They don't need so-called social science—
the pseudoscience of dodo heads of inferior birth
who have nothing better to do with their time.
Women are able to set a healthy direction for the world
by applying their natural gift of motherliness.
With this nature-given endowment,
women are able to take care of the society and the world,
devaluing no one except those who are lovers of war.
War will never end until all people recognize and value
the feminine principle of nature.

The development of the teaching of the Heavenly Way
came from the mother of Lao Tzu.
She transmitted the teachings of earlier women leaders:

Lao Tzu simply put their teachings into written form.
These teachings were the wisdom of ancient developed individuals
who searched for the Way.
They lived in close contact with nature.
By observing the lives of people and animals,
they discovered that the feminine principle
is superior to the masculine principle,
in personal, social, and worldly life.
When the feminine position is usurped by the male,
the world is set in turmoil.

Beloved sisters,
Will you teach your sons to be daredevils
and prepare them to be canon fodder
for the ambition of inferior world leaders?
War has never stopped war. War only creates war.
Can you watch this situation without offering your help to rescue
the world from the tar pit of the masculine impulsive force?
The world needs cooperation and harmony,
not aggression and competition.
Universal spiritual education,
with the goals of genuine spiritual growth
and development of all people is the only true antidote for war.
Teach your sons and daughters to find a better way
to help their own lives and the life of human society as a whole.
This is not the responsibility of a professional priesthood,
but of individuals.
Individuals are the true foundation of an improved world,
and the key to lasting improvement is the rediscovery
of feminine values.

Beloved sisters,

The world may not return to the old days

when women were supreme,

but wisdom can bring the world back to life.

You must renew your efforts

to prevent men from pushing the world to total destruction.

Some men have conceived of a paradise

where there is permanent peace for everyone,

but you have to die first before you can enjoy it.

Women are now being taught to be suicide bombers

as men prepare to turn everything into ash.

Beloved sisters,

Don't let them do it.

Coexistence is the ultimate law of Nature;

the T'ai Chi symbol expresses this deep truth of life.

Although there is not much that can be done

in a male-centered society to inspire social change,

women of the world can teach their sons good ethics when they are young.

Basic ethics are ignored by our super-tense commercial world

that is obsessed with competition.

You can transfer your natural abilities in managing family life

to take care of the big family of humankind.

The world should be cared for like a big family.

You need men and you love men.

You can show men how to live together in peace and harmony

instead of fertilizing the wilderness with their own blood and bone.

Cruelty should not be exalted as a heroic achievement.

Natural spiritual education should lead the world,

and women should make themselves fully available
for this meaningful and useful service.

Beloved sisters,
You have been social victims for over 3000 years.
What have men done to the world?
They have created a mess.
The world is no longer a safe place to live.
You must fulfill your duty to educate the culture
and reshape a better world that will become livable again.

Women invented the home,
while men promoted religions for their own social gain.
Home is as sacred as Heaven.
Heaven offers encouragement to the souls of men and women alike.
It is not a spiritually dark, alluring concept of some race or society
that your children should die for.

Beloved sisters,
Wherever you are,
whatever your racial background,
whatever your spiritual customs,
it is your responsibility to bring harmony,
cooperation, and love toward all
neighbors, families, and friends,
and whatever help others may need.

Beloved sisters,
There is no Heaven,
if there is no respect for the feminine principle.

There is no beautiful world, if the female principle is denied.

There is no real beautiful life, if the value of women is degraded.

There is no useful education, if the spiritual vision
of universal integrity is not taught.

There is no happiness of life, if a sense of aesthetics is not nurtured
in the intellect and its systems.

There are no true religions, unless the oneness of universal divinity
is recognized above all.

Beloved sisters,
As mothers and as women,
few of you have chosen to be spiritual workers of the world,
though some of you lived singly and spiritually.
May you all carry the knowledge to all people
that the Mother Universe is superior to all Gods
that have ever been created.

Beloved sisters,
You are born with the virtue to yield,
but in the realm of universal morality,
you should yield to no one.
While you do not need to compete with men,
you can still offer the message of the Heavenly Way
that was initiated by women
and that is still taught wherever there is a woman.

As women,
you have the responsibility for all life.
The life of the world is your natural concern.
This is not an exaggeration of the power of women.

It is a very simple thing: by giving love to your children and your men
you can develop the sense of love for all children and all people,
even men who are lost.

We hope you will all give this message some thought.
The Mother Universe does not want people
to end their lives with their stupid ways.

Love to you all:
to our own children,
to all children of the world,
and to all the mothers and fathers of the world.

— *OmNi and Maoshing*

Chapter 15

Encouragement to Wise Women for the Improvement of the Human Spiritual Condition

In recent centuries, women have been forced—through political campaigns, social movements, fashionable education, and for survival—to become manlike. Men, at the same time, have become weaker and unable to support their families single-handedly. Thus, in most modern families, both men and women need to be lifemakers. As a result of this trend, men may be unable to find comfort in their own homes and look for it elsewhere, while women may lack the security and stability that men can provide in their lives. Both may suffer emotionally from the instability of their life ties and the insecurity of their lives. Furthermore, the young ones of the family have little quality time with their parents. These situations have become the problems of modern life. What life progress has truly been made by this new trend of society? Can anyone answer us?

As well, modern education aims mostly at shaping people to become mere social tools or taxpayers to support society's massive social programs. This does not help the younger generation build a healthy personality, nor does it help them know the real purpose of life. World leaders are blind to the fact that amassing financial strength is not as useful as guiding society in a healthy, spiritual way toward a better future.

The conscious tools of liberty and independence that were used to open up society from the old ruling systems have been misapplied in individual life. At their worst, those slogans are used to justify erecting new, massive and interfering ruling systems, of the kind that human life has experienced in the last few centuries. Although people are provided with a sense of freedom and independence in the new open societies, the new educational trends have affected men and women negatively rather than positively, particularly in the areas of social morality and family unity. For instance, the overexaltation of personal freedom and independence has led to a shift in the words' real meaning. Freedom has come to mean an irresponsible life, and independence has become an excuse for shameless dependency on social programs. None of the younger generation perceives that true freedom and independence are high spiritual pursuits. In reality, there is a moral discipline that each individual needs to fulfill in the normal period of life.

The conceptions of freedom and independence are high projections of the mind, and to achieve their spiritual depths a great deal of personal refinement and adjustment needs to be realized. In contrast, when these high spiritual projections are used as social slogans, they bring more conflict and rebellion among the teenagers and young adults in family life. One needs to see the importance of a healthy human relationship, the truth of which involves interdependence. And the necessary conscious standards for this relationship are cooperation and equal duty in life. Additionally and equally important is the value of making a commitment to life. These thoughts have not been seriously explained to the young lives to prepare them for adulthood.

Social leaders have failed to see that cooperation, equal duty in life, and mutual commitment are the natural adhesives for a normal, sound human relationship. Those elements are what keep a good marriage together as a sound life unit in the greater society; the insistence on personal freedom and independence as political tools do not. Should conflict occur within family, school or general life, then mutual respect and mutual yielding are the most important practices to follow.

Throughout the world, the worst cultural influence in male and female relationships has been encouraging young women to imitate the male habit of social competition. Conflict is thus brought into the home and supported by those living under the same roof. A home is for married life, which is the basic sound pattern of human life. When men are scared and the hearts of women are broken, both genders suffer and end up going nowhere. A poor quality of life is the result. We have witnessed numerous marriage failures and relationship breakdowns caused by the inappropriate use of personal freedom and independence to support each partner's arrogance.

Women's great contribution is to assist the safekeeping of the world through maintaining peaceful, orderly, and loving societies just as they do so well when creating a home. Women have an important role in worldly life. They do not have to imitate and compete with men. This time can be a turning point for the world with its much needed improvement, if women stand up and perform the world's work with patience, persistence, and tolerance just like they do as wives and mothers in the family home.

As mentioned before, both freedom and independence have been the subject of political promotion, used to help society break away from colonial control. There is nothing wrong with the words' true meaning in those circumstances, however, once their meaning is overly extended they can be used for creating disharmony between partners and related couples. This is the politically negative side effect of the last two centuries. The meaning of these words should be correctly reviewed and appropriately used to serve the great life of all individuals and the wider society. At least it should be understood that these words are relative concepts and not absolute social standards. Each one of us needs to make a genuine and consistent effort to reduce the unnecessary friction and competition between men and women in our societies and within our families. Although, in some situations, freedom and independence can still be used to resist the potential evil abuse and persecution from any one side.

The harmony of family life is the basic foundation of human social life. Some social leaders have tried to replace this basic foundation with orphanages, clubs, churches, and political parties, but once this basic human relationship changes, the meaning of life changes also. Personal privacy and happiness is damaged by the new trend of shallowly connected interests such as those of finance and politics, as each side searches to take and to receive more. A normal personality cannot grow from such an environment. Although freedom and independence are, among many others, great spiritual qualities, and for some individuals they are the subject of serious pursuit, we should know that their partial and misguided exaltation can create real social problems.

The teachings of the Integral Way wish to correct the practice of promoting any single quality, such as exalting equality without seeing the natural need for differences. We are reminded of the importance of maintaining our lives with a practical sense of wholeness and balance amidst spiritual qualities overly promoted by both religions and political movements. A balanced and holistic view is needed for the healthy performance of life and the real leadership of society. We also need to understand the deep meaning of democracy. Democracy is the practice of tolerance and mutual acceptance of all differences. It should not be used to compete for superiority in any life circumstance.

People became ideological after the successes of the French and American revolutions and the Russian and Chinese communist revolutions. In those social events the untested new "medicine" was vigorously promoted to society as the miracle cure-all remedy. The evil root of socialistic religions can also be found in this promotion. The new ideologies incited radical revolutions and although some social progress was made, the natural harmonious and cooperative relations among individuals, families, and societies has suffered and been badly disturbed. In fact, new rivalries and confrontations have been established in society at all levels, such as the relationship between the workers and business management. In family life, a genuine improvement of living conditions is so much more helpful than ideological argument and fighting. That improvement should form the example for wider social improvement.

Ideological promotions have strained natural human relationships and negatively affected the quality of married life. In the aftermath of revolutions and big wars, some subnormal situations among people have become the norm. Sexual freedom encouraged irresponsible sexual attitudes leading to the rapid and fatal spread of sexual diseases and epidemics. Wise individuals value sexual prudence.

The virtues of a celibate and clean single life can be revalued. Mutual devotion and mutual support in marriage deserves the utmost respect. It is the basic relationship between men and women.

Traditionally, men were responsible for earning a living outside the home, while women were responsible for the internal management of family life. This basic pattern has helped human society develop steadily. Now, however, since both husbands and wives are intellectually educated they may fight over conceptual matters, arguing about who is right and how the children should be brought up. Intellectually, men and women have been educated to be the same; there is no respect for a feminine approach to problem solving. Women are made to be as rough and tough as the men.

Generally, men tend to be more ideological while women are more practical. Men tend to be good at the rough big outlines, while women are good at the details. When men get confused and make a mess in the big house of human society, it is usually women who clear it up and restore order to the house. But for a long while now, the real feminine function of practically working the details of life and mending the shortcomings of men has been overlooked. Without the feminine principle, family and social life cannot achieve harmony.

Today men and women are equally encouraged by the new ideological trends and concepts, and both are all too ready to fight and argue. Fighting for the louder voice is a new phenomenon that has arisen out of the last two centuries. It occurs everywhere: in public places, homes, schools, and workplaces. At the other extreme, people have no voice unless they praise the new adopted social ideology. The ideology sets the conditions for people's lives without any vision for the long-term natural health of society; it has disturbed the peace and harmony among people. It is more important that social efforts support the health of a society and the family life of all people.

Cultivation of the individual personality is completely ignored by the new social trend of the world. At the same time, the old religious ways with their poor spiritual quality have been shown unfit to guide and assist people, thus confusion within human society is everywhere and in every aspect. The Integral Way with its focus on the conscious health of society and the individual expects to take the lead as the voice of social conscience.

A practical family and social life should be the role model for a couple or a team. These things are a priority. Ideological fighting does not bring anything good into a family or a society. No one should compete to be the boss. Instead, we should help each other find the best solution in all of life's different situations.

Real spiritual progress of the world depends on people of conscience working together to create genuine improvement rather than merely scratching the superficial face of society. Any individual strength is too limited. At the beginning of this millennium, the Integral Way recommends that the public cooperate together to correct the past and to move forward to support a new and cleaner direction. It recommends that the feminine principle with its practical view of social management should be respected, particularly in performing spiritual work. At a time when the spiritual house of humankind has been so greatly disordered, the women of this greater family are encouraged to offer their help.

In modern times, there are a few genuine women who have not received the cultural deformation from the ideological fervent of the last century, but there are very few pure and nonconfused men. This situation is more a result of the cultural confusion than the individual nature of men and women. It is time for all people to respect their natural healthy condition and fulfill their natural and proper functions in life to make a genuine contribution to society's progress. Women are encouraged to replace competition with the human spiritual standard of cooperation for the greater benefit of the human family. We hope that women can attain the necessary objectivity to achieve such a task, for it seems that men are unable to loosen their breath from the tension of modern life.

The waste of social and political campaigns needs to be reduced. More progress can be produced by the spiritual work done by each individual, each family, and each society. Understanding the duty of personal improvement is more meaningful than engaging in competition for social positions, which is mostly motivated by self-serving reasons. These showy efforts express the lack of individual personal growth.

If you are interested in the cultural spiritual work of the Universal Integral Way, the spiritual benefit of which is for society and for your own personal support, we encourage you to choose it as a new type of career, especially for women. It is for your mutual spiritual help and is the new frontier for conscientious people. It suits people of heart. People who are attracted to things only by their senses may not be interested, though people of clear intellects can serve from both the heart and the senses.

Our interest is to assist people to develop wholeness and that is why we respect the *Integral* Way of Life. In the sphere of human life, all idealistic elements should be understood relatively; they should not be accepted absolutely, even those of freedom and independence. Those concepts are intended to mean that social stature is the natural birthright for all individuals. This is the foundation for the further development of human life. But, if these concepts are overly extended in any living unit, such as a family or marriage, their meaning shifts to signify that you need to be self-interested, self-opinionated, and self-indulgent.

In life, at some stages and in some relationships, you need to provide cooperation and commitment. At the same time, you can expect that the good things that come from freedom and independence involve some struggle. Realistically speaking, do not allow exaggerated thoughts of a good life and happiness to be a matter of being free and self-determining, as that can destroy your real quality of life. Overindulging in thoughts of freedom and independence can rival the real support you need for the achievement and accomplishment of your life. No ideology can replace your genuine, constructive, and effective efforts.

As a result of modern education and influence, people can be classified into three types. Type One: hardheaded with a hardened heart. This type of person represents the failure of life and experiences no real happiness. They have been brain-washed with all types of external learning and their minds are full of undigested knowledge. Their hearts have become hardened from the negative experience of life. Type Two: hardheaded with a soft heart. This individual has the same hard-headedness as Type One, but their heart is responsive to natural kindness without being self-opinionated. This type of person has difficulty balancing their life. Type Three: Open-minded with a soft heart. This type of person stays away from unnecessary struggles that can cause the brain to harden, and they take difficulties nonpersonally. Their minds are naturally flexible and their hearts are kept open to accept the light for their ever-new strength. They are kind and not opinionated. Among these three types you yourself know what to choose.

The first type of person represents the majority. Not only have these people changed the meaning of freedom and independence, but they have also changed the meaning of another important word—love. To them love equals fun, and having fun means making no commitments and taking on no emotional burdens. These hardheaded people deny the spiritual value of life, except to the extent necessary for taxation purposes. In this situation with these types of people, war is created to change the social focus or as a stimulation for industry. Who creates a human society like this? Ask the hardheaded wise guys. This has become the new trend of the world, which is continually being pushed further in that direction.

Constructive Suggestions to People Who Choose a Different and Consciously Healthy Way of Life

(1) Independence means your personal effort to attain a sense of value and dignity in your individual life.

(2) Freedom means your personal effort to produce broad options in your life that are not limited to being a mere biological tool of your physical body or a work-tool of society.

(3) A self-supported life is a sign of a healthy and responsible individual life.

(4) Family life is the human way of working as a team for its members' joint physical survival. Each partner needs to make a cooperative contribution to the team as the basic foundation of life.

(5) In family life, no one should make another person their slave. Individual independence should be respected. Respect for individual value and dignity is the correct form in which to raise children.

(6) The option to family life is a single spiritual life. In modern times, the benefits of a spiritually teamed life may be helpful for those modern spiritually interested individuals. Such a team should be recognized as a cooperative of spiritual individuals living and working together for the common cause of spiritual pursuit. If it is one's choice to live in such a manner (as an improvement upon the lifestyles of the early monks and nuns), particularly for those in their later years, then organized preparation can be made for services and living purposes. In this situation, there will be areas of mutual dependence and, therefore, suitable contributions by each team member may be made.

(7) The key spirit for achievement and the success of a better life is the commitment to a single or teamed life. This helps to expand and complete an individual's great qualities of independence and freedom.

(8) Whether in teamwork or in life, cooperation is necessary for accomplishing big and difficult situations in life.

(9) Under a reasonable ruler, democracy accepts different visions and values the multiple options of people to accomplish things for the mutual benefit

of all. It is illustrated by the good spirit and practice of a healthy, cooperative family life, which is unlike the practice of the wider society where party line politics dominates and becomes the obstacle for real democratic progress.

(10) Spiritually, being free from any type of dependency and conditioning is a worthy pursuit and real achievement. Yet in practical life, certain sacrifices need to be made by your responsible choosing.

(11) A dutiful and devoted family life or a teamed spiritual life is for the spiritual fulfillment of life, rather than a mere contractual relationship.

(12) Value your vote and use it prudently. It is an important social support to life that you can offer to modern society.

(13) Spiritual learning and development helps you develop above the emotional and social conflicts and the backwardness of old customs and religions. You can use those things as compost to grow real, beautiful, and fragrant flowers in the new and great energy field of your life and the lives of those you are connected with.

(14) The ability to share material strength and knowledge with those in need is the real value of any personal hard work.

(15) In the management of a society, a family, or indeed any life team, ideology should yield to practical and matter-of-fact improvements. One should never ignore matter-of-factness for the victory of ideological argument. The deep and far vision should be respected, always.

(16) Never be frustrated by seeing and experiencing a limitation as a matter-of-fact. You need to grow a clear vision from the situation before you make a move. Do not be confused by unrealistic dreams. Those things should never be accepted, adopted, and exalted as social visions because they prepare the ground for tragedy on a massive scale for all involved. Observing the limi-

tations of any individual and learning the lessons from the past is the way of truthful spiritual development of all people.

In these difficult times we have some understanding for women. In a woman's life, happiness or misery is 90 percent determined by their marriage decision and it is the same for men. Some women prefer not to marry because of the difficulty in finding the right life partner. They are also not interested in giving birth to a big group of children at a time when the world is already overpopulated and the quality of human life is degraded and low. In this situation, one option for women is to devote themselves to spiritual work, choosing to live in cooperative teams with the spiritual and emotional support of one another from the Heavenly Way.

The Heavenly Way forms the spiritual agreement of the team, and it also forms the way to reach out socially to assist and improve the much needed ethical condition of the world. An individual's or a society's conscious health is the important foundation for further growth. Those who choose it are wise to live on the safe and dry shore so they can give help to others who are drifting in the torrential flood of the world's bad culture.

Chapter 16

Who Would Do Better to Serve the World?

We have presented a puzzle to those of you who could have a clear understanding of what is good for humankind's future. We will now help solve the riddle and untie any knots for you.

The positive side of the life nature of both genders has made great contributions to human life and it will continue to be humankind's main strength. The negative side of the life nature of both genders has always been, and always will be, the cause of the world's trouble. It is the regressive force in human society's progress.

In the last three thousand years, the negative trend of the masculine principle, with its excessive and unhealthy competition, has become stronger than the positive trend. This one-sidedness has caused real problems for humankind, and now that it has become the controlling force of society, the situation has become subnormal. Old world religions have not provided any true and lasting benefit to serve universal justice, so what then is the true guidance of life?

Throughout many generations, some people have supported the positive power of both genders. We don't intend to change this, but in order to bring about a new situation in the future we encourage women within this vast human society to step forward and find a life expression that better suits their true feminine nature.

The foundation for a better and healthier future, which remains unalterable, is laid down in the *Book of Changes,* wherein we find an abundance of illustrations covering all situations and depicting the fact that in any situation human strength can be applied positively or negatively. Through the study of the *Book of Changes,* we can see how excessiveness leads to trouble and we can learn to act in a way that balances the two extremes or minimizes trouble.

Lao Tzu, in the *Tao Teh Ching*, continued the effort to show how two extremes can be balanced for great harmony. He taught that men would be wise to openly adopt the feminine principle, while women should strengthen their qualities of kindness and tolerance for the sake of human progress. The vision and prophecies contained within the *Book of Changes* and the *Tao Teh Ching* were formulated long before the development of human societies.

The *Heavenly Way* booklet was written to help people put the great human vision of harmony into practice. Instead of ideological disputes, universal ethical standards should be applied in private and public life. When all people accept universal ethical standards, men and women shouldn't be troubled whether society's leaders are male or female. When world leaders accept and use universal ethics to guide society and fulfill their private and public duties, the world would soon shift back to a healthy, benign, and normal condition.

Several times we have suggested giving women the opportunity to lead and repair a world that has been split apart by religious thought developed by leaders who lacked the depth and breadth of a complete worldview. A healthy, positive approach based on the feminine principle, together with young, ethically educated lives can help the world become a better and safer place for spiritual growth. The new female teachers should be committed to world harmony and cooperation. They should be persuasive, but not intimidating like that of the conventional religionists who threaten nonbelievers with hell. Other than the occasional natural disasters, the real hell is religious darkness, sociopolitical mistakes, and greed-driven modern healthcare systems. We've "changed our old tune" to present to you the possibility of a new direction for human society, one that promotes motherly love as the oldest, truest, and newest spirituality for a new human society.

No man should feel that they are being degraded by this new approach. We set the goal of Universal Divine Oneness for both men and women to achieve, and whoever sincerely endeavors to achieve such an important spiritual task are the real future leaders. But in our true hearts, we do wish to encourage giving women the opportunity to lead the world. They are the unreleased power that can correctly guide human strength. Like the selfless love of the ancient gentle mothers, they are able to serve all people spiritually.

We hope men will understand that they should either move in the new direction or offer their support to the new female spiritual teachers and workers to achieve a practical and much needed harmonious future for human society. This direction can bring about a softening of the male ego and achieve basic harmony and cooperation between men and women, which is the fundamental goal that should be joyfully attained. We are men and we extend our spiritual effort to uplift all men and women. The great goal of world harmony can be achieved through the positive strength of all women and men.

We have waged a challenge against the excessive masculine mentality of all people, which has been unable to achieve any real or lasting peace. Incapable male leaders have created a big mess of the world. We hope our writing can stimulate people to reflect on the world's troubles and encourage them to change their emotionally indulgent and riotous styles of behavior.

By reflecting on the benefit of the great and respectable feminine power, each one of us can guide the world to a better future. This approach is certainly less expensive and involves no great pain or sacrifice, unlike that required by an over-reliance on the masculine approach. This should be the high thought for the healthy progress of men and women and the entire world.

PART V

*Nurturing Universal Ethics
is the Foundation for Your Work*

"The Heavenly Way"

Chapter 17

Introduction to the Heavenly Way

Whoever rejects the Heavenly Way
is rejected by the Heavenly Kingdom.

The Everlasting Soul, via the Heavenly Way,
reaches the Heavenly Kingdom.

Heavenly Truth is revealed to none,
but those of Heaven.

Heaven is true when it is embodied
in real life and in the way one treats one's surroundings.
Heaven's Way is mysterious to the small minds of people.

While our parents gave us a body;
Heaven, as the teacher of all people,
helps us acquire a spirit.

Heaven fails no one of sincere pursuit.
Those of persistent sincerity
have no difficulty in reaching the Subtle Truth
of the universe.
Persistent sincerity in life is the subtle substance
of individual lives and of the everlasting life
of the universe.

The Way of Heaven has no partiality,
but it always associates with good people
who conduct their lives correctly.

People may wrong one another
or mistreat one another, but this is not Heaven
because Heaven never wrongs or mistreats anyone.

Heaven does not change,
nor does the Way of Heaven.

No trouble is constant, if we remain
with the constancy of decency in life.
No blessing is constant,
unless we know how to value it.

If troubles come from the outside,
we can do something to counter them.
If troubles are of our own inner making
then we will surely suffer.
Wickedness does not go altogether unreciprocated.

The webless but reactive network presents
the subtle sphere of the universe.
It connects all lives and things as one life.

The webless but reactive network of the universe is knowable.
It is the conscious energy of life that extends its connection
to other lives and things of the world as one life and one being.

That is the faith that the entire universe is one being
and all humankind is but one life.

The webless network is unseen by many.
People mistake its invisibility for loopholes,
and think that it offers escape from the responsibility
of wrongdoing, so they risk doing such things.
But it is the Subtle Truth that whatever people do to others
they do exactly to themselves.

By doing wrong we are falling away from the supportive network
of a secure connection with the universal life.
In a narrow sense, we are punishing ourselves by
tying our lives and souls tightly and making them
unable to reach the entirety of the universal life.
We take away the opportunity to smoothly stretch our lives
and souls to connect with the one universal everlasting life.

All wrongdoing comes from this loss of a broader vision.
We thus fall into the darkness of the soul
and create hell in our own lives.

Repentance in life helps the soul gain
an opportunity for self-improvement.
Repentance truly works to help restore our vision
to see the broad connection of life.
Repentance in our mouth gets approval from others.
Repentance in our heart turns our self around
to receive the real, healthy fortune.

Chapter 18

Your Life is Active Within the Webless Network (A New Elucidation of the Heavenly Way)

(Note: This is my [OmNi] new version of the traditional Tai Shan Kan Yin Pien, *which is one of the most simple yet most valuable of the ancient spiritual writings. It is a basic text on ethics and elucidates Lao Tzu's adaptation of the ancient teaching. Master Kou Hong of the Jing Dynasty [265–419 CE] collected* Tai Shan Kan Yin Pien *during his vast research into the society of his time. He added it to his collection, but gave no personal comment. The piece was reedited around the time of the early Sung Dynasty [960–1279 CE]. It was, along with other important spiritual books, the main spiritual discipline of my early youth.)*

My first English edition of *Tai Shan Kan Yin Pien* was published in 1975, as the *Heavenly Way* booklet. It was intended as a spiritual contribution to the health of society. But due to a lack of spiritual vision, people did not recognize the value of such a profoundly simple teaching. Instead, they preferred more complicated intellectual knowledge, so I published *Tao, The Subtle Universal Law and the Integral Way of Life,* and later, *The Key to Good Fortune.* These titles repeat the same material in different ways and are still valuable references. They offer important spiritual guidance, especially for modern people who are intellectually developed yet spiritually confused. With persistent study and healthy reflection, these books can help you clear away your spiritual confusion.

Spiritual vision may not be possessed by everyone but intellectual spiritual knowledge can be taught. That is why in the three decades since these publications, I have written books that satisfy the intellects of modern people in the hope of improving people's spiritual knowledge and understanding. However, if you don't make use of spiritual knowledge it becomes useless; it must be practiced to be effective.

Before the end of the last century, I published *Enrich Your Life With Virtue* intending it to provide a new spiritual direction for society. Recently I've come to realize that the *Heavenly Way* is still the best foundation from which people can learn and progress.

My personal wish is that people can still appreciate the plain spiritual truth of everyday living. That is why the simple teachings of our spiritually developed ancestors have been my unchanging focus.

Now I feel there is a greater need to have those simple spiritual instructions available to the modern world, which is why I have reworked *Tai Shan Kan Yin Pien*. I present it as a gift to my real spiritual friends. The most important points are:

(1)   As revealed by the highest one, Lao Tzu, and those of similar development, the deep truth of human life is that it contains latent conscious energy with great potential. This latent conscious energy is highly responsive and active and is what makes human life superior to all other forms of life. Internally, it activates life and, at the same time, is receptive to and passively activated by life itself. Externally, it is active and reactive as a complete connection with the human world and the entire universe.

In developed individuals, the entire universe connects with all aspects of their human nature, through this webless network that exists among all lives and nature. But for the majority of people this webless network may be difficult to perceive until they have refined their spiritual perceptivity. We should at least understand that what we cultivate on the inside is precisely expressed on the outside and, therefore, we should make serious efforts to keep our consciousness clean and healthy.

Our consciousness can be seriously damaged through our life experiences. Like fruit it can easily rot if left exposed to the wrong conditions. As described by the highest developed one, "There is no inlet to blessings or troubles.

They are invited solely by and correspond exactly to people's own energy, lifestyle, and deep mental frames." Like the shadow that follows our every movement, our consciousness constantly attracts a similar energetic vibration and reaction from the universal energy field.

(2) In the universe, there is a hidden webless network that is completely reactive and responsive to our own energy arrangement. People are able to indefinitely extend their lives on the healthy side, but not toward the unhealthy negative sphere. It has been said, "Once the healthy nature of life is damaged one can lose a nick *(a unit of 100 days)* or a similar amount of enjoyment from their life as a result of their unhealthy behaviors." It depends on how serious the mistake is and how deep the spiritual involvement. The suffering of one's life increases as more and more nicks are lost.

(3) When our lives begin to lose their benign nature, we suffer physically, psychologically, and spiritually. The healthy condition of these three aspects is weakened and troubles begin to manifest. General help and support in life begin to disappear, and disaster and punishment ensue. Blessings pass us by and abnormal problems increase until all the nicks of our blessed life are spent and an unnatural death comes to claim us.

(4) There is a natural order in the universe. The solar system and all of its planets can be considered one family. Together they spin with the North Star, and the North Star spins with the Weaving Maiden. There are many Weaving Maidens in the galaxy. They are the virgin daughters of the Mother Universe. Their job is to keep the webless network completely alive and responsive. This was perceived by the refined intuition of our developed human ancestors.

(5) Our lives are connected directly with the webless network from above our heads, and the condition of our lives is clearly described by the aura that exists there. Though we may see the bodily aura, only gods and spiritually

developed ones can perceive the aura above the head. No sin or guilt can be hidden in this aura from the eyes of gods and spiritually developed ones.

(6) In our human bodies there are different spiritual entities related to the genes and cells of the different organ systems. This is similar to the external system of nature. The three negative spirits of our human life are traditionally called:

(a) *Pong Chiu*: The overly expanded evil spirit of pride.
(b) *Pong Tsi*: The overly expanded evil spirit of self-interest.
(c) *Pong Jia*: The overly expanded evil spirit of greed.

These negative spirits reside in the upper, middle, and lower body respectively and lead to the depletion of our spiritual energy and the promotion of death energy.

During each *Geng Sheng* Day,[1] these negative spirits become active and ascend above our heads to reveal any wrongdoing. For this reason, *Geng Sheng* Day is traditionally a time to keep a peaceful mental and physical expression to protect the brain and allow the high spirit of life to control the negative spirits.

Another observance is appropriate each lunar month at the time of no moon, just before the new moon. At this time the Kitchen Spirit, representing the harmonious atmosphere of the family's collective lower level spirits, becomes active. These spirits provide for the nourishment of physical maintenance, and the family's collective aura will rise to the sky to be seen by the gods and spiritually developed ones. Since the kitchen is where we can prepare offerings to both the visible and invisible spheres of life, it should be kept

---

1. The double yang metal day that takes place once in every 60-day cycle. It is traditionally a day set aside for cultivation and renewal. For more information see the *Esoteric Tao Teh Ching* and *The Book of Changes and the Unchanging Truth*.

clean, peaceful, and nicely ordered, as should the physical aspects of our being.

Sins or transgressions against the normal, healthy condition of life can cause both big and small troubles. For big transgressions we may lose a complete 12-year cycle of life, while for smaller transgressions we may lose a nick. On the other hand, gathering spiritual merit can add units of time to our lives. Those of us who wish to attain an everlasting life, or at least a long and happy life, must avoid doing evil or making any conscious transgressions against the nature of life.

(7) We should move toward that which flows with the waves of the Way. It is optimal to maintain our freedom to respond appropriately to the webless network and not confine ourselves to rigid emotions, attitudes, or life situations. We should learn how to retreat from that which is against the flow of the Way, so as not to restrict our range of motion or evoke a tightening of the web around our lives.

(8) Examples of good and safe directions include:

Take no wrong paths.

Do not cheat.

Be kind and gentle with people and things.

Do not harm plants or any life thoughtlessly.

Be loyal to society and dutiful to your parents.

Love your brothers and sisters and respect your elders.

Care for the young and assist the widowed and helpless.

Straighten your own life, and then help others do the same.

Be happy with yourself and respect the progress and achievement of others.

Have sympathy for people in trouble.

Offer relief to people in an emergency.

See other people's gain as your gain and their loss as your loss.

Do not publicize the shortcomings of others.

Do not brag about your own advantage.

Take less and let others take more.

Do not hold resentment or take offense.

Be wary of being favored.

Ask no return for your good deeds.

Have no regret for offering your help to others.

(9) With good and safe behaviors we receive beneficial results and respect from others. Heaven sends blessings to us and evil spirits shun us. The spiritual realm protects us as we continue to accumulate merit and establish high spiritual achievement. To those of us who are searching for high spiritual satisfaction and the freedom of a Heavenly Being, 1300 good deeds should be realized. To those who wish to enjoy a trouble-free life on earth as an earthly spiritual superior, 300 good deeds should be accumulated.

(10) Those who aim for a good life and spiritual achievement must keep away from improper behavior. The most important factor to consider is ethical development. The health of our consciousness is of deep value to our lives and it is the root of our entire being. Our individual moral condition must therefore be the main spiritual concern above any type of religious preference or style. All behaviors that can negatively affect personal spiritual health must be removed like the rotten roots of unhealthy vegetation.

Until basic, universal moral standards are recognized by all people, there will be no resolution to worldly conflict. Universal morality should be the essential spiritual effort of the new generations. Let us develop basic universal ethics and reduce all tension between religions.

(11) We should not do anything that goes against the cause of righteousness. The cause of righteousness is based on the nature of God. Human nature is derived from God, but the general mind has forgotten this and replaced the real God with a conceptual god. For thousands of years, social religions have promoted a conceptual god, creating great confusion and conflict within society. Failure to recognize the true, living nature of God can lead to inhumane acts, cruelty, and all kinds of evil doing.

Other behaviors that should be avoided include:

Secretly causing harm to others.

Secretly disobeying the laws of society.

Disregarding the kind wishes of your parents.

Disrespecting your teacher.

Neglecting your duty.

Fooling those who are less learned.

Scandalizing others or punishing the innocent.

Stirring up trouble without concern for others.

Being overly assertive or headstrong.

Mistaking right for wrong and wrong for right.

Keeping the company of bad people and avoiding the company of good people.

Flattering superiors and punishing subordinates.

Not appreciating the help and kindness of others and maintaining resentment toward others.

Slighting the life of people or disturbing the social order.

Taking another's life for profit.

Undermining another's position for self-interest.

Fighting and competing for power and authority.

Killing people who have surrendered.

Demoting and degrading the upright and sincere.

Maltreating orphans or widows.

Taking bribes or abandoning laws.

Making the straight way crooked and considering the crooked way straight.

Sentencing light misdeeds with heavy punishment.

Raging around or taunting people who are being executed.

*Failing to admit mistakes or to change your mistaken behavior even
  with clear knowledge.*

Abdicating your responsibility to others.

Hiding good and useful discoveries for selfish reasons.

Slandering sages and virtuous people.

Persecuting moral and upright people.

Creating danger or trouble for others.

Reducing other's possessions for your own profit.

Exchanging unworthy goods or deeds or failing to maintain fair trade.

Undermining public benefits for selfish gain.

Stealing credit for another's achievements.

Concealing the talents of others and exposing their shortcomings.

Disclosing another's secrets or consuming their goods.

Assisting others in doing evil.

Using power to satisfy unworthy desires.

Disgracing others for personal gain.

Damaging people's crops.

Destroying people's marriages.

Becoming wealthy by improper means and remaining proud of it.

Evading punishment for shameful acts.

Attributing misfortune to others and hiding your own misdeeds.

Concealing your own shortcomings.

Vainly gathering name and social position by crafty, cunning, or deceptive means.

Threatening others with force.

Indulging in violence and killing.

Breaking into other people's homes and stealing.

Setting fire to or vandalizing another's property.

Creating obstructions to the success of others or destroying their tools or means of livelihood.

Hoping for the failure of others who are doing well.

Working to have dutiful people exiled.

Evading or wishing harm upon your creditors.

Cursing others because they have denied your wishes.

Enjoying the failures or shortcomings of others.

Repressing the talented.

Making fun of another's appearance.

Wrongfully trying to attract people for negative purposes.

Taking another's property by force.

Robbing others to become rich.

Scheming for promotion.

Being unjust in delivering reward or punishment.

Overindulging in physical pleasures.

Being overly critical of subordinates.

Threatening others for fun or profit.

Fanning the flames of other people's arguments.

Engaging in mob behavior for evil doing.

Being unfaithful to your superiors.

Creating unfavorable situations or making groundless, bad comments about others.

Defaming others behind their backs.

Maintaining self-righteousness while slandering others.

Striving for excessive personal gain.

Using untruthful teachings to attract others.

Giving up what is good and true to support wrongdoing.

Conducting business unfairly for profit.

Deceiving the undeveloped to build your own strength.

Maintaining the appearance of kindness while harboring cunning intentions.

Mixing falseness with truth.

Denying people's good faith in life.

Promoting narrow-mindedness or guiding others on the path of disintegration and death.

Special Considerations for Family Life

For men:

Be faithful and loyal to earn the cooperation and respect of your spouse and to maintain good relations.

Refrain from the habit of overly boasting or disrespecting women and children.

Refrain from getting drunk or behaving against the natural morality of life.

Always strive to be creative in doing your best to provide for all your family members.

For women:

Remain soft and gentle.

Maintain sincere respect for your men and avoid competing with them.

Refrain from jealousy.

Refrain from unnecessary cursing or swearing.

Remain respectful to your in-laws.

Refrain from pushing your men for more power, wealth, or social influence to feed your own vanity.

For both men and women:

Refrain from disrespecting your ancestors. (They did their best to continue the family line as you are doing now for future generations.)

Remember all useful learning from your elders.

Always seek to maintain the harmony and prosperity of your family.

Do not cling to selfish intentions.

Hold no hatred or resentment for others nor curse them in private.

To maintain your personal energy field in life avoid:

Shooting birds and driving animals away for mere emotional pleasure.

Disturbing hibernating animals or disrupting flocks of birds for no good reason.

Toppling the nests of birds or plugging up the holes of animals.

Harming pregnant animals or breaking birds' eggs.

To maintain the natural cycles in the human spiritual sphere avoid:

Blaming God for human failure.

Blaming other people for personal failures.

Cursing the weather for personal unhappiness.

Using the image of Heaven and Earth to support personal ambition.

Quoting holy sayings to prove your righteousness, especially in trivial circumstances or matters.

Jumping over wells or earthen ovens. *(You need to respect the public water sources and places of food preparation to avoid their unnecessary contamination.)*

Striding over food, cooking utensils, or people.

Terminating unwanted babies or babies with defects. *(Farmer's families in the countryside did these things in earlier times. Today birth control should be used in advance.)*

Engaging in strange behaviors secretly.

Making merry or being emotional during the end of the lunar month, in the early morning hours, during the seasonal transitions, or at the end of the year. *(These times should be kept for silent renewal, reflection on what has occurred, and preparation for the time ahead.)*

Spitting or urinating while facing north, especially in the remote outdoors or wilderness. *(This would show disrespect to the North Star, which represents the spiritual direction of all humans. It is also important to avoid exposing yourself to the wind.)*

Singing or crying while facing the oven and when cooking. *(This is to avoid contact with smoke or ash and to avoid disrespecting the symbol of the household's peace.)*

Using the oven or stove to light incense. *(The oven fire is for the cooking of food, which serves the body, while incense serves as a symbolic offering to spirit, which is the light of life.)*

Using improper fuel for cooking. *(For instance, in some places dried animal waste is used for cooking. This is disrespectful of life.)*

Exposing your nude body to cold winter weather or during outdoor camping, especially at night.

Engaging in negative or destructive activities during:

	Northern Hemisphere	Southern Hemisphere
The beginning of spring	(Feb. 4th or 5th)	(August 4th or 5th)
The beginning of summer	(May 6th or 7th)	(Nov. 6th or 7th)
The beginning of autumn	(August 8th or 9th)	(Feb. 8th or 9th)
The beginning of winter	(Nov. 7th or 8th)	(May 7th or 8th)
The vernal equinox	(around March 21st)	(around Sept. 21st)
The summer solstice	(June 21st or 22nd)	(Dec. 21st or 22nd)
The autumnal equinox	(Sept. 23rd or 24th)	(March 23rd or 24th)
The winter solstice	(around Dec. 22nd)	(around June 22nd)

Spitting at shooting stars. (In the East, people used to spit at shooting stars because they believed they were bad omens. This is ignorant behavior. In the West, the image of a witch riding a broom was similarly treated as a bad omen, but this is just superstition.)

Pointing fingers at rainbows, as this is disrespectful.

Pointing fingers or excessive staring at the sun or the moon.
(This is disrespectful and can damage the eyes.)

Hunting creatures or burning grass and bushes in the wilderness in the spring, as this is the mating and reproductive season.

Cursing while facing north or unnecessarily killing turtles or snakes. (Turtles and snakes are the spiritual symbols of the northern sky energy and the seven constellations that reside there. These seven constellations form the shape of a reptile. In earthly life, north represents the head and is the source of heaven and spiritual life. Because the head is related to the north, it should be kept cool, while the body, which relates to the south, should be kept warm.)

The above unhealthy behaviors cause negative effects in our lives. The seriousness of a transgression determines whether we lose a nick or a complete 12-year cycle. Once our individual account is emptied by spiritual transgressions, we will die an unnatural death. If the spiritual debt is more than can be repaid by our individual life, the suffering will be passed on in the form of unhealthy genetic material to our descendants. Though the new life must endure some suffering, there is still an opportunity to awaken spiritually and purify the unhealthy genetic legacy.

Those who make a living out of the suffering of other people will pay by their own lives and possibly those of their spouse and children. Even if death is not immediate, they will incur different types of suffering, such as flooding, fire, robbery, theft, loss of possessions, disease, and conflict. The repayment must equal the amount of wrongdoing. Those who take another's life without justification will incur similar disasters and those who make money by improper means are only creating poison to quench their thirst. The thirst of these people, however, is never quenched and death follows them closely.

On the other hand, those whose intentions are good, even if their good deeds do not succeed, will gather good energy into their lives. The healthy spiritual sphere, which is interrelated to their lives, gives support accordingly. But, for those whose intentions are bad, even if the bad deeds are not successful, they will gather evil energy into their lives as an invisible vibration, and lower spiritual entities will jump at the chance to join such a life.

Constructive and destructive spirits have no physical strength unless they attach to a human life. This is why our human life energy is so precious. Our lives must be kept clean and pure to attract good spiritual energy and repel negative energy. Those who have done bad deeds, but later repent thoroughly and purify their spirits can, through persistent and constant good deeds, bring about a positive change in their lives. This is how to change troubles into blessings, misfortunes into good fortunes, and misery into rejoicing.

Good people, therefore, speak about good things, look at things in a positive light, and fulfill goodness at every turn. When we practice these three actions in our everyday lives, we can strengthen the subtle vibration of our minds within three years. This in turn will attract goodness into our lives and Heaven will extend blessings to us. Bad people, on the other hand, who speak evil, view things as evil, and fulfill evil activity, will naturally attract negativity into their lives.

Though the Way is easy to practice most of us make it difficult for ourselves. True heavenly blessings are free, such as peace, safety, prosperity, and a long happy life. There is no charge for these high blessings in life, and they are not difficult to achieve; most of us just don't see their true value. Instead we constantly trade these blessings for temporary excitement and all kinds of suffering. This is how angels transform into devils. Unfortunately, even devils have the power to create exactly what they choose in their lives. Do not trade your precious life energy for devilish activities. Be an angel in life and enjoy true blessings.

A *Summary of the* Heavenly Way

(This piece is contributed by a student of the College of Spiritual Science and Art at the Yo San University of Traditional Chinese Medicine, Los Angeles, California.)

Dear OmNi,

I want to thank you for assisting me in bringing my awareness back to the soul, the center of all my searching and spiritual pursuits. It is with me always, and simply by me living a virtuous life with joy and happiness my soul will naturally rest in its shell. Through my self-cultivation and living a virtuous life, within the guidelines of the *Heavenly Way,* I wish to create the most suitable environment for my soul to rest in.

The *Heavenly Way* is a guide to living an integral life within this world and following it enables me to protect and maintain a healthy soul. This first step to spiritual integration is where one's body, mind, and soul become one in everyday life. The *Heavenly Way* gives practical guidance by listing worldly pursuits that negatively impact on my soul and create further obstacles to my development. We are swimming in a sea of *chi* and every thought and deed sends out ripples of energy into the vast ocean of consciousness. As I accept the truth of living within the sea, my awareness of the waves and their impact grows. I see how my thoughts and deeds create my life's experiences, delivering fortune and misfortune.

How to live my life is my responsibility. By sincerely embracing the truth that is described within the *Heavenly Way* and applying its lesson in my life, I can reform my destiny and remove the self-created obstacles. Through my cultivation, I weed out the negative influences: the thoughts, actions, and relationships that create negative ripples within my life.

My purpose in life is to cultivate my purest, innermost nature. This means supporting myself through activities that help society, while uplifting my own development. My chosen direction to pursue this goal is through practicing Traditional Chinese Medical healing and teaching. I am grateful for having found this path and the tradition that is the Integral Way, and for your role in gently guiding me toward the truth that is my own eternal soul. Thank you again for your patience and understanding.

Love from Your Friend and Student

Chapter 19

The Hidden Spiritual Responsibility of Personal and Social Behavior

God and the Individual Soul

The good souls of living human life comprise the human spiritual world, and these good souls converge to be God. All good souls are deeply related to nature and make nature their background while they serve the human world. Why? When a soul is backed by nature it means there is no more narrow-mindedness or prejudice in play. These good souls have dissolved the contamination and limitation from worldly living and achieved universal Godly nature.

There is another part to human spirituality in which God represents the spiritual progress of people. At a different level of human spiritual stature, spirituality is projected. In truth, God is the projection from all good souls that appreciate and join with one another to be God. But when a different spiritual quality is projected, an image of God is presented as the spirituality. Thus the spiritual life of humanity is also the spiritual growth of its people.

Your Life and Soul

An individual life is both biologically and spiritually based and its core is the soul. The spiritual energy of the soul is the core of the physical existence of all individual lives. As a result, your soul is necessarily involved in your life's activities and behaviors that, individually and collectively, cause the strengthening or weakening of your soul. In other words, your hardworking, normal, and circumstantial behaviors form your soul's condition. And, though you may not see it or feel it, the good or bad health of your soul will be reflected exactly in your physical condition. Thus your general health is one aspect of your external life that is affected by your internal condition.

In modern terms this means that once you damage your soul, even though you may have a good insurance policy or good medical care, these external things can't really help since your ill-health comes from the deep internal sphere of your life—your unhealthy or suffering soul. Thus a long life, short life, healthy life, unhealthy life, happy life, and unhappy life reveal the condition of your soul's development in relation to your physical life partner. Though not as obvious as the physical and mental spheres of your life, the health of your soul does determine the quality and length of your life.

The Modern Condition of General Souls

The problem with modern life is that it overexalts personal freedom. It even interprets freedom to mean self-indulgence rather than its deep sense of spiritual and personal freedom.

In overpopulated places such as crowded cities, the pressure of life is unnaturally heavy and people easily ignore moral problems. Due to the benefit of an improved level of education however, some modern people do pay attention to their behavior, and suffer less from bad choices and their moral consequences. But this benefit is often lost through overindulgence, such as overeating, excessive sex, and all kinds of extreme physical and social activities, for mere emotional excitement. Overindulgence is a bigger problem than ever before. The modern cultural tendency of overexternalizing life has caused life to lose its all-important balance.

It is the old fashion in social spiritual promotion to apply morality mostly to personal social behaviors. But early people of the Way also considered it immoral to treat their bodies poorly, because life is an endowment from Nature. Thus overeating, excessive sex, and other overdone emotional and physical activities were considered immoral as they caused one's life to weaken. Based on the teaching of the Way, the balanced view of life should be accepted for the health and safety of your life and as the basic moral obligation toward your physical life.

The Way is the Discovery of the Ageless Experience of Human Life

Unlike the conventional lip service from the external religions, the Way or Ageless Truth of Life is the accumulated wisdom from human life experience through endless generations. The people of the Way closely observed that cultural or social trends either lead people to good health or to poor health. As a part of your personal spiritual duty you need to be aware of this and self-correct to limit any negative influence. Since the conventional priesthood has neglected its professional duty to alter the course of troublesome trends and has actually added to modern problems, the old religions have lost their important social function.

To pursue good health, it is not enough to merely exercise and take vitamins. Your choice of lifestyle and vigilance over your moral behaviors are just as important for your long, happy, and healthy life.

The Spiritual Service from One Outstanding Individual

There is an old treatise written by an outstanding individual that relates to spiritual responsibility in personal and social behavior. It points out that your soul's health is the strength of your life's survival. Though short, it carries a powerful message to people of high conscience.

The Strength of Spiritual Survival by Chang O

(Originally Presented as Yin Chi Wen— *"The Quietest Way of Internal Strength Building")*

According to generations of study, *Yin Chi Wen,* "Tract of the Quietest Way," appeared to the public no later than the early Tang Dynasty (618–906 CE). My family favored this teaching and adopted it as part of my youth education. During my childhood, probably no village or family in China was without it. Its social influence was almost equal to the earlier writing of the *Tai Shan Kan Yin Pien.* That spiritual treatise points out the moral consequences of your personal behavior, while the *Yin Chi Wen* points out the moral consequences of both personal and social behavior. Both treatises show that there is a spiritual responsibility for improper behavior.

We are convinced that the long-lived China has survived because of the moral condition of its society. Different politics bring turmoil to a society in various generations, but the moral strength of the general people has maintained China as a vast society with a unique culture that outlived all ordeals. Deeply learned Westerners like Dr. Paul Carus of early last century said: "We cannot help granting that the character of the Chinese maxims ranges very high; and we must confess that among all the nations of the world there is perhaps none other so seriously determined to live up to the highest standard of ethical culture."

We appreciate what he observed. As natives and pupils of a long Chinese history, we can see that the moral strength of the people is the only thing that ensures real happiness in life. Nothing good comes from the external establishment, though it can provide better social connections among people.

This moral foundation of Chinese social strength characterized most individuals and their families, even if a few cunning ones found ways for temporal social success. Unlike societies outside China's natural boundary, whose social foundations were the churches of organized religions, in China you see few churches, but if you take some time you will understand the hidden power of respect for the virtues of life.

The main theme of the *Yin Chi Wen* is the strong testimony to the secret blessings that come from the enduring spiritual strength in personal life rather than from any other source. As an individual, your personal moral condition still expresses the real spiritual strength of life.

Chang O was the author's secular name. For many lifetimes, he lived a life that exemplified the most truthful doctrine: that social struggle may bring external victories and temporal needs, but it is through the power of an upright character that the soul endures. His spirit has been respected as the Authority of Civil and Moral Power. After serving as a royal official of the Tang Dynasty, he lived simply as a recluse. During his official career he exercised moral power over the people and his moral influence still has a tremendous unconscious influence on the Chinese people. He was also respected for his natural personality that was filled with spiritual nobility and piety. The people of Tzu Tung district of Shu (now a place in the Shih Chuang province), where Chang O lived, showed respect and affection for him, and after he died they built the Temple of Prevailing Civil Power in his honor. People near and far came to pray and pay their homage to the sage of Tzu Tung.

Here is what he revealed.

> For 17 lifetimes, I have been incarnated as a learned person and lived a respectful life. The secret strength I hold within, over my many lifetimes, is that I have never oppressed or maltreated anyone. I helped people in misfortune, rescued people from poverty, shown compassion to orphans, and forgiven people for their mistakes. I have extensively practiced the hidden virtuous fulfillment of good deeds without proclaiming credit, in order to attune my being with the nature of Heaven above.

If you are able to keep your heart as I have kept mine, Heaven will surely bestow blessings upon you. Therefore here I reveal the secret source of these blessings. This will enable you to attain a better life, internally and externally, in this lifetime and in future lifetimes, from the Everlasting One.

Let any individual who wants to expand the field of happiness lay the foundation of it in the depth of their heart.

Practice kindness wherever you find a suitable and correct opportunity, and let your deeds of spiritual merit go unheeded.

Do good at all times and secretly practice many meritorious deeds to acquire spiritual strength.

Benefit all living creatures and all human beings by cultivating goodness and happiness.

Be honest like the nature of Heaven in conducting your affairs, cheating no one, including yourself.

Be compassionate in the administration of your state affairs, which must be devoted to the salvation of people.

Let your heart be impartial and wide of range.

Fulfill your four obligations: Be faithful and reverential to the order of the global human society. Be filial and obedient to parents and elders. Be congenial and friendly to all people. Be sincere in your relationships with your life partners.

Impartially observe the highest doctrines of spiritual unity within and without, but let people have their different stages of growth.

Let all people know to worship the truthful oneness of the universal
divinity. Be mindful that some spiritual teachings in specific
locations may carry this highest truth too.

Discourse on morality and righteousness and convert both the
cunning and the dull.

Preach on the canonical books and histories and enlighten
the ignorant.

Relieve people in distress as speedily as you must release a fish
from a dry rill, so it will not die.

Deliver people from danger as quickly as you must free a sparrow
from a tight noose.

Be compassionate to orphans and kind to widows.

Respect the aged and help the poor and the poor in spirit.

Promote good and recommend wisdom.

Be lenient with others and exacting with yourself.

Save your spare clothing and provisions so that you may give them
to those in need.

Give away coffins so the dead among the poor will not be exposed.
However, have a coffin for yourself in which to bury your own ego
and the past.

Build charitable graveyards for unclaimed corpses.

Set philanthropic instructions for the education of young ones.

If your own family is well provided for, extend a helping hand
to your relatives.

If the harvest fails, then help your neighbors and friends.

Let measures and scales be accurate, and be neither chary in selling nor exacting in buying. Above all have accurate scales for your virtues too.

Treat your employees with fairness and consideration.

Do not expect perfection nor be too strict in your demands.

Publish and make known good works and sacred scriptures to upgrade people's spiritual condition and the healthy knowledge of life. The best is not said with words, but with subtle virtues.

Build and repair temples and shrines as many people need symbols of the spiritual sphere of life. But do not neglect the temple and shrine within yourself.

Distribute medicine to alleviate the suffering of the sick.

Offer tea and water to relieve the distress of the thirsty.

Light lanterns at night to illuminate the path where people may walk.

Keep and build boats to ferry people across rivers. Be a "ferry" for those who are unable to cross life's troubled waters.

Buy captive creatures and set them free.

Abstain from taking life by your own hand or with your command; it is not a privilege for humankind to slaughter others.

While walking be mindful of ants, insects, and the like.

Be cautious with fire. Do not set mountain woods or forests ablaze. Also do not set "fire" among people.

Do not go into the mountains to catch birds in nets nor to the water to poison fish.

Do not butcher the ox that plows your field.

Do not throw away your writing, and respect the writing of others.

Do not envy others' accomplishments, but sharpen your own to better serve people.

Do not sexually harm anyone. Sexual violation only results in self-destruction and has no benefit.

Do not initiate litigation nor stir others to litigate.

Do not injure the reputation or interests of others.

Do not meddle with the conjugal affairs of others.

Do not, on account of personal malice, create disharmony between brothers.

Never take advantage of your power, nor set father and son at odds. Do not misuse your power to disgrace good and law-abiding people.

Do not be presumptuous if you are rich, nor deceive the needy and suffering. Instead, offer them opportunities for survival and better living.

While attending to your duty, be humble and modest.

Live in harmony with your relatives and among your fellow people.

Let go of hatred and forgive malice.

Be close and friendly with good people that will help you practice virtue with your body and soul. Keep a distance from the wicked; this will protect you from evil.

Pass in silence over things wicked, but broadcast all that is good.

Do not assert with your mouth what your heart denies.

Always have in mind helpful sayings.

Cut the brambles and thorns that obstruct the road. Remove sticks and stones that lie in the path.

Repair the roads and passes that have been unimproved for many years, since they help to smooth your own life's road.

Build bridges over which thousands of people may travel.

Expound moral maxims so others can correct their faults. More importantly, leave your subtle virtuous merits for generations to come.

Supply the means to help others of talent complete their good deeds.

Let your work conform to the Heavenly Law, and let your speech express humaneness.

Keep the ancient sages before your eyes even when eating or while looking over the fence.

Be mindful when you are alone in the shadow of your blanket.

Perform all good deeds and restrain from doing evil, so you will be released forever from the influence of evil, and always be surrounded by good guardian angels.

Immediate rewards will come to you, and later rewards will reach your posterity depending on how you treat others. Your close descendants not only carry the genes from you and through you, but before the age of 30, they reflect your own spiritual condition. A hundred blessings will come to you in loads like a chariot pulled by rushing horses; a thousand fortunes will surround you like a mass of clouds gathering above. Do not all these things accrue in the heart of the quiet Heaven?

Reflections from the Later Generations

The work of Chang O represents the moral awakening of all deeply learned people. Many evaluations of his work have been made in later generations by those who deeply studied the *Yin Chi Wen*. Some even show their appreciation by expressing their sincere intention to follow Chang O's spiritual example. The following spiritual reflections were presented as attachments to the Tract when it was published for the public.

Only the True God Represents Spiritual Oneness

The True God inspires Chang O to take compassion on the ignorance of all sentient beings that cannot liberate themselves from the curse of their accumulated spiritual responsibility. So he proclaims these moral instructions, thereby opening the way to enlightenment for generations to come. His love is greater than that of a father who instructs his children, and his discipline is greater than that of a master who trains his disciples. How sincere, surely, is the road that leads to sainthood and enlightenment, the best method that avoids misfortune and rescues us from evil. May people who receive these instructions exert all their mental energy to actualize them and to attune themselves to the boundless love of the True God of Spiritual Oneness to save themselves and their world.

Heaven and Earth

Heaven, as the *yang* principle of the Lord of the Universe, and Earth, as the *yin* principle of the Lord of the Universe, are both the functions of the Lord of the Universe. They constantly work to regenerate the ten thousand things. That is their purpose. If the thought of a person is bent on benefiting others, then that person becomes The Lord of *Yang* and *Yin*, the Heaven and Earth in life, not merely appearing in the form of a male or a female.

It is not sufficient for people of high social stature to refrain from coveting promotion and seeking wealth. They should employ benevolence to benefit all fellow people. Otherwise, the purpose for which Heaven created us will be altogether lost.

A Heavenly Judge

A Heavenly Judge is someone who straightens their own life to live according to the Heavenly Subtle Law. Through your good example, you can bring good influence to others. May you be a Heavenly Judge of the quality described by Lord Chang O.

Humaneness Rewarded

The Way of *yin* and *yang* in life can be illustrated by the law of cause and effect among your behaviors in life, such as what you sow so shall you reap. The reward may manifest either in this life or in succeeding lives. The Heavenly Network is vast and hangs loosely, but it never permits any thing to escape. You must harbor no doubt about this.

Save as Many Lives as You Can

The closest life to save is your own. You need to save yourself from life's excesses such as overeating, oversleeping, excessive sex and greed, and the exaggerated arrogance of thinking you know it all, as well as the many other things beginning with the prefix "over."

The Double-Headed Snake

The movement of both human society and individual life is like the movement of a double-headed snake. Most of the time, the two heads move in the same direction with double standards and double practices, so there are individuals with two faces, forked tongues, and insincere minds. At other times, the two heads move in self-contradictory ways. Sometimes both heads move in the same negative direction, thus evil assists evil. Very rarely do the two heads join together to move in one constructive direction for the benefit of all.

The Foundation of Bliss

All deeds originate in the heart. All the good acts that are enumerated above begin in the heart and are completed in the heart. The heart's innermost recess is the very spot where there is Heaven and where there is Hell. The difference between the wise ones, such as Niao and Shun (the ancient wise emperors), and the wretched, selfish ones, such as Jey (the last emperor of the Hsia Dynasty) and Jou (the last emperor of the Shang Dynasty), pivots around this very small thing. The latter two emperors abused their powers for personal enjoyment.

In the heart's innermost recess unexpected blessings grow, as if they were in an actual field. Though spiritual and mysterious, it possesses a solid, tangible soil that can be watered and tilled. The soul of a true, earnest, and gentle person has its root in this obscure recess, which one examines and purifies in solemn silence and privacy. The way of self-purification and the sure foundation of bliss lie simply in a heart that respects others, not in one that makes light of the world or in one that nurses personal indulgence and self-delusion.

Seek Truth for the Salvation of the Soul

If a respectable individual is disposed toward loving kindness, they cannot help doing things to benefit others. If a villain is bent on selfishness, he will surely do things harmful to others. People who think about and care for others are those of superior personality, and people who think only of themselves are those of smallness. The difference lies in one's own fundamental thought, whether it is of the ego or not. Some incessantly accumulate evil, while others gather good deeds; when we see the result, the difference is as clear as the sky and earth.

A strange, saintly personage once warned an eminent truth seeker: "I see you are seeking the truth. But if you would have it for your private self, saints and gods will have no regard for you." Are not gods and saints as well as sages and holy people bent on saving the world? Some seek saintliness in their pursuit of everlasting life and immortality, but if their heart is tainted with a single thought of egotism, they are grievously at fault. This is so even though it may be hidden and they do not know it. There is no chance of their ever attaining sainthood.

The Disease of Egotism

When others do good, fall in line as if it were your work and be sure to bring it to completion. Treat others' property as if it were your own, so you will be thoughtful in using it. Some people have thousands of troubles because they cling to the idea of self. Therefore they scheme and contrive in ten thousand different ways. They alone want to be rich, they alone want to be happy, they alone want to enjoy life, they alone want to be blessed with longevity; and to others' poverty, misery, danger, or suffering, these people are altogether indifferent. It is for this reason that they disregard the life-will of others and neglect the Heavenly Subtle Law. The only cure for this disease is the vastness of infinite space, so that wealth, honor, happiness, comfort, health, and longevity can all be enjoyed. Everyone will have his or her natural longings satisfied, and the Heavenly Subtle Law will be displayed with untold exuberance.

Filial Piety

Filial piety, the duty of children, is the guide of all actions. It is the ultimate root of humaneness. Is it possible that the root can be rotten while the branches and leaves grow luxuriantly?

The four essential elements of filial piety are:

(1) To be established in virtue in order to extend your life to be helpful for others.

(2) To keep up the family.

(3) To keep your body unimpaired.

(4) To cultivate your character so as not to disgrace your genes and spiritual essence.

Pious children will not:

Let their parents' heart be roused to thoughts of cold indifference.

Let their parents' hearts be annoyed or harassed.

Let their parents' hearts be alarmed or filled with fear.

Let their parents' hearts be aggrieved or embarrassed.

Let their parents' hearts be perplexed.

Let their parents' hearts feel ashamed or indignant.

Notice the difference between the early Chinese and those people outside of China, all of whom may respect God: those outside China established faith in God as their spiritual ruler, but the early people of China respected the sky or Heaven as the common source of their lives. Thus their attitude toward the sky is practiced in exactly the same way as their filial duty toward their parents in life.

All Good Ways Reach the Same Goal

Without the universal divine heart, all people might not be induced to goodness. The True God of Spiritual Oneness inspires people differently. They may pay homage at a sanctuary or a temple, they may worship the sky, or they may bow before statues of deities or sages and recite the classics or sutras. If they do so with single-mindedness and sincerity of heart, all of these roads will lead to goodness; but there should be no thought of attaining blessings or acquiring rewards.

Practices Vary

What is to be avoided most in your life is vacillation and frivolity, and what is most excellent is a reverential heart. Therefore, endeavor to preserve sincerity of heart and consider reverence as most essential. Sincerity and reverence make you a companion of Heaven, Earth, Gods, and Spirits.

There are individuals, however, amongst the crowds that adopt various religions as their guidance, who bow before statues and recite the sutras, always bent on preserving reverence and awe. They will hardly relax their vigilant guard over the heart, which will by degrees become pure and bright, free from evil thoughts and ready to do good. This enlightenment is called the "most happy land." Here, too, avoiding vacillation and frivolity remains essential for the religious follow-ers and the people of the untainted truth, for those things render you unreliable. Always keep your heart restrained with reverence and awe. Otherwise, what is the use of doing all the required rituals, such as the recitation of Buddhist sutras or the discourses of Confucius?

A Sympathetic Heart

The great virtue of Heaven and Earth is to create. All living beings, humankind, and animals alike, derive their vitality from this one and same source. Nowhere under the sun is there a being that dislikes life and embraces death with joy.

To respect all lives, set unneeded, captured animals free. Do not abuse the lives of animals or your own. Some people, in a sympathetic outburst of the heart, buy caged animals to set them free: there are more meaningful things to do with your spare money. Thoughtless people make light of small creatures such as ants, spiders and so forth. They kill them for wanton or no reasons at all. Another way is to cage them, having no thought of pity or remorse; but pious hearts refrain from such cruelty.

The Voice Within

The Heavenly Reason consists of two words, but they are in your own heart. If when you do a thing and in your heart there remains some misgiving, then your deed is against Heaven and contrary to Reason. A virtuous individual scrupulously guards himself or herself when alone, solely to retain Heaven's Reason and to calm human desires. That is to say: "Attend to your duty and do not scheme for gain. Look after what you ought to do and do not measure your merit."

The source of good and evil is in the heart, and the best method of controlling it is a reverential attitude of the heart. Ever turbulent is the heart of the one who does evil; ever wakeful is the heart of the one who does good.

The teachings of spiritually focused people are written in many books. There are a thousand gates and ten thousand doors, but through which shall you enter? The main point is to guard yourself when alone so you do not go astray. Then you will see how your strength grows.

Proceed in goodness for a thousand days and that will not be enough; proceed in evil for half a minute and it will be too much.

The Law Behind the Moral Law

You should be selective about the conditions of your life that impact on you. Worldly heroes are conditioned by their society and time. In contrast, the masters of life—the true heroes of moral victory—select their own conditions; they are above the control of conditions. When you understand that people are subject to conditioning, you know to first observe the conditions before making a selection. The value of your spiritual growth is to learn to be selective and not give mastery over your life to the conditions of your life. Rather, it is better to create your own conditions.

Human life was created by the most harmonious conditions, as are the rewards of a good life. Spiritual self-cultivation is your life's spiritual education. The truth is you need to carefully choose the spiritual conditions for your soul's nutrition to avoid the degradation and suffering that comes from worldly culture and other conditions of life. This can assure your spiritual success. Please refer to the book *Stepping Stones for Spiritual Success*, which can help you form the foundation of your great life being.

Chapter 20

Imminent Salvation for the Present Time

The Way means how to live a life correctly according to nature.
It can be applied to an individual or to all people collectively.

The Way is Universal Nature itself.
It is flexible, above broadness or narrowness.

We have the choice to live our lives narrowly
and burn out fast, or to live the far-reaching
and long enduring way.

Though the matter can be understood relatively,
it brings forth the possibility that
we can join in the decision making of our own destiny.

A living life can be perceived as an open opportunity.
The opportunity has no fault.
What matters is our personal growth
in shaping our fortune.

To make the high choice we need to grow our wisdom.
We can fail, however, by overly attempting to search
for wisdom outside of our lives.
Truly useful wisdom is installed in life itself.
It shines through clouds in our daily life.

Intellectual knowledge requires wide reading, learning,
studying, and researching.
Wisdom appears by living normally and peacefully even in difficulty.

Rush and haste block the good flow of the natural mind.
While living a quiet and calm life allows
life's wisdom to identify with our life being.

Wood or metal can be shaped and reshaped,
when their natural good foundation still exists.
We too can be conditioned and reconditioned,
but only when our natural condition remains unharmed.
From this simple fact, we should see that
developing the natural potency of our lives is far more important
than gathering all the adhesives along the way.

We can be conditioned to be good or bad.
We can be conditioned to be smart or foolish.
And we can be conditioned to be rich or poor.
Most of us are subjected to all conditions.
Often we proclaim our ideas and expectations
without seeing how our conditioning made us behave.

We can be conditioned to be good,
and by acting on those good conditions
we are recognized as good.
True virtue, though, is the normalcy of nature which makes us so.

We can be conditioned to be bad.
We merely execute the conditions to produce wrongdoing.
Proudly mischievous,

we cannot see that we are victims of our own conditioning.
There is no pride in being so.

Our parents conditioned us far before we were born.
They and their surroundings conditioned us in our early lives.
They shaped the pattern from which we learnt to react to life's situations.
At the beginning that may not strip us of joy.
Gradually we lose our natural angelic being,
by subjecting our life to conditions,
some of which we cannot refuse, while in others we have a choice.
We subject our life to the conditions mostly for external reasons.

I met three jugglers of life some time ago.
"A" said he would be happy if he had a million dollars.
"B" said he would be happy if he earned a Ph.D. degree.
"C" said he would happy if he married a beautiful woman.

Years passed by.
I met them again.
"A" said he would be happy if he possessed many millions.
"B" said he would be happy if he could win the Nobel Prize.
"C" said he would be happy if he could be with more beautiful women.

Each got what he once wanted so desperately.
The more they got, they more restless they became.
Having more has become the condition for wanting more.
The good life is consumed by having more.
The direct and balanced proportion has been ignored.
The ladder to living externally has no end.
Observe objectively:
Does striving for life cause the loss of life's naturalness?

If being good or bad comes from acting on the conditions of our lives,
then from where and from what comes our sense of responsibility for life?
We need to ask ourselves, "On what do we weigh the value of life?
Do we value life on the externals or on life itself?"

If we are willing to pull down the smoky curtain,
we may see that the responsibility of life is to nurture life's naturalness.
All the externals are far from the essence of life.

Why can't we see this by ourselves?
Before the growth of life, we habitually gather things,
both material and nonmaterial, without cultivating discernment.
After a while, our lives become occupied with garbage.
We see and think the garbage is our life's identity.
We have lost the vision to see that the purity or health of life is above all.

Living the deep and natural Way, we are the disciples of life.
But living unnaturally we become the pupils of death.
We must learn to persistently empty the garbage gathered
since our conscious minds began to grow.

Living in the world, we pay a price.
We hold the toxic garbage of the world as our achievement.
This poisons our lives and the many lives around us.

Natural disasters such as earthquakes, volcanoes, flooding,
and storms are bad enough.
Tornadoes, hurricanes, and tidal waves cost lives.
But human society itself can be conditioned by immature religious or political beliefs,
which costs an even greater enormity of lives.

People incautiously fall prey to the social fantasies promoted by cunning leaders.

These leaders, themselves, were initially the victims of social vanity.

They once were considered saviors of the society or of the world.

But they saved no one.

They only made many people the fertilizer of their own vain fantasies.

The original sense of life to all individuals is an opportunity.

Each individual has a duty to life.

If we so choose we can refuse to live with a sense of duty for a natural life.

We can even be encouraged by some conventional religious teachings

to escape the duty of life.

However, the truthful teaching of life is the normalcy and decency of life itself.

To maintain our own health, there are natural duties to fulfill.

The number one duty of the attentive student of a natural life

is to cultivate high discernment among the things one expects to take in.

It is not a big deal to learn to collect.

High taste can be cultivated along life's way.

But one important thing that we often neglect is

learning to unload.

Our lives should not be made into a garbage container.

Thus for natural health,

we have to clean out our conscious store often.

We also have a duty to cultivate emotional peace.

That means to peacefully face all the emotional stress that comes

from supporting our lives, the lives of our young ones, and

the lives of our elderly parents, when they are in need.

We must learn not to support a social leader with ambiguous character.
If we do, we may pay a heavy price or make others pay a heavy price
for our unselective support.
It is our duty not to become the fertilizer of our own or anyone else's vanity.
Similar tragedies, big and small, have occurred repeatedly throughout history.

Further, it is our human duty to examine the accuracy of religious promotions,
intellectual knowledge, and the information imparted by others.
It is our duty to meditate on the conventional faith we inherited and
the common interests of our society to decide if we are misleading ourselves,
or if we are being misled by leaders.
The standard for this investigation and inspection is the consideration
of the well-being of individual life and that of society.

Generally, when trouble comes, undeveloped people give their lives to panic.
But the wise ones support a calm, clear mind and therefore endure.
In troubled times such as now,
we should know how to behave and support one another.

Thank you for considering this humble advice
and thinking over the duties of a natural life.
May we benefit our society and ourselves
by letting go of the things that do not truly serve us,
and by fulfilling our duties of a natural life.

Love to you all.

PART VI

*Examples of Great Individuals Who Achieved
Themselves Through Feminine Virtue*

"Feminine Virtue"

Chapter 21

Seven Great Especially Achieved Ones

(Note: It is our personal wish that achieved female leaders develop from the spiritual effect of this book and that this book may mark a new stage of human social development. In other words, we expect women to become the new balanced leaders of society. The following examples of great lives come from a time when men dominated society and women dominated the family home: a time when society was superficially or loosely connected and it was in family life that great personalities were prepared and nurtured.

Men had already made the world their playground, an arena for hunting and killing. Very few men were developed enough to maintain the upright direction of the healthy humanistic nature of love, thus there are scarce examples of true spiritual leaders in worldly life.

From the following individuals mentioned below, you can see that a great personality is neutral and balanced in life. These individuals contain the beauty and the healthy side of both masculine and feminine nature. To put it more accurately, these men were students and embodiments of a balanced life nature. They fulfilled themselves through the use of the feminine principle. This is why we choose to present them here in this book: for their pure interest in developing a balanced life, not because they were famed as great hunters or conquerors or figures of hero worship.

Few individuals can see that the greatness of people is in developing the balance and harmony of both male and female characteristics as aspects of the same life essence.

Feminine virtue and motherly spiritedness are the source of high civilization. Very few men exemplify such achievement. We wish that successful women in the future, who leave their names in history, are not those who attempt to defeat others like their male counterparts have done. Rather, they are individuals who have helped the world become a healthier and safer place to live, thus providing great examples of a true and balanced personality.)

The Yellow Emperor

Although the Yellow Emperor began his life in primitive society, he set the cultural direction for many generations to come. One reason he achieved so much was because he never tired of humbly seeking people with special development and learning from them. From him we can learn to embody the initiating spirit of life.

Lao Tzu

We should learn from Lao Tzu's ageless depth of heart and the way he responded with great serenity in a time of turmoil.

Fang Rei

Fang Rei was a talented businessman and strategist. Even though we are only very poor students of such things, we know to pay respect to such a teacher. We can all learn from his great example.

Kou Hong

Kou Hong chose a path of spiritual pursuit. Although that does not necessarily lead to a big fortune, it is important to all human life. We are encouraged to follow his direction and not worry or feel regret about moving steadily along the spiritual path.

Master Lu, Tung-Ping

Master Lu was a great swordsman and poet. We should appreciate these abilities of Master Lu as expressions of his spiritual learning. We can see from his life that there are many refined talents and pursuits that can become important elements of a life lived with immortal joy.

Chen Tuan

Master Chen Tuan could sustain himself alone in the mountains without needing to eat or even breathe. We can follow his example and way of studying the *Book of Changes*, so that we too may be able to solve the riddle of eternal life within nature.

Kwan Yin

We have included the example of *Kwan Yin*. Although she was not an actual person, she represents the universal spiritual nature that exists in the depths of all people.

Kwan Yin refers to a spiritual educational system that can help an individual develop inner vision. Through the gradual growth and attainment that comes from this practice we can guide ourselves to live in the light. *Kwan Yin* also indicates the principle of combining spiritual self-cultivation with the external rituals of worship. This is our approach based on the principles from the *I Ching* and the ancient commentary of Confucius. Through his in-depth study of the *I Ching*, Confucius was inspired to see that the Way may be achieved through uniting the internal essence with external ritual. This was his ultimate attainment from years of experience as a great educator.

Praise to the Yellow Emperor

You were one of the great humanistic leaders. You were born unspoiled. Your parents never used alcohol or drugs to damage your unborn life. You were never culturally twisted and you did not allow any unhealthy elements to be held within your personality. You were born fortunate and are worthy of the admiration of all people.

At your birth, there were no negative social conditions to pull you down, but there were a lot of social challenges awaiting you in your young life. Because my (OmNi) parents practiced the same way as your parents, my humble life was also blessed with good fortune. Both our families are ancestors of the one big family.

Your greatness was achieved by undertaking all things, both big and small, with the utmost dedication and due attention. By taking care of problems before they became noticeable or of concern, your great accomplishments naturally accumulated. You never waited for negative trends to grow in size. That was how you ruled society peacefully. That is also the main principle for the care of health in life. The dutiful maintenance of a healthy life and a healthy society is your practical legacy. That is the healthy approach that is passed down in our tradition.

You were never discouraged when you were weak and you were never arrogant once you became strong. You moved freely, both forward and backward. All your moves were based on righteousness and universal principle. You did not live within the confines of any ideological bondage. You conducted your affairs in broad daylight. The natural organic health of people and society was your main priority.

You downplayed differences among people and absorbed all the best knowledge and wisdom for use in your service to the world. You seemed to be blessed by Heaven. People helped you because you kept yourself humble and always ready to learn. You always let others be wiser than yourself. That was how you continually grew.

Your spiritual legacy is far-reaching. You happily embraced the perfect naturalness of all things. Marvelous was your ability to insist on no particular style in managing the affairs of the people. The principle of *Wu Wei* was developed as a result of your naturalness. From you, people learned to do nothing extra. They learned not to encumber the perfection of The Centermost Way in their lives.

There is no way to attain real peace and happiness in life, other than the way of naturalness that you exemplified. You learned from the developed ancestors how to behave simply and unfettered. Unfortunately, the foolish leaders of later generations could not comprehend this as easily as you.

For the less intelligent people of our generation, the Way is in aligning with the perfection of life. Constant improvement is the real practice. It is the greatness of the path of spiritual self-cultivation.

Yellow Emperor, you were once the very image of the sun. In a single lifetime you brought so much to the world. You were the manifestation of the sun's energy on earth, and for this we salute you. As a human individual, you exemplified the utmost completeness of being. All the wise ones acknowledge your greatness and your achievement as a human ancestor who came forth from Great Nature.

Praise to Lao Tzu

You were the first to continue the Way following Fu Shi, Shen Nung, and the Yellow Emperor. You showed the Way as the development of humanistic culture that remains true to the healthy side of human nature.

You did not work for personal ambition or fame. Your teaching was purely the light that radiated from your being, from the wellspring of knowledge that you embraced. You had no interest in social favoritism. You simply encouraged all people to seek the essence of life.

You showed clearly that it is one's work that gives spiritual meaning to life and that no matter what one's duties are, they are to be done thoroughly. You taught that all meaningful work becomes spiritual practice when faithfully and correctly attended to, and that worldly position offers no basis for pride; only virtue can add real value to life.

You used the example of the water buffalo to demonstrate the virtues of steady persistence and gradual growth in our lives. True progress doesn't come in any single great leap. Haste makes waste, and life is damaged by too much speed. Rather than flashy, superficial gain, you showed the way of safety in plainness.

At the check point of Hung Ku, you were recognized as an achieved one by the dutiful keeper who requested your teaching. You left us with only a very thin book written on a handful of leaves, showing that nature does not need any thick books to present the plain and simple truth.

Since the time your book was handed down, many interpretations have been written. Although each writer presented their attainment, few of them could see the truth that exists beyond the words. Books are just descriptions for communication and a passage for information. They are not something that should ever cause a fight or dispute.

You took nothing from the society of your time, yet you left us with the most valuable instructions. You plainly showed us the way of doing nothing against the nature of life. As you have passed it down, The Great Principle of Doing Nothing Extra contains four meanings. They are:

(1)   Do not be hypocritical or hypercritical.

(2)   Hold no bias whatsoever.

(3)   Do not seek or hunt for social favor.

(4)   Never tire of living simply and uprightly with good health.

You lived to be 200 years old by your emphasis on healthy living. You did not identify with time; you put all worries aside. You showed us how to be at ease in the eternal greatness of the universe. Where will we ever find another teacher like you? You are free from the contamination of past, present, and future. Such is your life. You live with all space and time.

Praise to Fang Rei

You were born in The Warring States Period at the end of the Chou Dynasty, in a time when there was strong competition to be the number one ruler of the battling kingdoms. You were endowed with the wisdom to learn and achieve the Way and you chose to assist those who had been defeated, ruined, and humiliated. Throughout your life you followed the way of helping people rebuild their lives.

As a result, you restored the Kingdom of Yu. You taught people the virtue of tolerance and how to quietly rebuild themselves following setback or defeat. I was also born in Yu and have learned the value of tolerance that you taught.

While the people of Yu were regaining their strength, the Kingdom of Wu was being weakened and destroyed by its people's own arrogance and negligence. They became careless in celebration following their military victory.

Tse Shue was the general and strategist from Tsue who helped the Kingdom of Wu become the strongest of all kingdoms. The King of Wu did not learn, however, to value his faithful and capable assistants. He preferred that people should try and please him, and so he sowed the seeds of future defeat.

You used strategy to undermine King Wu's trust in Tse Shue. As a foreign born individual, Tse Shue was forced to flee the country when he lost King Wu's favor. The King was negligent and did not recognize Tse Shue's great spiritual quality. As is usually the case, the truly faithful and capable people were persecuted due to the jealousy of the vulgar-minded.

Once the main beam of the building was sagging to breaking point, you caused the house to fall and helped bring the Kingdom of Yu to victory. Though the victory was great, you did not share in the glory. Instead, you simply withdrew after helping free the people of Yu from tyranny. It was a spiritual errand perfectly done. After such an errand, an achieved one would naturally choose to leave.

You then began sailing and conducting trade with many different people. You ventured to all of the different inland waterways, and your ships carried goods to the places where they were needed most. In this way, you became the first great businessman. You amassed great fortunes several times over and dispersed all your treasure to help the poor and needy.

You laid down the main principles of business and showed how offering the right goods for the right price with good service would inevitably bring success. You used business as a means of practicing universal love, fulfilling the principle of the Heavenly Way that the more you give, the more you have.

You never used your intelligence to compete with people or cause anyone trouble. You always gave people your help. You also kept your promise to save Shee Sze: the most beautiful woman of the time. She was the one who had helped you weaken the militarily aggressive kingdom of Wu.

You implemented the principles of the Way that you learned from your teacher, Wen Tzu, who had personally learned the Way from Lao Tzu. You illustrated the Way in a very unique manner: achieving with success and activity rather than passivity.

You always insisted on fairness and righteousness in both business and life. For all these things and more, you have become a hero of life's natural science for generations since that time. You accomplished your life in the Way completely and accurately. You are a true master: a torch-carrier of the Heavenly Way.

Praise to Kou Hong

Everything you learned was self-taught because your father had already passed away. Although you were born into a family of scholars, the family fortune had already declined. You had to make your own way, both in life and in learning. When you were young, you had to borrow books to read. You copied the good ones with your own hands to use again and again. You were also skilled in spear and battlefield combat. According to your record, the art of using the spear was in the movement of a small circle. No opponent could escape the tip of your spear. From your circular art form came the inspiration for Push Hands in T'ai Chi Chuan. You also studied the art of commanding armies in war.

The Governor of the South Ocean recognized your virtue. He gave his only daughter to you in marriage and recommended you as an advisor to the Army General. As the General's advisor, you capably assisted him in quelling the rebellion of the uncivilized tribes of the south.

You advised the General not to kill the rebels, but to tame them. You calmed the riots and established social order through the use of superior fighting skills and strategy. For this the Emperor of the Jing Dynasty gave you the position of Duke of the Interior Region. You thanked the Emperor for his kindness and then devoted yourself to spiritual cultivation along with your wife and father-in-law.

A generation earlier, Governor Bao Chien was the commander-in-chief of the entire central army. He was a disciple of Master Tsue Tzi, who challenged the authority of Emperor Tsau. At that time, the Han Dynasty was declining, having long since lost its power as the real center of society. Cunning politicians had seized the central administrative power and were using the old social image as a cover for achieving their political ambitions.

Prior to the Han Dynasty, after the fall of Tong Tsou, Tsau rose in power amidst other ambitious leaders. He took command of the central government in order to contain any competition and became head of one of the most powerful kingdoms of the Warring Period. But Tsau was arrogant and could not bear to be insulted or challenged.

Your granduncle's teacher Tsui Tzi was once a guest of Tsau. During his visit, he taunted and ridiculed Tsau, showing him great disrespect. Tsau ordered Tsui Tzi's arrest, but to no avail as Tsui Tzi had the power to become invisible and to multiply his image into numerous replicas. In this way Tsui Tzi showed Tsau that his immense political power did not make him a sovereign ruler. He showed him that no one in the world is outside the Law of the Universe. By teaching Tsau this good lesson, Tsui Tzi stopped Tsau from his continual military and territorial expansion. The Yang-Tze river region was thus saved from further destruction by Tsau's northern forces.

Your granduncle Kou, Shah-Sheng was the disciple of Tsui Tzi. He enjoyed popularity for his spiritual art in the Kingdom of Wu. You were expected to inherit the achievement of your granduncle and so you studied under his disciple, Master Yin Zheng, who had inherited all of Kou's achievement and spiritual art.

You were the fourth generation in your family's line of spiritually achieved ones, as well as a serious scholar. You led the spiritual direction away from magical craft and toward the pursuit of health and longevity for all people. You also diminished the use of spiritual endeavor for military and political purposes and refocused it on positive spiritual service for the benefit of all people.

You gathered many past teachings that had previously been scattered, to test them and prove their validity. As a result of your good work, these priceless teachings are available today. You separated spiritual pursuit from politics and promoted spiritual, mental, and physical health for everyone.

You organized your spiritual efforts in the book titled *The Man Who Embraces Simplicity*. This great work has real academic value and represents the accumulated effort of four generations of serious spiritual research and attainment. Master Dao Hong-Jeng and other leaders continued in your direction. They also cultivated themselves in the spirit of research, but not as deeply and broadly as you.

In the fresh air between wars, the scholars began to express their romantic side and the literary nature of southern Taoism grew. But they discarded your spiritual scientific approach and with their emotional focus they soon created another religion.

New leaders such as Lu Shui-Jing were major contributors to the movement of southern Taoism. Mao Mountain became their spiritual and social center. It was used as a vehicle for spiritual worship and the development of a safe and prosperous life. This social approach was merely a more religious mutation of the northern tradition. Its social style was copied from people living outside of China. The good influence of your practice, however, continued to be felt in the south and along with the new social religious approach, the teachings spread widely among the people living south of the Yang Tze River.

We appreciate the serious and responsible manner in which you approached spiritual matters. Your initial ambition was to combine Confucius's learning with the natural spiritual discoveries of the later generations. Your spiritual example shows that the movement toward cultural and spiritual integration should be the effort of each generation.

Some Further Words To Thank You

As humans we all live with the simple natural essence. In this regard everyone is the same. Some individuals misapply their simple essence by creating loud splashes that can disturb people for generations; while others value their simple essence and apply it in the direction of helping others. You were one such model. Your simple essence lit up the world in your time. Though you did not completely achieve your worldly goal, your spiritual direction will be appreciated for all time. You did not seek to make a splash. You just quietly devoted yourself to all of humankind. You are a great model and example of a spiritual researcher. You also gave direct guidance to people to help them with their spiritual development.

Your life has given us encouragement to carry on our work and helped us broaden the range and focus of our endeavors. With your example, we continue to monitor the spiritual work of the Integral Way.

Through the Integral Way, people are able to clearly see through the emotional foundation of religions. They are also able to see that the true power and knowledge of life resides in a healthy intelligence rather than pure emotion. Separating the two weakens the power of life, while integrating the two strengthens life and brings blessings. True progress for humankind may be achieved by following the light of rational faith. This is the direction offered by the Integral Way.

Praise to Master Lu, Tung-Ping

Your life was not easy. You were born into a noble family that had fallen into decline. You were under pressure to restore the family name and were pushed to study hard to earn a position at the royal court. This, however, was not your personal interest. You searched for the meaning of life and the attainment of a peaceful mind. You wished to achieve angelic immortality above the confusion of worldly life.

Your personal wish was to be a traveler and be free to go wherever you liked. With the ample money you kept in your deep sleeves, you did exactly that. You spent freely for charity and the enjoyment of travel, and with a sword on your back and a gourd in your hand you enjoyed the natural beauty of the earth.

Master Lu, you were a talented poet, but you were not so good at socializing with the influential officials who could have given you great status. You preferred to be like the wild crane flying freely wherever it wished. To be caged by name and position in a meaningless governmental dream would not do. This was your family's desire; it held no interest for you.

From Zhan Buddhism, you thoroughly attained the meaning of life and self. From Taoism, you learned the secrets of longevity, and from natural spirituality you achieved the freedom to live unbound by the human shell. You attained the power to instantly solidify in form or to scatter yourself to be invisible particles in the air. In more than a thousand years, you have never tired of helping people in the world. You respond with your immortal essence when and where and for whom you see fit.

Dear Master Lu—You have our admiration. Who else had the determination to so easily give up pursuing the vanity of worldly life? Your interests were so different. You pursued the art of immortality. People who think that such things are mere fiction keep themselves away from the high truth of life forever. And those who have a strong desire to become an immortal are led astray by their own emotion. Emotions are not suitable material for building an everlasting life. Living by impulse blocks the road to achieving immortality one way or another.

Dear Teacher—How does one follow your lead? What is the correct way to learn immortality? You would laugh and say that your immortal life is just a game of proving the high truth of subtle reality. If people were serious they would know to keep their lives clean. They would purify their physical, mental, and spiritual genetics to restore everlasting life. For those who are serious, do not miss the opportunity of restoring your eternal life. Lifting yourself above all worldly contamination enables you to find immortality in this very lifetime.

Dear Teacher—You would say: "The secret of my immortality doesn't cost a penny, but for those who prefer to stay in the mud, immortality is impossible, even though it is free." At least the majority who choose to stay in the mud can still pay the church to take them to the Blissful Heaven of Ignorance.

Praise to Chen Tuan

Is there anyone who would choose to be born without the care and love of a mother and father? There is one such child. Its name is humankind. Though the sky is its father and the earth is its mother, from the beginning, humankind had to learn to be independent.

A long time ago, a baby boy was wrapped in cloth and abandoned in a small boat. He was found and adopted by an old, poor fisherman named Chen. The old fisherman always fed the boy fish soup, but occasionally a lady passerby in dark clothes nursed him with her breasts. This was no ordinary woman; her milk helped enlighten the boy.

The boy raised by this fisherman was Chen Tuan. When he was older he went to school in the village. The old fisherman dreamed that his son would one day be a high official in the royal court. He hoped that his son's success would allow him to enjoy his winter years in glory. Chen Tuan had no difficulty learning the routine schoolwork, which delighted all the people of his village, but there was something that weighed heavily on his young heart. He questioned, "How a boy could be born without parents?"

One day the lady in dark clothes reappeared and gave Chen Tuan a book. She told him, "Study the book diligently and you shall find how and where life comes from." With this riddle and task, his other cares were forgotten. This book was the *I Ching*. It is a great treasure that serves as a master key to most other knowledge. From its study, many different systems of knowledge were developed. Within the symbols of this book are contained the secrets of the entire universe.

At school, Chen Tuan was still under the same pressure as the other boys to prepare for the general scholarly path, but as a result of a massive social upheaval their world suddenly changed. The upheaval ended the social order of the Tang Dynasty, which had lasted for almost four hundred years. The society was thrown into great turmoil and during the next 50 years there were ten short-lived dynasties. Although Chen Tuan had become a profound *I Ching* scholar and was renowned for his prediction skills, he refused to do readings for the new emperors on questions of military competition. Even so, each emperor in turn still invited him to become involved in his new regime.

One day, while Chen was walking through a tide of refugees, he saw a mother carrying a bamboo pole on her shoulder. At each end of the pole there was a basket and in each sat a little boy. Upon closer examination, Master Chen was greatly surprised and announced to the mother, "You are carrying two emperors-to-be on your shoulders."

The boys were brothers of the Chu family and the woman was the wife of a low ranking military officer. As the boys grew, Master Chen met them now and again under various circumstances. When the elder boy had become a strong man, Master Chen invited him to play a game of chess. The game was set with an interesting wager: If the boy lost the game, he would exempt Master Chen's home of Hua Mountain from having to pay any tax. The boy agreed, thinking this simply to be a joke. Later, when the boy turned out to be the first emperor of the Sung Dynasty, he kept his promise. Though Master Chen remained his close acquaintance, Master Chen preferred not to be involved in political decision making. He was invited to give advice on a few occasions and that was good enough. He had earned the right to live on Hua Mountain tax-free.

Some people live on the wealth of their relatives. Under such conditions it is hard to avoid bondage or slavery. This type of life held no interest for Master Chen. He knew that the world needed the advice of someone who lived in quietude. Even great leaders like the Chu brothers had to be kept at some distance. Being too close to people brings the risk of being pulled into the whirlpool of their lives and one could lose one's spiritual growth. On the other hand, being too remote shows a lack of love and compassion and makes it difficult to help others.

The human spirit lives in the world with the sky as its father and the earth as its mother. Each person is a child of the earth and the sky, yet each must live with independence. Master Chen embodied the true independence of the Human Spirit. He did not cry for lack of love from a mother and father or brother and sister, as most children would do. His life was a great example of the spirit of independence. His spirit was connected directly with Mother Earth and Father Sky. Master Chen lived in between heaven and earth with dignity and poise. He made himself an example of the proper relationship between heaven, earth, and all humankind.

The Most Responsive Internal *Kwan Yin*

In earlier times, the natural projection of people's emotions about the unknown aspects of life held a kind feminine image with motherly characteristics. Organized religion appeared when people shifted their worship from a feminine image of gentleness and kindness to a masculine warrior image. That change in emotional projection spawned a paternal society to serve the social needs in a new stage of life.

While the feminine side of nature accomplishes things in a subtle and almost invisible way, the masculine warrior nature has a more outward and active presence. Yet, the image of a feminine deity gives a closer description to the truthful spiritual function of nature.

At the centermost core, the real spiritual essence of nature is above any sense of gender. What is called "spiritual" is simply the potency of nature before it develops into individual lives and things. But, because modern people have been confused by religion and overly intellectual education, they do not realize the simplicity of this.

As the masculine influence grew around 4000 years ago, the previous feminine household leadership declined, surviving only in some parts of the rural country-side. This trend also carried over to religious activity, where only a few names of the formerly popular feminine deities survived in the new community spiritual worship. The most powerful mythological deities became male, as did all the heroes in folklore, songs, and stories. Respect for such feminine attributes as peacefulness, caring, and harmony gradually faded.

In Babylonian myth, the creator of the world was a jobless male bachelor. Paternal Babylonian society created that story around 4000 years ago and the Jewish people later adopted it. In contrast, China's creation myths are much older and show a distribution of power between the male and female aspects. One story tells about Pan Gu, the first male, who shaped the world using his axe. The other story tells about Nu Wu, the first female, who created people by using mud and water from a pond. These two myths clearly imply that in Chinese creation mythology, the beginning of the universe was attributed to both the male and the female.

An early social practice of people in China was the worship of Queen Nu Wu, who personified Mother Nature. Later this practice was replaced by the worship of the sun, which held the popular image of a male social leader in the sky. As people's literary capability grew many more creations followed and, as a result, the female deities became less and less popular in the religious market.

Kwan Yin became popular in the Tang Dynasty, partly due to the influence of Empress Wu. Although the background of *Kwan Yin* is superficially related to Buddhism, it was essentially a return to the feminine worship of ancient times. Truthfully, *Kwan Yin* was the image of many goddesses combined into one new goddess. Her image became widely accepted as the female image of divinity. Tracing back through the different regional histories and their corresponding styles of worship, we can see many associations between *Kwan Yin* and the old forgotten goddesses.

In Chinese, *Kwan* means the power of deep perception and insight. *Yin* means sound, tone, vibration, and a wavelike movement of energy. Taken together, *Kwan Yin* means to observe how life vibrates and how life vibrates in oneself. As a specific image, *Kwan Yin* represents beauty, purity, and perfection. She also represents the process of sublimation that one can practice in life to reach such purity and perfection. *Kwan Yin* worship has its own independent connotation, which is the pursuit of perfect beingness of life. At the general cultural level, *Kwan Yin* simply relates to spiritual truth.

Kwan Yin can also be considered one of the three aspects of mind, body, and spirit of an individual life. *Kwan Yin* relates primarily to the aspect of mind. To people of self-development, *Kwan Yin* is a symbol for the work of self-improvement and the refinement of one's spiritual self through internal practice. To undeveloped people, however, *Kwan Yin* is just an image of external worship.

At the general level, *Kwan Yin* is the subconscious mind, expressed as the Maiden Messenger in Muni's teaching.[1] From this viewpoint, *Kwan Yin* is the Maiden Messenger who moves between the upper, or higher self, and the lower self. This is discussed further in the book *The Story of Two Kingdoms,* where you may find the esoteric meaning behind the set of metaphors. With spiritual practice, *Kwan Yin* can help you attain harmony between the lower and higher aspects of your self.

The worship and practice of *Kwan Yin* is a useful starting place to help you in the process of sublimation. *Kwan Yin* can also be expanded to cover the entire process of integrating your individual life with the entirety of Great Nature. Your spiritual nature is not like the apparent physical sphere of life and nature. Without spiritual practice, your spiritual nature and each aspect of it remain hidden and latent. The spiritual energy of life can be evoked and will respond to an individual who cultivates and moves toward self-improvement.

---

1. Muni, a Persian prophet whose teaching was known as Manichaeism, was active around 300 CE. His teaching carries some relics of the early westward people, and has been adopted and inherited by Tibetan Buddhism.

The Ageless Teacher is the highest aspect of human life and Great Nature; it is the Way. In general life, access to this teacher is blocked unless the function of the Maiden Messenger is first enhanced. With sufficient development through self-cultivation, the Maiden Messenger teams up with the Ageless Teacher to help the pupil through life. In general undeveloped life, this function is the subconscious mind. Its health is not assured unless correct spiritual guidance is accepted and followed.

Particular invocations, sounds, and vibrations are useful for self-cultivation. In our tradition, these practices and that of *Kwan Yin* can transform the restless hearts and minds of the young life, who do not know how to manage their lives, into civilized individuals. In my time, there were many wars to draw the interest of restless boys, but thanks to the traditional practices my mother offered, I did not rush to join them. These practices may not seem as necessary for modern boys in a time of less drastic social upheaval, but they can still be helpful by redirecting them away from excessive disturbances.

PART VII

*The Reality of Jesus's and Buddha's Teachings
Can Help You Choose the Truthful Lifestyle*

"The Way of Compassion"

Chapter 22

The Source of Jesus's Teachings

Long before human history began, there was the attained wisdom of the Way that developed before the religions created by the contaminated and conceptually overexpanded mind. The *I Ching* is one book that records that wisdom. The book is the light of human nature passed down by our ancestors. It is such a treasure to all of humanity.

Much later, around 2500 years ago, before human societies became strongly competitive, Lao Tzu worked to stop the deterioration of people's quality of life. In the *Tao Teh Ching*, Lao Tzu restored the wisdom of long ago by teaching that lowliness in life is the spiritual fulfillment of kindness and love to all people.

Around 2000 years ago, Jesus's teaching had much to do with the Way. He embodied and continued the teaching that spiritual lowliness fulfills the spiritual nobility of life. He used his own fleshly life to exemplify and demonstrate this high spiritual virtue. Early people knew that the quality of one's being is the real value of life. There is no need for cosmetic coverings. The religionists, however, used Jesus to establish social control. As the spiritual rulers of people, they went against the virtue of Jesus.

Chien, Hexagram 15 of the *I Ching*, gives the message: "Benefit goes to the humble, while failure awaits the arrogant." All six lines of the hexagram express the same natural trend that the modest receive benefit, while the conceited reap failure. This has been clearly interpreted to the public by Jesus's Sermon on the Mount. You can compare these simple lines to Jesus's sermon.

You may find this truth in your own life that people who are ignorant or who have not reached maturity are thorny, provocative, aggressive, and bossy; whereas people who have grown into maturity are not bossy but self-effacing and considerate of others. Hexagram 15 shows the essence of the Way, which Jesus demonstrated.

Jesus used singular expressions when referring to his life being, never plural. This was to carry the teaching of the Way that all people are one life. He also used the titles of "Son of God" and "Son of Man" when referring to himself in public, in order to express the Way's teaching that God and all people are one.

Jesus realized that the truth, the life, and the light are one. He realized the Universal Truth of life. He was not a scholar who theorized but never lived life. Jesus proved his universal personality—the union of God and all people.

Chapter 23

The Teaching of the Way by Jesus

What Jesus offers to the world
is to benefit all people universally.

Jesus teaches the Way to Eternity.
It was the West that set the style of public service.
We hope people have understood him through the generations.

The Way cannot be elaborated merely by words.
The words only convey the meaning.
The Way can be comprehended by its directness and simplicity.

Sometimes people cannot get the meaning.
They have become confused and complicated by worldly life
and their own style of thinking.
Their minds are also obstructed by the heavy pressure
that comes from society's many false establishments.
Some people's conscious condition is worse than others'.

All people are on the Way.
The Way is the universal flow of life.
No one can live without the Way.
But when people lose their spiritual vision
they cannot see the broad truth of life,
and they fight and strive for things out of narrow interest and desire.
Fewer people are able to keep their original life nature.
For those that do they enjoy the simple essence of life.

Though our work presents the Way,
Jesus, as the pioneer, did much to bring the Way to the public.
If he could be correctly understood,
we wouldn't need to write so many books.

It is not that his or our work is hard to understand.
Truthfully, it's not a matter of language,
it's a matter of the mentality that is naturally formed
and flows with the Way.
Whoever reaches the direct sense between the lines
can touch the meaning of the Way.
We don't compete with how the West shaped Jesus,
and though we offer a new service to people of open spirit,
the common source is the Way.

For your spiritual benefit we directly present the Truth.
The spiritual source of life is the Divine Light
of the Heavenly life-giver—the sun.
You too can live like the sun.

Our learning and training is from the Way.
Some differences may be seen between Jesus's teachings and ours,
but the real difference is that we face a different public today.

In early times, few people had education.
Today, most are intellectually educated.

Jesus's teaching, without Lao Tzu's, may not reveal the depth.
Likewise, Lao Tzu's teaching, without Jesus's, does not show examples.
Uniting both, a better public service can be given.

The Heavenly Way as Presented by Jesus to the West

(Commentary by OmNi, the Son of Unity)

The Demands

Be merciful, just as your Father is merciful. (Luke 6:36)

The sun in the sky is kind. You create your own trouble by being unkind toward one another.

Blessed are the merciful, for they shall receive mercy. (Matthew 5:7)

Whatever behavior you present will attract its likeness in return.

All those who take the sword will perish by the sword. (Matthew 26:52)

The sword is not the means to fulfill the Heavenly will.

The poor you always have with you, but you do not always have me. (John 12:8)

Merely being kind to the poor cannot improve their lives or yours, but the fresh life spirit in you from Me is the way of evergreen life.

For all who exalt themselves will be humbled, and those who humble themselves will be exalted. (Luke 14:11)

Read the *Tao Teh Ching* by yourself.

For those who have more, more will be given, and from those who do not have, even what they think they have will be taken away. (Luke 8:18)

The spiritually receptive will receive more, and those who refuse to be spiritually benefited will be denied credit by the bank in Heaven.

The light is with you for a little longer. Walk while you have the light so that the darkness
may not overtake you. If you walk in the darkness, you do not know where you are going.
(John 12:35)

Read the book, *The Unchartered Voyage Toward the Subtle Light,* as well as
our more recent books. These books contain material from the unpublished book *The Path of Subtle Light,* which was written before the terrorist attacks of September 11. The Subtle Light means the Will of Heaven.
It is the wisdom to see the Will. The Path of the Subtle Light is a non-
verbal spiritual pursuit that is above the conscious and conceptual levels.

The eye is the lamp of the body. So, if your eyes are sound, your whole body will be full of light;
but if your eyes are not sound, your whole body will be full of darkness. If then the light in you
is darkness, how great is darkness. (Matthew 6:22–23)

The same supplement applies as above.

You shall love the Lord your God with all your heart, and with all your soul, and with all
your mind. This is the greatest and first commandment. And a second is like it: You shall love
your neighbor as yourself. On these two commandments depend all the law and the prophets.
(Matthew 22:37–40)

Heavenly Father,
Your Divine Light in me is the ruler of my life.
I follow and obey your Divine Light only.
It guides me to live with the Universal Truth
that is impartial to all people.
It is the great balance of the universal nature itself.
It guides me to conduct my life with the Way of Heaven.

When I live my life in health,
my head reaches the highest Heaven, and

my belly button maintains the needful gravity in life on earth.

Uprightness is the backbone of my being.

Righteousness is my left hand and Virtuous Fulfillment my right.

Progress is my left foot and Temperance is my right foot.

The centeredness of my being balances all my desires and imaginings in life.

Thus, the Way in my life is straightened and gives me support.

I love and respect all the teachers and students of great devotion in the past, present, and future, and I move forward for growth and development.

Discipleship

Follow me, and I will make you fishers of men. (Matthew 4:19)

I have merged my life with the Heavenly Father and you can do the same. Whoever follows me, I will make them fishers of people that you may bring them to the Heavenly Kingdom. "Me" as I understand means Person of Eternity.

Do to others as you would have them do to you. (Luke 6:31)

Do not do to others what you do not want them to do to you.

Whoever of you does not renounce all that you have cannot be my disciple. (Luke 14:33)

The world's trouble comes from people having too much self-interest. Unless you denounce the "me" of self-interest, you cannot be a disciple of the everlasting life of Heaven.

Whoever serves me must follow me, and where I am, there will my servant be also. (John 12:26)

The Heavenly Father is the light of my Divinity. I, and all you, as my disciples, have to transform our beings into the being of the Father.

Behold, I send you out like sheep into the midst of wolves; so be wise as serpents and innocent as doves. (Matthew 10:16)

Since you live among the masses of undeveloped people, good intentions may not be fulfilled unless suitable tactics are applied.

Preach as you go saying, "The kingdom of heaven is near at hand." Heal the sick, raise the dead, cleanse the lepers, and cast out demons. (Matthew 10:7–8)

Medicine has multiple forms. The highest medicine has no form, as it is the life spirit itself, but it has to be suitably evoked with various approaches. This pure and natural form is the best because it causes no harm to life, and it should be applied even if only as a supplement.

Truly I say to you, many prophets and righteous men longed to see what you see, and did not see it, and to hear what you hear, and did not hear it. (Matthew 13:17)

The teaching of prophets and righteous people were reactions to rough situations. They mostly expressed the subnormal situations in life, instead of the regularity and normalcy of everyday life. Most people, however, cannot see in the ordinary and normal the most important truth that cannot be presented by the teaching of doing. This miraculous power is prestored in all lives. The power of miracles is in your life: it comes from the good foundation of your own normal life. But people prefer to make other people perform miracles for them. That is the old and the new ignorance.

Do not labor for the food that perishes, but for the food that endures for eternal life, which the Son of Man will give you. For it is on him that God the Father has set his seal. (John 6:27)

There are two kinds of food: one feeds the temporal being of formed life; the other feeds the spirit of life, enabling the spirit to enjoy everlasting life. Tze, or Tzu, means Son of Man. It is an honor, unlike the son of a confused birth. Son of Man is not merely any person, but those who present the humanistic spiritual effort such as Lao Tze, or Tzu, Chuang Tze, or Tzu: they present teachings for the health of society and individual life. The key point of a healthy individual life and society is that people conduct their life away from social competitions that can cause rivalries and produce hatred and hostility in the world. Another, Sun Tze, or Tzu, wrote *The Art of War*. The art there is to reduce the sacrifice of lives to zero, or the bare minimum. That also needs to be the principle of government and business.

Blessed are you when men revile you and persecute you and utter all kinds of evil against you falsely on my account. Rejoice and be glad, for your reward is great in heaven, for in the same way men persecuted the prophets who were before you. (Matthew 5:11–12)

Merge your life with the Divine Light of the Heavenly Father, with all your thoughts, words and behaviors; nothing should be left out. There is no dark force that can triumph over the light. There is nothing that can really damage you. The persecutors have to persecute their own soul before they persecute your form. Their price is high.

As you enter the house, salute it. And if the house is worthy, let your peace come upon it; but if it is not worthy, let your peace return to you. And if any one will not receive you or listen to your words, shake off the dust from your feet as you leave that house or town. Truly, I say to you, it will be more tolerable on the Day of Judgment for the land of Sodom and Gomorrah than for that town. (Matthew 10:12–15)

Heavenly Father,
Your benevolence in Heaven is also on Earth.
As the true source of the light,
You are the power in life that shows the Way.
Hallowed be thy name in each good, clean life.

Thy kingdom of peace and happiness come.

Thy will be done on earth as the imminent focus.

May our daily needs receive inexhaustible providing

and our trespasses be forgiven.

Because the high life energy we possess can attract its likeness,

the abundant grace of life can come from our own merit,

but you provide the capability to do so.

From you we learn to forgive the trespassers

who may attempt to harm us and others.

Even in his late years, Mao Tse-Tung, the leader of China's communist revolution, kept studying the book, *The Heavenly Kingdom of Great Peace* that came from the *Tai Ping Ching* of the Han Dynasty. But it was too late for him to correct himself.

Disclosure

For their sakes I consecrate myself. (John 17:19)

The world is a confused place. You and I have to consecrate the common life.

My Father is still working, and I also am working. (John 5:17)

The Heavenly Father never ceases to give light and neither do those people of Heavenly birth who have upgraded their life spirit from the general level of other people.

Judas, would you betray the Son of Man with a kiss? (Luke 22:48)

Judas is a type of person. They can be in any place and in any group.

Why do you call me good? No one is good but God alone. (Luke 18:19)

The good excuse themselves from being called good because they expect to be better. The evil ones refuse to be called evil because they expect to be noticed.

I am the good shepherd. The good shepherd lays down his life for the sheep. (John 10:11)

A kind, voluntary protector needs reciprocal protection from the protected.

I am the way, and the truth, and the life. No one comes to the Father, but by me. (John 14:6)

"Me" refers to Jesus as a man who presents high virtue in a humble but straight manner. Truthfully it means the magnificent essence or the high spiritual potential in all high life. According to the *Tao Teh Ching,* the one of the Way identifies their life with the Way, the one of Heavenly Virtue identifies their life with the Virtue of Heaven, and the one of the lost identifies their life with the lost. Here Jesus means that the one who follows the Way and the Virtue of Heaven is merged spiritually and totally with the Way and the Virtue of Heavenly Life.

A prophet is not without honor except in his own country and in his own house. (Matthew 13:57)

Even the high truth may go unnoticed when presented in an undistinguished manner.

I am the bread of life. Whoever comes to me will not hunger, and whoever believes in me will never thirst. (John 6:35)

The teaching of the Way is flavorless and not attractive enough to those who only run after physical and emotional gain. But the Way instantly satisfies all travelers on the Path of a Constructive Life once they recognize the normality, constant peace, and support of nature, and live with it accordingly. People deviate from the Way, however, by running after all types of fantasies thereby expressing their individual lack of earnestness with respect to normality and health.

The Son of Man will be delivered into the hands of men, and they will kill him, and three days after being killed, he will rise again. (Mark 9:31)

 The innocent are defamed and the righteous are killed. The world may pull them down, but the Heavenly Father will raise them high.

The Counselor, the Holy Spirit, whom the Father will send in my name, will teach you all things, and remind you of all that I have said to you. (John 14:26)

 Dear Heavenly Father,
 Most people see you as the physical force, the sun,
 but there are some who can see you as the
 true spiritual source of all enlightened and illumined souls.
 Heavenly Father, please allow this little one,
 your smallest child, to embrace your light,
 to break off the darkness inside and outside of my life,
 and to follow your light and guide my life to eternity.
 With your light, my life is guided.
 With your light, my life is protected.
 And with your light, my life is nurtured.

Faith

It is I; do not be afraid. (John 6:20)

 People can be afraid of the presence of their conscience.

Father, into your hands I commit my spirit! (Luke 23:46)

 Join the Heavenly Father with your spirit.

All things are possible for the one who believes. (Mark 9:23)

 Believing is the mother of merit.

Go your way; your faith has made you well. (Mark 10:52)
> The one who is equipped with faith cannot be defeated by illness.

Blessed are those who have not seen and yet believe. (John 20:29)
> Blessed are those who can sense the possibility of finding the cure in life.

Take heart daughter; your faith has made you well. (Matthew 9:22)
> Faith can straighten and cure the ill-life.

Blessed rather are those who hear the word of God and keep it! (Luke 11:28)
> God blesses people with the light. People, however, may value words higher than the light.

Believe me that I am in the Father and the Father is in me; or else believe me for the sake of the works themselves. (John 14:11)
> Believe that the life that joins the Heavenly Father is eternal.

Peace I leave with you; my peace I give to you; not as the world gives do I give you. Do not let your hearts be troubled, and do not let them be afraid. (John 14:27)
> Peace is the greatest blessing among all blessings. But people look for minor blessings, ignoring the greatest one in their life as the real gift from Heaven.

If you have faith as a grain of mustard seed, you will say to this mountain, "Move from here to there," and it will move and nothing will be impossible to you. (Matthew 17:20)
> Faith is powerful in any circumstance even when wrongly applied, but it bears sweet fruit in the life that applies it correctly.

Forgiveness

Father, forgive them, for they don't know what they do. (Luke 23:34)
>   Innocence requires the encouragement of higher growth, but it should
>   not receive unsuitable punishment.

I have come to call not the righteous, but sinners to repentance. (Luke 5:32)
>   The biggest sin of life is ignorance.

I tell you, there is joy before the angels of God over one sinner who repents. (Luke 15:10)
>   People can be joyous over the success of their mischievous doing, but the
>   joy of the angels of God is for those who know when to stop and return
>   to normalcy in life.

Receive the Holy Spirit. If you forgive the sins of any, they are forgiven; if you retain the sins of any,
>   *they are retained. (John 20:23)*
>   The Holy Spirit in life is the Spirit in you that dares to forgive whoever
>   offends you, while the Evil Spirit is any hatred you hold on to until death.

Therefore I tell you, people will be forgiven for every sin and blasphemy, but the blasphemy
>   *against the Spirit will not be forgiven. (Matthew 12:31)*
>   You can be forgiven spiritually for what you do and say, but you can
>   never receive forgiveness from the Spirit of Life for the damage you
>   cause to yourself.

I tell you, there will be more joy in heaven over one sinner who repents than over ninety-nine
>   *righteous persons who need no repentance. (Luke 15:7)*
>   When many people are righteous, the repentance of one sinner is pre-
>   cious. When many people are evildoers, one righteous person is the Godly
>   beloved.

Why do you question thus in your hearts? Which is easier, to say to the paralytic, "Your sins are forgiven," or to say, "Rise, take up your mat and walk?" (Mark 2:8–9)

It is easier for religionists to say "God bless you," by looking at your wallet, than to say, "sincerity in conducting your life correctly can save your soul."

Truly, I say to you, people will be forgiven for their sins and whatever blasphemies they utter; but whoever blasphemes against the Holy Spirit can never have forgiveness, but is guilty of an eternal sin. (Mark 3:28–29)

Life is holy, when it is in peace.
Life is good, when it is in peace.
Life is true, when it is in peace.
Life is beautiful, when it is in peace.
Eternal sin is the behavior that denies life.
Thus, the Holy Spirit of eternal life is denied
when exchanged for momentary gain.

It is written that Christ is to suffer and to rise from the dead on the third day, and that repentance and forgiveness of sins is to be proclaimed in his name to all nations, beginning from Jerusalem. (Luke 24:46–47)

Whatever people establish can be ruined if it has caused disputes. Whatever name carries the teaching of forgiveness for one another has manifested the correct function of spiritual teachings among people and that cannot die.

For if you forgive others their trespasses, your Heavenly Father will also forgive you; but if you do not forgive others their trespasses, neither will your Father forgive your trespasses. (Matthew 6:14–15)

The Subtle Law of the universe responds to life correspondingly with no bias.

Judgment

Do not judge so that you may not be judged. (Matthew 7:1)

Being judgmental, while not seeing your own great faults, is the black spot of human nature.

I came to cast fire upon the earth, and how I wish it were already kindled. (Luke 12:49)

In the darkness of the earth, there the fire needs to glow.

Do you think that I came to grant peace on earth? I tell you, no, but rather division. (Luke 12:51)

Among all people there should be no class division. Different spiritual qualities, however, make people deeply divided. Spiritual education should bring them closer together.

Strive to enter through the narrow door. For many, I tell you, will seek to enter and will not be able. (Luke 13:24)

To those who carry too much, the Heavenly door is too narrow. For those who carry nothing—no conscious burdens—the Heavenly door is wide open.

Woe to you, Pharisees! For you tithe mint and rue and every herb, and neglect justice and the love of God. (Luke 11:42)

Spiritually there is no established authority, but in each moment there is a new spiritual challenge that needs a correct response. That is the Heavenly Way. It is not dead, but forever alive.

I came into this world for judgment so that those who do not see may see, and those who do see may become blind. (John 9:39)

Spiritual vision is not a free gift. It is the accumulation of spiritual self-discipline and cultivation.

And this is the judgment, that the light has come into the world, and people loved darkness rather than the light, because their deeds were evil. (John 3:19)

Indeed, people do not want to hear the truth about themselves. They prefer to gossip about others.

Of that day or that hour no one knows, neither the angels in heaven, nor the Son, but only the Father. Take heed, watch; for you do not know when the time will come. (Mark 13:32–33)

The world has its pattern of ups and downs,
but time is in its own timeless procession.
It is not the timing of what would happen,
be prepared and make ready for whatever may happen.
The useful preparation is never to be disappointed or excited
when nothing or something happens.
Simply live your life normally.

For nation will rise against nation, and kingdom against kingdom, and there will be famines and earthquakes in various places: all this is but the beginning of the birth pangs. Then they will deliver you up to tribulation, and put you to death, and you will be hated by all nations for My name's sake. (Matthew 24:7–9)

The greatest challenge to the individual lives of human beings is to know the will of God. God wills balance, God wills harmony, God wills safety, and God wills happiness for you. You may refuse all of them, but to try them out would do you great benefit. If you make mistakes, do not panic like young monkeys after being mischievous. But rather behave as human beings, and afterwards return to the God of Health, the God of Peace, the God of Safety, and the long-lived God of Prosperity. (From Chapter 14 of *The New Universal Morality: How to Find God in Modern Times*.)

The Kingdom

Repent, for the kingdom of heaven is at hand. (Matthew 4:17)

Blessed are the poor in spirit, for theirs is the kingdom of heaven. (Matthew 5:3)

No one who puts a hand to the plow and looks back is fit for the kingdom of God. (Luke 9:62)

The time is fulfilled, and the kingdom of God is at hand; repent, and believe in the gospel. (Mark 1:15)

Let the children come to me, do not hinder them; for it is to such as these that the kingdom of God belongs. (Mark 10:14)

Leave the dead to bury their own dead; but as for you, go and proclaim the kingdom of God. (Luke 9:60)

Unless your righteousness exceeds that of the scribes and Pharisees, you will never enter the kingdom of heaven. (Matthew 5:20)

Every scribe who has been trained for the kingdom of heaven is like a householder who brings out of his treasure what is new and what is old. (Matthew 13:51–2)

The kingdom of heaven is like a treasure hidden in a field, which someone found and covered up; then in his joy he goes and sells all that he has and buys that field. Again the kingdom of heaven is like a merchant in search of fine pearls, who, on finding one pearl of great value, went and sold all that he had and bought it. (Matthew 13:44–46)

All these verses above are simple statements introducing the Heavenly Kingdom of Great Peace and Harmony.

Love

Simon, son of John, do you love me? (John 21:17)

There are two kinds of love: emotional love and spiritual love. Knowing the difference between the two is a sign of growth. It is important never to confuse emotional love with spiritual love. Emotional love is out of personal need; it is self-centered. Spiritual love, however, is Godly love. It is not self-centered, but offers and gives. Emotional love should be based on the growing knowledge of life. Love without true knowledge leads to long remorse, whereas the love towards God is the love for the eternity of life. For the love of God, you love people. In this case, the more you give the more you have. That love lasts long, growing strong and tall in your spiritual life.

If you love me, you will keep my commandments. (John 14:15)
Those who love the eternity of life give Godly love to all. That is the commandment of eternal life.

Greater love hath no one than this, to lay down one's life for one's friends. (John 15:13)
In worldly life, all relationships are subject to change except true friendship. Although true gold can be obtained, true friendship cannot be exchanged for gold.

The Father himself loves you, because you have loved me and have believed that I came from the Father. (John 16:27)
One who attaches to what is visible usually neglects the deep source.

Those who love me will keep my word, and my Father will love them, and we will come to them and make our home with them. (John 14:23)
For the love of the house, one would also like to shelter the birds with the house. In other words, if one loves the Father then one loves all of creation. And as the *Tao Teh Ching* guides us: Love the son *(the product)* and keep to the source *(the Mother)*.

For the Father loves the Son, and shows him all that He Himself is doing; and greater works than these will He show him, that you may marvel. (John 5:20)

There is no greater love than the love between parents and their off-spring. It is love with inexhaustible support. It is the same as the close connection between the formed life and the Spirit of life, the offspring and the Source of spiritual life.

For he whom God has sent utters the words of God, for it is not my pleasure that He gives the Spirit. The Father loves the Son, and has given all things into his hand. (John 3:34–35)

There is God, the Father, you may not see.

He can be the spiritual reality of humanistic love.

There is the son—the human people and their world

where all types of temptations lie.

The Father loves the son,

but when the son is attached to worldly temptations

he is lost.

That is the pain of the Father.

Because the son does not understand the deep love of the Father,

he keeps wandering farther and farther away.

And so he could lose the spiritual root of life.

As the Father has loved me, so I have loved you; abide in my love. If you keep my commandments, you will abide in my love, just as I have kept my Father's commandments and abide in His love. (John 15:9–11)

Both the soul of life and the form of life are creations of Father Nature. But when the form of life attaches to the world, separation occurs, and the price of that is death.

If the world hates you, know that it has hated Me before it hated you. If you were of the world, the world would love you as its own; but because you do not belong to the world, but I have chosen you out of the world, therefore the world hates you. (John 15:18–19)

Love and hatred is a pair of twin brothers in life.
The world and your life are a pair of twin sisters.
The unity is your life with God, the Father,
who is the root of life.

Confrontation between the two is the ignorance.
Ignorance in life is the devil.
It is caused by the conflicting emotions and desires
of the different interests from the low sphere of your life.
That is the reptile known as the serpent.

You did not choose me, but I chose you. And I appointed you to go and bear fruit, fruit that will last; so that the Father will give you whatever you ask Him in my name. This I command to you, so that you may love one another. (John 15:16–17)

The "me" refers to the spiritual aspect of yourself, the high self, while the "you" is the physical aspect, the low self. For a correct relationship to exist between the two, the high self should choose what to support, while the low self should simply obey and cooperate. When God is allowed to rule your life, the Kingdom of Heaven is there.

The correct and great fruit of life comes from careful cultivation with well-selected conditions. Those conditions should be the choice of the high self, the me, rather than the low self, the you, which is cluttered with short-lived interests and desires for immediate satisfaction. Without the cooperation of the two—the spiritual me and the physical you—life is fruitless and meaningless.

Prayer

And whatever you ask in prayer, you will receive, if you have faith. (Matthew 21:22)

What is granted must be coherent to the will of God.
What is not granted must be protection from God.

Pray for a small seed that will grow into a complete tree
with abundant fruit in life.
Do not ask for a twig or a branch of an already grown tree
or whatever attracts you for now.

For faith, though it is such a tiny seed, contains the whole life of a tree.
With your careful cultivation it can grow into a strong and tall life
that can last a long time.

Where two or three are gathered in my name, there am I among them. (Matthew 18:20)
Where there is harmony and unity, My spirit is there too. Jesus stands
for Justice Eternally Serving Universal Spirituality. That is the quality
of a divinity. It is more than a mere name. Hasn't there been enough
evildoing using Jesus's name for irrational support? Always examine
the divine purpose for gathering, as wolves can be in sheep's clothing.

It is written, "My house shall be called a house of prayer;" but you make it a den of thieves.
(Matthew 21:13)
Each life has an inner room that should be used for praying only. However, thieves occupy most people's sacred room. It is not hard to get rid
of the external thieves, but it is hard to eliminate the internal ones. This
is the work that each life must always do.

My Father, if it is possible, let this cup pass from me; not as my will, but as Your will.
(Matthew 26:39)

> The divine quality in life is exhibited on occasions where you do not
> rush for profit that is not yours, nor do you avoid trouble or suffering
> where you have a duty.

Watch and pray that you may not enter into temptation; the spirit indeed is willing, but the flesh
is weak. (Matthew 26:41)

> It is not that temptation is always strong, rather that your flesh can be
> weak without spiritual discipline in your life.

I do not pray that You should take them out of the world, but that You should keep them from the
evil one. (John 17:15)

> The world is the Kingdom of Heaven, but it has been degraded by a
> declining human spiritual quality. It has been made into an arena of
> cunning ones. Make room for God in your heart. The ruling of God will
> first be to all individuals, then, to the entire world.

Beware of practicing your piety before others to be seen by them; for then you will have no reward
from your Father in heaven. (Matthew 6:1)

> Spiritual fulfillment is not for show; it is to realize in your personal life.
> If spiritual work is for show it loses its purpose.

Pray that it may not happen in winter. For in those days there will be such tribulation as has not
been seen from the beginning of the creation that God created until now, and never will be.
(Mark 13:18–19)

> There are four seasons in a year—winter, spring, summer, and fall. Each
> season is a good season, when God is with your life. But no day can be
> right when the element of God is absent.

I will pray to the Father, and he will give you another Counselor to be with you forever. This is the Spirit of Truth, whom the world cannot receive, because it neither sees him nor knows him. You know him, for he dwells with you, and will be in you. (John 14:16–17)

The Counselor seems to be replaceable, but each individual life needs God. This fact cannot be replaced and it also applies to the world. God is the light in an individual life and the light in the human world. Seeing the light, you see God, you see the spiritual counselor. The three partners are always there in a life of sincere piety.

The hour is coming, and now is, when the true worshippers will worship the Father in spirit and truth, for the Father seeks such as these to worship Him. God is spirit, and those who worship Him must worship in spirit and truth. (John 4:23–24)

The followers of a Constructive Life worship the Father (the Source) in spirit and truth.

Salvation

Even the hairs of your head are numbered. (Matthew 10:30)

Though the Heavenly network appears to lack density, no one can escape from it. (*Tao Teh Ching*)

Truly, truly, I say to you, whoever keeps my word, will never see death. (John 8:51)

There are few who know my Word, therefore the preciousness is unknown. (*Tao Teh Ching*)

This is eternal life that they may know You, the only true God, and Jesus Christ whom You have sent. (John 17:3)

My Word has the source. My Work carries the purpose. (*Tao Teh Ching*)

As Moses lifted up the serpent in the wilderness, so must the Son of Man be lifted up, and whoever believes in him may have eternal life. (John 3:14–15)

The life of the serpent is not to be disregarded, but it needs direction and refinement. How precious then is your spiritual life?

I am the resurrection and the life. Those who believe in me, even though they die, will live, and whoever lives and believes in me will never die. (John 11:25–26)

Have faith in life's ability to regain life. It is different to the faith that you only live once. People who believe that tend to live without any deep concern for life and may even live irresponsibly.

For this is the will of my Father that all who see the Son and believe in him may have eternal life; and I will raise them up on the last day. (John 6:40)

Life is eternal for everyone, both the good and the bad. You have to know that the rewards and punishments of life are eternal too. The real matter of life is what you carry and what you continue for.

Whoever drinks of the water that I will give him will never thirst; the water that I will give him will become in him a spring of water welling up to eternal life. (John 3:14)

Jesus, a true spiritual person, reveals that the fountain of everlasting life is within. But people look outward to formalities, rituals, and artificial doctrines. All those attempts are like looking for fish from trees.

My sheep hear my voice. I know them, and they follow me. I give them eternal life, and they will never perish. No one will snatch them out of my hand. (John 10:27–28)

Spiritual protection comes from the Virtuous Power of life. Trouble can be invited by living or behaving without virtue, thus keep close to the model of True Virtue.

The cup that I drink you will drink; and with the baptism with which I am baptized you will be baptized; but to sit at my right hand or at my left is not mine to grant, but it is for those for whom it has been prepared. (Mark 10:39–40)

The way to prepare yourselves is to be centered, not right or left sided. (Refer to the book, *The Centermost Way.*)

And everyone who has left houses or brothers or sisters or father or mother or children or lands, for my name's sake, will receive a hundredfold, and inherit eternal life. But many who are first will be last, and the last will be first. (Matthew 19:29–30)

Live for the important goal of life. Do not be scattered all the time by mere trifles. As the *Tao Teh Ching* guides: The big use of the instrument *(life)* is not to be segmented. This means that the Way is the purpose and your life is the vehicle, vessel, and instrument in which to fulfill the purpose of the eternal Way.

The purpose of the teaching of the Heavenly Way is to introduce the Heavenly Kingdom.

Chapter 24

The Divine Buddha

In early times, out of the nature of human sensibility, all types of nature worship was developed. Some people worshipped the sky, sun, moon, and stars, while others the mountain, lake or ocean. And some worshipped the stone and tree. Such worship reflected humankind's feeling for nature, rather than mere superstition. It added a poetic feeling to the living surroundings. It was a benign practice and was not harmful to the normality of life. If something called Taoism or a naturally expressed religion existed, it was just real spiritual life among people. It has been practiced throughout all time, long before written history.

As a result of the overly free conditions of those early times, much low level worship was also active, such as animal worship and all types of superstitions. Those were harmful to normal society. Even in these modern times we can still find traces of their existence in later created religions.

Around 3000 years ago, as people's minds started to grow, cunning-minded individuals began using conceptual creations to influence others. Some people succeeded by making a living using religions, while others succeeded by playing an influential social role. When people grew to a new stage of life, around 2500 years ago, some individuals awoke from the religious mischief of others and began to develop new teachings. Buddhism was one. It grew from observing life's troubles. It turned away from the older artificial religious enticements with their conceptual deities that are believed to make you rich, famous, and grant your wishes. The effort to awaken from religious control brought forth the important understanding of attaining peace of mind, which became the respected key practice and solution to life's troubles.

Attaining peace of mind, if practiced without stiff religious control, can be considered a growth of the mind. The religionists, however, placed it back into a religious framework and the awakened one was newly decorated in gold. He was made into a new social tool to suit the emotional needs of those who could not see the truth. Though Buddhism was a new creation, it perpetuated the customs of old. As a result, the lazy-boned and cunning-minded individuals became a special class, similar to the modern politicians that ride on the shoulders of others and enjoy special privileges.

Also around that time, Alexander the Great introduced the art of statue making into Asia. Statue worship marked the shift from natural worship to worship of the human form, and helped to eliminate the practice of animal worship. We can understand that some people need symbols to help their emotional lives. Symbols can also be used for the practice of spiritual concentration. People can even use them to express their own chosen spiritual shape. From the perspective of living art, we may have sympathy for those who need these things. But that worship is not as refined as the clear awareness of the high truth of spirituality that is formless and unable to be defined.

Many statues of Buddha are made in gold in various positions of sitting, lying or standing. If we correctly understand that the spiritual value of life is internal, then each statue can symbolize one good virtue of human life. Though external, statues can express real internal qualities to which worshippers can offer their respect. In fact, it is the valuable virtues of life that are actually being exalted. In this respect the new Buddhism causes no harm, but from another perspective it also offers the lazy ones an excuse to be propped up by social support.

The new religion makes Sakyamuni into an almighty being to which people pray for riches and the granting of personal wishes. Yet these very pursuits were what Sakyamuni renounced in his physical life! In truth people do not follow Buddha's way. They attempt instead to twist his arm to obtain things of a value different from what he originally set. That's the funny side of human nature.

Buddha worship reflects the worshipper's condition of life. Asking help from the one who has renounced any interest in worldly pursuits is not Buddha worship;

it is merely statue worship, which serves the superficial, not the deep and true nature of life. Who is in charge of one's destiny? Is the statue or the one who worships it?

A life that overly devotes itself to worship and neglects its real improvement becomes irresponsible. This is what really happens to those who worship statues under the name of Buddhism. A statue can never answer our needs of life. A statue remains untouched and unmoved. It is the image and quality of calmness that can create the power to face life's turmoil. This type of worship may help our personal growth, if our reflective mind starts working. It can be more effective than buying the expensive services of a psychologist who lives in similar darkness. But with calm reflection, you and your psychologist may see the light of life together. What this means is that life's questions need no answers. They should mostly be left alone to allow for a natural solution. Wisdom comes from hindsight, after the real happening or experience. Isn't that the real achievement Buddha pursued in his life? Should other lives engage in that same pursuit? The real Buddha has achieved his own spiritual magnificence by being low.

People call the statues in gold, Buddha. They burn incense for them and bow to them. They pray to them and ask what can be done for them. They keep circling around them year after year, making them into their personal caretakers. Yet who is the one who should eventually care for their life? Is it the one worshipping or the one sitting motionless?

The Real Divine Buddha

The Divine Buddha is where our active conscience is.
Our conscience activates the Divine Buddha.
Away from our conscience, there is no Divine Buddha.
And away from the Divine Buddha, there is no clear and active conscience.

Both our conscience and the Divine Buddha exist.
With Divine Light we can see them merge into one.

But when the heart is no more the heart,
there is no more Divine Buddha either.
Nor is there any trace of becoming Divine Oneness,
or being able to identify with one another.

Where there is conscience, there is the Divine Buddha.
Where there is no conscience, there is no Divine Buddha.
Do not go against the conscience for the sake of mere convenience.
The Divine Buddha and our conscience are always there with us.

The Great Way of Life is not far away.
There is no need to search for it.
It is near at a distance that we can touch, feel, hear, and see,
although it cannot be objectified.

The Great Way of Life is not far away.
There is no need to search for it.
It can be seen everywhere.

Simply, love the pure life always.

Chapter 25

Do Not Give Up the Way of a Good Life

Dear Friends,

The world needs your help.

People do not know emotionally how to live a healthy life.

People do not know how to attune their minds.

They may have money and they may have power,

but they live poorly or madly,

and may even be in a dark alley.

You are intelligent and you are talented.

Thank you for learning from us.

We encourage you to follow the Path of a Constructive Life

and use the gentle feminine approach

in working to reedit the world culture.

Today there are things either too old or outdated

or too new and untested.

Choose the constructive cultural influence for yourself and others;

respect what is great and promote it to the world.

Life is full of interesting things, if people learn to live simply.

Life can be miserable, if people overextend themselves

and push to the verge of destruction.

Learn the natural rites performed in the big hall of life

that reflect the grandness of life.

Learn to use the good music that takes you to the realm of beauty.

We have plenty of good teachings that have been

communicated through philosophical discussions,

lecturing, and our books.

You can put them into practice in your lives.

The world does not need much,

and it also does not matter where you are.

But you have to be artful in delivering the meaning to people.

You are the new stars.

You can do well.

What you need to do is find a new and effective way

to deliver the message.

Look at the depth of life.

The best means of making a living is to be helpful to others.

You may also find that you are being helped by what you do.

Reach out.

Try things out.

The learned can help the ignorant.

Your way should be a new way.

There should be no more fooling people,

no more manipulation,

and no more corruption in spiritual work.

Be courageous with a high sense of morality.

The world needs a guiding light.

This does not come merely from our books,

but from those people who embody and exemplify

the truth carried in the books.

In some people there is prejudice or hatred,

but there should be something else there too.

You are the right people.

You are the new hope of the world.

Do not give up on us easily.

You will be there to guide people on the Way.

Chapter 26

Lyn Chi—*The Mother of Wisdom*

In the vastness and profundity of the universe,
something exists.
This something can be here, there,
somewhere and someplace.
But there is no way to catch it, describe it
or hold onto it.
What can be described is not this something.

Throughout generations a few people
may have reached it.
They used their talent to describe it.
Different names are therefore given,
but none carry the truth of it.

This something cannot be created.
Creations are of the mind and hand.
They are second or thirdhand productions.
This something is far beyond the
perception of mind and capability of hand.

All creations move in the opposite direction
to reach this something that is generally understood
as spiritual or soul energy.
Soul energy is in the natural mind before
it is shaped by conditions.

In the West, some people call it God.
Some write books about it,
but no book can hold the essence of God.
Some gather people to create religions out of it.
Formalities can be set,
but this something is far away from any form.

Religious testimonies tell the experience of God
with certain shape or form.
Once the subtle experience enters the describable,
no matter how accurate or true to
the momentary real experience,
there exists a big distance from the Reality.

The subtle potency of the universe
has no shape or form.
God is beyond shape and form
though people attempt to make one.

Temples and cathedrals were built as houses for God.
But no God can be kept there nor visits such places.
Once a dead structure is presented,
the real God dwells far away.

No matter what people do with their high artistry
there is no way to produce God.
The more we do and try, the less opportunity there is that
Lyn Chi or the Efficacious Subtle Potency can be approached.

In the East, similar things are done.
People hope to contain that something

for their daily consoling and consulting.
Numerous statues, sutras, and mantras were created,
but the more people do, the more confused they get.
Eventually, people are unable to see the Reality beyond
the substitutes they made to worship.

Twenty-five hundred years ago, someone honestly stated that
the existence of this something is evasive and illusive.
It is the Subtle Reality of universal nature.
It is the source of the universe with all beings and things.

This Subtle Reality is beyond our senses,
and it cannot be held by our thoughts.
Just as when an essence is taken,
what is leftover and can be held
is just a dreg.

Those who try to hold this Spiritual Reality
as descriptions of the mind
destroy its beingness of Subtle Truth.
A universal standard of spirituality can be set,
but even that is still a relative way of speaking.

The Universal Subtle Reality is the wonder beyond
the mind that appreciates it.
And, at the same time,
the Subtle and Absolute Existence exists among all wonders.
Like the big muscles
that can be trained to produce physical strength,
and like the healthy mind
that can be trained to produce intelligence,

machines can be created,

and the moon and planets can be reached.

But most times, people are unable to reach the depth of themselves.

Soul energy is higher than the mind.

The mind in its natural condition is higher

than the intellectual mind shaped

by intellectual training.

The great mind cannot be demanded.

No great mind can be forced to produce

inspiration, enlightenment, and special vision.

Those things just happen spontaneously and naturally.

They cannot be forced.

Good vision can be produced by living a quiet life,

as described in the *Tao Teh Ching*.

The more force you use,

the more stagnant the mind becomes.

What wisdom can people produce in a structure

that offers no freedom?

A storm in the brain only produces low products

because it exercises within certain established frames.

How can exquisite things be produced?

The Universal Subtle Reality is not God, Buddha,

or any other divinity.

Those are conceptions produced by the human mind.

The Subtle Truth is integral; it cannot be expressed.

We can only view it as a whole.

The Subtle Reality is the source of our physical being.
Though efficacious, it is beyond our imagination.
How do I present it?
I can merely say that the Subtle,
but Efficacious Reality of the universe and our lives
is something within us and beyond us;
it is within our minds and beyond our minds.

In my writing,
I simply call it the Subtle Energy or the Subtle Essence.
Whether my writing carries the deep sense to any of the readers
depends on the growth of their own minds.

When we exhaust ourselves from whatever
we are capable of being and doing,
we are close to thinking of help from the Subtle Reality.
This is what money cannot buy,
power cannot seize, and
talent cannot apply.
What is there may come,
if we do not squeeze our lives or the lives of others
and let the tightness of our minds go.

Language has its limitation.
This is not my personal failure or yours.
It is the failure of humanity.
Imagine: when we quit the physical beingness
where do we go?
We may join the entire Subtle Reality.

The Subtle Reality is not one single being
we know as the self.
It is the nondistinguishable entirety
or as I term it, the Integral Truth.
The Subtle Truth is that non-being;
it doesn't disappear with us.

To the Subtle Truth, all people are equal.
But the development of each individual is unequal
and cannot be unified,
though religions attempt to do so by
leaders who imagine it is the answer for all.

Worldly religions have created a new reality
where most people are made to chase their own shadow.
But they leave *Lyn Chi* to be something and someone else.

People do not see that although they are
capable of making money, creating businesses,
governments, and religions—
that despite all types of external effort—
they cannot produce even a little of *Lyn Chi*.

Scientists work on the sphere of the measurable,
but *Lyn Chi* is far beyond that.
Lyn Chi cannot be made to come or go.
Lyn Chi cannot be made to be near or far.
One may not know her existence,
but she exists to those who do not doubt her,
who just be with her and not compete with her.

A rough boy I have been,
my parents taught me to learn from the
gentleness and softness of the natural female.
They helped me learn from the tenderness and flexibility
of the new born babe who is beyond gender confusion.
Gentleness, softness, and tenderness are the conditions
for witnessing *Lyn Chi*.
These are the conditions that enable the witnessing of
the Subtle Truth of life and the universe.

My parents guided me to study books.
They also denied the subtle truth in those books.
Finally they told me that all people, no matter who they are,
have to surrender to *Lyn Chi*—the Knowable Unknown One
or the Unknowable Knower.

The Great Knowable but Unknown Reality is simply with people.
I call it *Lyn Chi*.
It calls me *Lyn Chi*.
I call it God,
but it calls me God.

Who is who?
It takes a lifetime, or maybe more, to unite with *Lyn Chi*.

Appendix A

Explanation of Terms

Less common terms that appear only once or twice in the text are explained each time they are used. The scope of this list is therefore limited to those terms which appear often in the text and which are more likely to be unfamiliar to the reader.

I n t e g r a l W a y S o c i e t y (I W S)

The *Integral Way Society* is a service and community organization of the *Universal Integral Way*. Its members serve the modern world through sharing the natural wisdom of Lao Tzu and the ancient spiritually-developed ones, as transmitted by the Ni family. The purpose of the IWS is to cultivate balance, health, harmony, and virtue within each life and all society.

R e l i g i o n

An intermediate step on the path to spirituality. Early human beings established an external object in which to believe. Religious worship, including offerings and sacrifices, were originally intended to harmonize the relationship between human beings and the unseen spiritual realm. The choice between religion and spirituality is that of looking for help from an external spiritual authority or discovering one's own internal spiritual reality through self-cultivation processes.

S p i r i t u a l i t y

The achievement of the subtle essence of the universe through self-cultivation and individual spiritual realization. As one's spirituality develops, deeper levels of reality unfold. Externally, this is expressed through good self-management and harmony with other people and one's environment.

Sisters of the Universal Heavenly Way (SUHW)

The SUHW is an informal network of women who are inspired to learn from and transmit the natural wisdom of the Universal Heavenly Way. The sisterhood encourages women to respect, value, and strengthen their natural feminine virtue and subtle spiritual power, so they may gently guide themselves, their families, and wider communities to ethical and balanced growth. The sisterhood is open to any sincere woman in search of support in their process of restoring their true nature.

Universal Integral Way or Universal Heavenly Way (UIW or UHW)

The UIW is the culmination of thousands of years of human spiritual effort, experience, and learning. It is the plain universal wisdom of life offered by our ancient spiritually developed ancestors that manifested during the long prehistorical stage of feminine-centered society. This effort continues through the work of the Ni family and their spiritual friends. It continues to evolve and adapt to the different stages of humanity. It is practically served by the living of a natural, constructive life as guided by the Path of Constructive Life (PCL).

The spiritual learning of the UIW helps us reach for and restore the naturalness of life. It is a complete life-education that supports our entire well-being and spiritual growth.

Appendix B

Chinese History Timeline

3852–2738 BCE	Fu Shi
3218–2078 BCE	Shen Nung
2698–2598 BCE	Yellow Emperor
2207–1766 BCE	Hsia (or Shah) Dynasty
began Hsia	The Great Yu
last emperor of Hsia	Emperor Jey
1766–1121 BCE	Shang Dynasty
last emperor of Shang	Emperor Jou
1122–249 BCE	Chou Dynasty
active around 1154 BCE	King Wen
active around 1104 BCE	Duke Chou
active around 571 BCE	Lao Tzu
551–479 BCE	Confucius
403–221 BCE	Warring States Period
372–298 BCE	Menfucius
221–206 BCE	Chin Dynasty
246–206 BCE	Emperor Chin
206 BCE–219 CE	Han Dynasty
220–264 CE	Three Kingdoms
265–419 CE	Jing Dynasty
618–906 CE	Tang Dynasty
617–650 CE	Emperor Tai Chung
684–705 CE	Empress Wu
907–959 CE	Period of Disorder
960–1279 CE	Sung Dynasty
1280 BCE–1368 CE	Yuan Dynasty (Mongol)
1368 BCE–1643 CE	Ming Dynasty
1644 BCE–1911 CE	Ching Dynasty (Manchu)

INDEX

The Path of Constructive Life: Embracing Heaven's Heart—Unveils the new vehicle of the Integral Way known as the Path of Constructive Life. It gives fresh direction and effective self-practices to achieve sexual harmony, emotional well-being, protection from harmful influences and a universal soul.

#BHEART—315 pages, softcover. $19.95

The Power of the Feminine: Using Feminine Energy to Heal the World's Spiritual Problems—The wise vision of the feminine approach is the true foundation of human civilization and spiritual growth. When positive feminine virtues are usurped in favor of masculine strength, violence and aggressive competition result, leading the world to destruction. In this book, Hua-Ching Ni and Maoshing Ni touch on how and why this imbalance occurs, and deeply encourage women to apply their gentle feminine virtue to balance masculine strength and reset the course of humanity.

#BFEM—270 pages, softcover. $16.95

The New Universal Morality: How to Find God in Modern Times—An in-depth look at living in accord with universal virtue; particularly relevant with the disappointing failures of conventional religious teachings and the degraded condition of modern morality. Authors Hua-Ching Ni and Maoshing Ni Ph.D. reveal a natural religion in which universal morality is the essence, the true God that supports our lives and all existence. A direct discussion of the nature of God and the process of becoming a spiritual coach to serve both our community and ourselves.

#BMOR—280 pages, softcover. $16.95

The Majestic Domain of the Universal Heart—By Hua-Ching Ni and Maoshing Ni Ph.D. This book examines the power of universal love and wisdom and shows you how to integrate these life forces into your life through deepened spiritual awareness. In addition to drawing from the teachings of Lao Tzu and Chen Tuan, Hua-Ching Ni offers his own inspiring guidance for all who are seeking spiritual growth through an integral way of life.

#BMAJ—115 pages, softcover. $17.95

The Centermost Way—Hua-Ching Ni has written an inspiring account of human spiritual development, from its earliest stages, through the course of the last two millennia, up to today. It is a guidebook for those seeking a way of life that includes family, work, social activities and interests, scientific and religious pursuits, art, politics, and every other aspect of existence that we know and experience in the course of a lifetime on earth.

#BCENT—181 pages. $17.95

Enrich Your Life With Virtue—By Hua-Ching Ni. By embracing a life of natural virtue, one reduces conflict in the world. However humble this may seem, its personal spiritual and social implications are far-reaching. By examining the history of human relationships from this perspective, Hua-Ching Ni offers a broad study of human nature and draws on a centuries old tradition of natural life that transcends cultural and religious difference.

#BENR—173 pages. $15.95

Foundation of a Happy Life—By Hua-Ching Ni. A wonderful tool for making spiritual life a part of everyday life through instructive readings that families can share together. The future of the human world lies in its children. If parents raise their children well, the world will have a brighter future. A simple family shrine or alter, and regular gatherings to read the wisdom and advice of spiritually achieved people, can contribute profoundly to the development of strong characters and happiness.

#BFOUN—190 pages. $15.95

Secrets of Longevity: Hundreds of Ways to Live to be 100—By Dr. Maoshing Ni, Ph.D. Looking to live a longer, happier, healthier life? Try eating more blueberries, telling the truth, and saying no to undue burdens. Dr. Mao brings together simple and unusual ways to live longer.

#BLON—320 pages, softcover. $14.95
Published by Chronicle Books

Strength From Movement: Cultivating Chi—By Hua-Ching Ni, Daoshing Ni, and Maoshing Ni. *Chi*, the vital power of life, can be developed and cultivated within yourself to help support your health and your happy life. This book gives the deep reality of different useful forms of *chi* exercise and why certain types are more beneficial for certain types of people. Included are samples of several popular exercises.

#BSTRE—256 pages, softcover with 42 photographs. $17.95

Internal Alchemy: The Natural Way to Immortality—Ancient spiritually achieved ones used alchemical terminology metaphorically to disguise personal internal energy transformation. This book offers prescriptions that help sublimate your energy.

#DALCH—288 pages, softcover. $17.95

The Time Is Now for a Better Life and a Better World—The purpose of achievement is on one hand to serve individual self-preservation and also to exercise one's attainment from spiritual cultivation to help others. It is expected to save the difficulties of the time, to prepare ourselves to create a bright future for the human race, and to overcome our modern day spiritual dilemma by conjoint effort.

#BTIME—136 pages, softcover. $10.95

The Way, the Truth, and the Light—This is the story of the first sage who introduced the way to the world. The life of this young sage links the spiritual achievement of East and West, and demonstrates the great spiritual virtue of his love to all people.

#BLIGP—232 pages, softcover. $14.95
#BLIGH—Hardcover. $22.95

Life and Teaching of Two Immortals, Volume 1: Kou Hong—Master Kou Hong, who was an achieved Master, a healer in Traditional Chinese Medicine, and a specialist in the art of refining medicines, was born in 363 A.D. He laid the foundation of later cultural development in China.

#BLIF1—176 pages, softcover. $12.95

Life and Teaching of Two Immortals, Volume 2: Chen Tuan—The second emperor of the Sung Dynasty entitled Master Chen Tuan "Master of Supernatural Truth." Hua-Ching Ni describes his life and cultivation and gives in-depth commentaries that provide teaching and insight into the achievement of this highly respected Master.

#BLIF2—192 pages, softcover. $12.95

Esoteric Tao Teh Ching—*Tao Teh Ching* expresses the highest efficiency of life and can be applied in many levels of worldly and spiritual life. This previously unreleased edition discusses instruction for spiritual practices in every day life, which includes important in-depth techniques for spiritual benefit.

#BESOT—192 pages, softcover. $13.95

The Uncharted Voyage Toward the Subtle Light—Spiritual life in the world today has become a confusing mixture of dying traditions and radical novelties. People who earnestly and sincerely seek something more than just a way to fit into the complexities of a modern structure that does not support true self-development, often find themselves spiritually struggling. This book provides a profound understanding and insight into the underlying heart of all paths of spiritual growth, the subtle origin, and the eternal truth of one universal life.

#BVOY—424 pages, softcover. $19.95

Golden Message, A Guide to Spiritual Life with Self-Study Program for Learning the Integral Way—This volume begins with a traditional treatise by Daoshing and Maoshing Ni about the broad nature of spiritual learning and its application for human life. It is followed by a message from Hua-Ching Ni. An outline of the Spiritual Self-Study Program and Correspondence Course of the College of Tao is included.

#BGOLD—160 pages, softcover. $11.95

Mysticism: Empowering the Spirit Within—For more than 8000 years, mystical knowledge has been passed down by sages. Hua-Ching Ni introduces spiritual knowledge of the developed ones, which does not use the senses, or machines like scientific knowledge, yet can know both the entirety of the universe and the spirits.

#BMYSM—200 pages, softcover. $13.95

Ageless Counsel for Modern Life—These sixty-four writings, originally illustrative commentaries on the *I Ching*, are meaningful and useful spiritual guidance on various topics to enrich your life. Hua-Ching Ni's delightful poetry and some teachings of esoteric Taoism can be found here as well.

#BAGE—256 pages, softcover. $15.95

The Mystical Universal Mother—An understanding of both masculine and feminine energies are crucial to understanding oneself, in particular for people moving to higher spiritual evolution. Hua-Ching Ni focuses upon the feminine through the examples of some ancient and modern women.

#BMYST—240 pages, softcover. $14.95

Harmony, The Art of Life—Harmony occurs when two different things find the point at which they can link together. Hua-Ching Ni shares valuable spiritual understanding and insight about the ability to bring harmony within one's own self, one's relationships and the world.

#BHAR—208 pages, softcover. $16.95

Moonlight in the Dark Night—The difficulty for many people in developing their spirituality is not that they are not moral or spiritual enough, but they are captive to their emotions. This book contains wisdom on how to guide emotions. It also includes simple guidance on how to balance love relationships so your life may be smoother and happier and your spiritual growth more effective.

#BMOON—168 pages, softcover. $12.95

Attune Your Body with Dao-In—The ancients discovered that Dao-In exercises solved problems of stagnant energy, increased their health, and lengthened their years. The exercises are also used as practical support for cultivation and higher achievements of spiritual immortality.

#BDAOI—144 pages, softcover. $16.95
Also on VHS & DVD. $24.95

The Key to Good Fortune: Refining Your Spirit (Revised)—"Straighten your Way" (*Tai Shan Kan Yin Pien*) and "The Silent Way of Blessing" (*Yin Chi Wen*) are the main guidance for a mature, healthy life. Spiritual improvement can be an integral part of realizing a Heavenly life on earth.
#BKEY—135 pages, softcover. $17.95

Eternal Light—Hua-Ching Ni presents the life and teachings of his father, Grandmaster Ni, Yo San, who was a spiritually achieved person, healer and teacher, and a source of inspiration to Master Ni. Deeper teachings and insights for living a spiritual life and higher achievement.
#BETER—208 pages, softcover. $14.95

Quest of Soul—Hua-Ching Ni addresses many concepts about the soul such as saving the soul, improving the soul's quality, the free soul, what happens at death, and the universal soul. He guides and inspires the reader into deeper self-knowledge and to move forward to increase personal happiness and spiritual depth.
#BQUES—152 pages, softcover. $11.95

Nurture Your Spirits—Hua-Ching Ni breaks some spiritual prohibitions and presents the spiritual truth he has studied and proven. This truth may help you develop and nurture your own spirits, which are the truthful internal foundation of your life being.
#BNURT—176 pages, softcover. $12.95

Power of Natural Healing—Hua-Ching Ni discusses the natural capability of self-healing, information, and practices which can assist any treatment method and presents methods of cultivation which promote a healthy life, longevity, and spiritual achievement.
#BHEAL—143 pages, softcover. $14.95

Essence of Universal Spirituality—In this volume, as an open-minded learner and achieved teacher of universal spirituality, Hua-Ching Ni examines and discusses all levels and topics of religious and spiritual teaching to help you understand the ultimate truth and enjoy the achievement of all religions without becoming confused by them.
#BESSE—304 pages, softcover. $19.95

Guide to Inner Light—Drawing inspiration from the experience of the ancient ones, modern people looking for the true source and meaning of life can find great teachings to direct and benefit them. The invaluable ancient development can teach us to reach the attainable spiritual truth and point the way to the inner Light.
#BGUID—192 pages, softcover. $12.95

Stepping Stones for Spiritual Success—In this volume, Hua-Ching Ni has taken the best of the traditional teachings and put them into contemporary language to make them more relevant to our time, culture, and lives.

#BSTEP—160 pages, softcover. $12.95

The Complete Works of Lao Tzu—The *Tao Teh Ching* is one of the most widely translated and cherished works of literature. Its timeless wisdom provides a bridge to the subtle spiritual truth and aids harmonious and peaceful living. Also included is the *Hua Hu Ching*, a later work of Lao Tzu, which was lost to the general public for a thousand years.

#BCOMP—212 pages, softcover. $13.95

I Ching, The Book of Changes and the Unchanging Truth—The legendary classic *I Ching* is recognized as the first written book of wisdom. Leaders and sages throughout history have consulted it as a trusted advisor, which reveals the appropriate action in any circumstance. Includes over 200 pages of background material on natural energy cycles, instruction, and commentaries.

#BBOOK—669 pages, hardcover. $35.00

The Story of Two Kingdoms—This volume is the metaphoric tale of the conflict between the Kingdoms of Light and Darkness. Through this unique story, Hua-Ching Ni transmits esoteric teachings of Taoism that have been carefully guarded secrets for over 5,000 years. This book is for those who are serious in achieving high spiritual goals.

#BSTOR—223 pages, hardcover. $14.00

The Way of Integral Life—This book includes practical and applicable suggestions for daily life, philosophical thought, esoteric insight and guidelines for those aspiring to serve the world. The ancient sages' achievement can assist the growth of your own wisdom and balanced, reasonable life.

#BWAYP—320 pages, softcover. $14.00
#BWAYH—Hardcover. $20.00

Enlightenment: Mother of Spiritual Independence—The inspiring story and teachings of Master Hui Neng, the father of Zen Buddhism and Sixth Patriarch of the Buddhist tradition, highlight this volume. Hui Neng was a person of ordinary birth, intellectually unsophisticated, who achieved himself to become a spiritual leader.

#BENLP—264 pages, softcover. $12.50
#BENLH—Hardcover. $22.00

The Gentle Path of Spiritual Progress—This book offers a glimpse into the dialogues between a master and his students. In a relaxed, open manner, Hua-Ching Ni explains to his students the fundamental practices that are the keys to experiencing enlightenment in everyday life.

#BGENT—290 pages, softcover. $12.95

Spiritual Messages from a Buffalo Rider, A Man of Tao—Our buffalo nature rides on us, whereas an achieved person rides the buffalo. Hua-Ching Ni gives much helpful knowledge to those who are interested in improving their lives and deepening their cultivation so they too can develop beyond their mundane beings.

#BSPIR—242 pages, softcover. $12.95

8,000 Years of Wisdom, Volume I and II—This two-volume set contains a wealth of practical, down-to-earth advice given by Hua-Ching Ni over a five-year period. Drawing on his training in Traditional Chinese Medicine, Herbology, and Acupuncture, Hua-Ching Ni gives candid answers to questions on many topics.

#BWIS1—Vol. I: (Revised edition)
Includes dietary guidance; 236 pages, softcover. $18.50
#BWIS2—Vol. II: Includes sex and pregnancy guidance; 241 pages, softcover. $18.50

Footsteps of the Mystical Child—This book poses and answers such questions as, "What is a soul? What is wisdom? What is spiritual evolution?" to enable readers to open themselves to new realms of understanding and personal growth. Includes true examples about people's internal and external struggles on the path of self-development and spiritual evolution.

#BFOOT—166 pages, softcover. $9.50

Workbook for Spiritual Development—This material summarizes thousands of years of traditional teachings and little known practices for spiritual development. There are sections on ancient invocations, natural celibacy and postures for energy channeling. Hua-Ching Ni explains basic attitudes and knowledge that supports spiritual practice.

#BWORK—240 pages, softcover. $14.95

The Taoist Inner View of the Universe—Hua-Ching Ni has given all the opportunity to know the vast achievement of the ancient unspoiled mind and its transpiercing vision. This book offers a glimpse of the inner world and immortal realm known to achieved ones and makes it understandable for students aspiring to a more complete life.

#BTAOI—218 pages, softcover. $16.95

Tao, the Subtle Universal Law—Most people are unaware that their thoughts and behavior evoke responses from the invisible net of universal energy. To lead a good stable life is to be aware of the universal subtle law in every moment of our lives. This book presents practical methods that have been successfully used for centuries to accomplish this.

#BTAOS—208 pages, softcover. $12.95

Concourse of All Spiritual Paths—All religions, in spite of their surface differences, in their essence return to the great oneness. Hua-Ching Ni looks at what traditional religions offer us today and suggest how to go beyond differences to discover the depth of universal truth.

#BCONC—184 pages, softcover. $15.95

From Diversity to Unity: Return to the One Spiritual Source—This book encourages individuals to go beyond the theological boundary to rediscover their own spiritual nature with guidance offered by Hua-Ching Ni from his personal achievement, exploration, and self-cultivation. This work can help people unlock the spiritual treasures of the universe and light the way to a life of internal and external harmony and fulfillment.

#BDIV—200 pages, softcover. $15.95

Spring Thunder: Awaken the Hibernating Power of Life—Humans need to be periodically awakened from a spiritual hibernation in which the awareness of life's reality is deeply forgotten. To awaken your deep inner life, this book offers the practice of Natural Meditation, the enlightening teachings of Yen Shi, and Hua-Ching Ni's New Year Message.

#BTHUN—168 pages, softcover. $12.95

Internal Growth Through Tao—In this volume, Hua-Ching Ni teaches about the more subtle, much deeper aspects of life. He also points out the confusion caused by some spiritual teachings and encourages students to cultivate internal growth.

#BINTE—208 pages, softcover. $13.95

The Yellow Emperor's Classic of Medicine—By Maoshing Ni, Ph.D. The *Neijing* is one of the most important classics of Taoism, as well as the highest authority on traditional Chinese medicine. Written in the form of a discourse between Yellow Emperor and his ministers, this book contains a wealth of knowledge on holistic medicine and how human life can attune itself to receive natural support.

#BYELL—316 pages, softcover. $24.95
Published by Shambala Publications, Inc.

The Eight Treasures: Energy Enhancement Exercise—By Maoshing Ni, Ph.D. The Eight Treasures is an ancient system of energy enhancing movements based on the natural motion of the universe. It can be practiced by anyone at any fitness level, is non-impact, simple to do, and appropriate for all ages. It is recommended that this book be used with its companion videotape or DVD.

#BEIGH—208 pages, softcover. $17.95
Also on VHS & DVD. $24.95

The Gate to Infinity—People who have learned spiritually through years without real progress will be thoroughly guided by the important discourse in this book. Hua-Ching Ni also explains Natural Meditation. Editors recommend that all serious spiritual students who wish to increase their spiritual potency read this one.

#BGATE—316 pages, softcover. $13.95

Entering the Tao—Traditional stories and teachings of the ancient masters and personal experiences impart the wisdom of Taoism, the Integral Way. Spiritual self-cultivation, self-reliance, spiritual self-protection, emotional balance, do's and don'ts for a healthy lifestyle, sleeping and dreaming, diet, boredom, fun, sex and marriage.

#BENT—153 pages, softcover. $13.00
Published by Shambala Publications, Inc.

The Tao of Nutrition—By Maoshing Ni, Ph.D. with Cathy McNease, B.S., M.H. Learn how to take control of your health with good eating. Over 100 common foods are discussed with their energetic properties and therapeutic functions listed. Food remedies for numerous common ailments are also presented.

#BTAON—214 pages, softcover. $14.95

Revealing the Tao Teh Ching: In-Depth Commentaries on an Ancient Classic—By Xuezhi Hu. Unique, detailed, and practical commentaries on methods of spiritual cultivation as metaphorically described by Lao Tzu in the *Tao Teh Ching*.

#BREV—240 pages, softcover. $19.95
Published by Ageless Classics Press

Chinese Herbology Made Easy—By Maoshing Ni, Ph.D. This text provides an overview of Oriental Medical theory, in-depth descriptions of each herb category, over 300 black and white photographs, extensive tables of individual herbs for easy reference and an index of pharmaceutical names.

#BHERB—202 pages, softcover. $18.95

101 Vegetarian Delights—By Lily Chuang and Cathy McNease. A lovely cookbook with recipes as tasty as they are healthy. Features multicultural recipes, appendices on Chinese herbs and edible flowers, and a glossary of special foods. Over 40 illustrations.

#B101—176 pages, softcover. $15.95

Chinese Vegetarian Delights—By Lily Chuang. An extraordinary collection of recipes based on principles of traditional Chinese nutrition. Meat, sugar, dairy products, and fried foods are excluded.

#BVEG—104 pages, softcover. $7.50

The Power of Positive Living—By Hua-Ching Ni. Ideas about simple improvements and changes in attitude that can be made in everyday life to increase our positive energy and health. Attain real internal peace while attaining external success and security.

#BPOWE—65 pages, softcover booklet. $8.50

Self-Reliance and Constructive Change—By Hua-Ching Ni. Being attached to cultural and religious fashions can hinder personal health. Hua-Ching Ni presents the Integral Way of spiritual discovery that is independent of cultural, political or religious concepts.

#BSELF—54 pages, softcover booklet. $7.00

The Universal Path of Natural Life—By Hua-Ching Ni. Study the ancient spiritual practices of *Yin Fu Ching*, a predecessor of the *Tao Teh Ching*. Connect with the natural unity and balance of the universe to nurture our spiritual essence and natural vitality.

#BPATH—109 pages, softcover booklet. $9.50

POCKET BOOKLETS & MISCELLANEOUS

Progress Along the Way: Life, Service and Realization—The guiding power of human life is the association between the developed mind and the achieved soul, which contains love, rationality, conscience, and everlasting value.

#PPROG—64 pages, paperback. $4.00

The Light of All Stars Illuminates the Way—Through generations of searching, various achieved ones found the best application of the Way in their lives. This booklet contains their discovery.

#PSTAR—48 pages, paperback. $4.00

The Heavenly Way—"Straighten Your Way" (*Tai Shan Kan Yin Pien*) and "The Silent Way of Blessing" (*Yin Chi Wen*) are the main sources of inspiration for this booklet that sets the cornerstone for a mature, healthy life.

#BHEAV—42 pages, softcover. $2.50

Harmony T'ai Chi Short Form (DVD)—By Maoshing Ni, Ph.D. Easy to learn 18 steps *t'ai chi*. Simplified from the regular 108-step T'ai Chi Chuan Parts I & II Harmony Style Form. Graceful movements for balance, peace and vitality.

#DSTEP—DVD, 28 minutes. $24.95

T'ai Chi Sword Form (DVD)—By Maoshing Ni, Ph.D. A short, instructional 10-minute sword form to help sweep away emotional obstacles and enhance protective energy. Excellent for developing spiritual focus.

#DSWORD—DVD, 19 minutes. $24.95

Crane Style Chi Gong (VHS, PAL & DVD)—By Daoshing Ni, Ph.D. Crane Style standing exercises integrate movement, mental imagery and breathing techniques, and are practiced for healing purposes. They were developed by ancient Taoists to increase energy and metabolism, relieve stress and tension, improve mental clarity, and restore general wellbeing. We are thrilled to also offer a reshoot on DVD of this incredibly beautiful old classic.

#VCRAN—VHS video, 120 minutes. $24.95

#VPCRAN—PAL video, 120 minutes. $24.95

#DCRAN—DVD, 120 minutes. $24.95

Attune Your Body with Dao-In (VHS, PAL & DVD)—By Hua-Ching Ni. The ancient Taoist predecessor to T'ai Chi Chuan. Performed sitting and lying down, these moves clear stagnant energy. Includes meditations and massage for a complete integral fitness program.

#VDAOI—VHS video, 60 minutes. $24.95

#VPDAOI—PAL video, 60 minutes. $24.95

#DDAOI—DVD, 60 minutes. $24.95

Taoist Eight Treasures (VHS, PAL & DVD)—By Maoshing Ni, Ph.D. Unique to the Ni family, this 32-movement *chi* form opens blocks in your energy flow and strengthens your vitality. Combines stretching, toning, and energy conducting exercises with deep breathing.

#VEIGH—VHS video, 46 minutes. $24.95

#VPEIGH—PAL video, 46 minutes. $24.95

#DEIGH—DVD, 46 minutes. $24.95

#DEIGHOriginal—DVD, 120 minutes. $24.95

T'ai Chi Chuan, An Appreciation (VHS)—By Hua-Ching Ni "Gentle Path," "Sky Journey," and "Infinite Expansion" are three Taoist esoteric styles handed down by highly achieved masters and are shown in an uninterrupted format. Not an instructional video.

#VAPPR—VHS video, 30 minutes. $24.95

T'ai Chi Chuan, Parts I & II (VHS & PAL)—By Maoshing Ni, Ph.D. This Taoist style, called the style of Harmony, is a distillation of the Yang, Chen, and Wu styles. It integrates physical movement with energy and helps promote longevity and self-cultivation.

#VTAI1, #VTAI2—VHS videos, 60 minutes each. $24.95
#VPTAI1, #VPTAI2—PAL videos, 60 minutes each. $24.95

Self-Healing Chi Gong (VHS, PAL & DVD)—By Maoshing Ni, Ph.D. Strengthen your own self-healing powers. These effective mind-body exercises strengthen and balance each of your five major organ systems. Two hours of practical demonstrations and information lectures.

#VSHCG—VHS video, 120 minutes. $24.95
#VPSHCG—PAL video, 120 minutes. $24.95
#DSHCG—DVD, 120 minutes. $24.95

Cosmic Tour Ba-Gua (VHS, PAL & DVD)—By Hua-Ching Ni. Cosmic Tour Ba-Gua has healing powers similar to T'ai Chi, but the energy flow is quite different. Ba-Gua consists of a special kind of walking which corrects the imbalance and disorder of "having a head heavier than the rest of the body."

#VCOSM—VHS video. $24.95
#VPCOSM—PAL video. $24.95
#DCOSM—DVD. $24.95

T'ai Chi Chuan: The Gentle Path (VHS)—By Hua-Ching Ni. The movements of *The Gentle Path T'ai Chi* guide us to follow the gentle, cyclical motion of the universe. By gathering energy in the lower *tan tien*, the root center, the movements will change our internal energy and guide us to a peaceful and balanced life.

#VGENP—VHS video. $24.95

COMPACT DISCS

Tao Teh Ching—This classic work of Lao Tzu has been recorded in this two-disc set that is a companion to the book translated by Hua-Ching Ni. Professionally recorded and read by Robert Rudelson.

#CDTAO—104 minutes. $15.95

Invocations for Health, Longevity and Healing a Broken Heart—By Maoshing Ni, Ph.D. "Thinking is louder than thunder." This cassette guides you through a series of invocations to channel and conduct your own healing energy and vital force.

#CDINVO—30 minutes. $12.95

Pain Management with Chi Gong—By Maoshing Ni, Ph.D. Using visualization and deep breathing techniques, this cassette offers methods for overcoming pain by invigorating your energy flow and unblocking obstructions that cause pain.

#CDPAIN—30 minutes. $12.95

Meditation for Stress Release—Dr. Mao's breath/mind exercises help us counter the ill effects of our stress filled lives by awakening our protective healing mechanisms. Learn to calm your mind and restore your spirit with ten minutes of simple meditation practices.

#CDSTRESS—30 minutes. $10.95

The Five Clouds Meditation—With James Tuggle. Three important practices from the Shrine Ceremony of the Eternal Breath of Tao and the Integral Way of Life. Beginning with a guided relaxation to increase your receptivity, you are then guided through the five energy systems and related organs to help thoroughly cleanse and balance your internal energy. It ends by refining your energy through the deeply potent Golden Light Meditation and Invocation.

#CD5CLOUDS—60 minutes. $12.95

Meditations to Live to Be 100—By Maoshing Ni, Ph.D. This two-disc set includes cleansing, rejuvenating, and harmonizing meditations for fueling yourself with vital universal *chi* and for living a longer, richer and more satisfying life.

#CDLON—120 minutes. $19.95

Published by Sounds True, Inc.

BOOKS IN SPANISH

Tao Teh Ching—*En Espanol.*
#BTEHS—112 pages, softcover booklet. $8.95

THE INTEGRAL WAY BOOKS, DVDs AND CDs

The books, DVDs and CDs of the Integral Way are published by Tao of Wellness Press, an imprint of SevenStar Communications. If you would like to find out more about us, order a catalog, or place an order for books or other items, please contact us at:

Telephone: 1-800-578-9526
Website: http://www.sevenstarcom.com
E-mail: taostar@taostar.com

SPIRITUAL STUDY THROUGH THE COLLEGE OF TAO

The College of Tao was formally established in California in the 1970s, yet the tradition from which it originated represents centuries of spiritual growth. The College values the spiritual development of each individual and offers a healthy spiritual education to all people.

The College of Tao is a school without walls. Human society is its classroom. Your own life is the class you attend; thus students grow from their own lives and from studying the guidance of the Integral Way.

Distance learning programs, based on the writings of Hua-Ching Ni and his family, are available for those who do not live near an Integral Way of Life center. For more information, visit http://www.taostudies.com or http://www.sevenstarcom.com. For further information and updates on correspondence courses being offered, please contact: info@taostudies.com. For regular mail, please contact the College of Tao at: 3362-141 Street, Surrey, B.C., Canada V4P 3L7.

It is recommended that all Mentors of the Integral Way use the self-study program to educate themselves. Anyone who wishes to teach the practices contained in Hua-Ching Ni's books must apply to the College for certification.

INTEGRAL WAY SOCIETY (IWS, formerly USIW)

❑ I wish to receive a list of registered Mentors teaching in my area or country.

❑ I am interested in joining/forming a study group in my area.

❑ I am interested in becoming a Mentor of the IWS.

❑ I am interested in subscribing to the IWS quarterly newsletter.

Name: _____

Address: _____

City: _____ State: _____ Zip: _____

E-Mail Address: _____

Mail this request to: IWS, P.O. Box 1530, Santa Monica, CA 90406-1530

And you can visit our website at: http://www.integralwaysociety.org

YO SAN UNIVERSITY OF TRADITIONAL CHINESE MEDICINE

"Not just a medical career, but a lifetime commitment to raising one's spiritual standard."

In response to the growing interest in Taoism and natural health care in the West, in January 1989 we formed Yo San University of Traditional Chinese Medicine, a nonprofit educational institution under the direction of founder Hua-Ching Ni. Yo San University is the continuation of 38 generations of Ni family practitioners who have handed down the knowledge and wisdom of ancient Chinese healing from father to son.

The foundation of Traditional Chinese Medicine is the spiritual capability to know life, to diagnose a person's problem, and to know how to cure it. We teach students how to care for themselves and others, emphasizing the integration of traditional knowledge and modern science, but the true application of Traditional Chinese Medicine is the practical application of one's own spiritual development.

The purpose of Yo San University is to train practitioners of the highest caliber in Traditional Chinese Medicine, which includes acupuncture, herbology, and spiritual development. We offer a complete Master's degree program which is approved by the California State Department of Education and which meets all requirements for state licensure.

We invite you to inquire into our program for a creative and rewarding career as a holistic physician. Classes are also open to persons interested in self-enrichment. For more information, please fill out the form below or visit our website at: http://www.yosan.edu.

Yo San University of Traditional Chinese Medicine
13315 W. Washington Boulevard, Suite 200
Los Angeles, CA 90066
Phone: (310) 577-3000   Fax: (310) 577-3033

❑ Please send me information on the Masters degree program in Traditional Chinese Medicine

❑ Please send me information on health workshops and seminars.

❑ Please send me information on continuing education for acupuncturists and health professionals.

Name: _____

Address: _____

City: _____ State: _____ Zip: _____

Phone: (daytime) _____ (evening) _____

MOVEMENT TRAINING & TEACHER CERTIFICATION

Chi Gong (also known as *qigong* or *chi kung*) is "energy work" and involves various methods of developing the *chi* or life energy of the body as the foundation of a healthy and happy life. The Ni Family Chi Movements Arts encompass a variety of Chi Gong forms that incorporate specific methods of breathing, meditative focus, physical movement, and energy guidance. The major benefits are general strengthening, enhanced flexibility and tone, relaxation and stress reduction, increased mental clarity, and the balancing of mind, body, and spirit leading to overall improved health, well-being, and increased longevity. These movement arts are an excellent complement to a healthy lifestyle.

The Ni family has gathered, developed, and passed down these useful Chi Gong forms through many generations, continuing their family's ancient spiritual tradition of Esoteric Taoism from the time of the Yellow Emperor and before. The Ni Family Chi Movement Arts include varieties of T'ai Chi, Eight Treasures, Dao-In, and many health and meditative practices. Please refer to *Strength from Movement: Mastering Chi* by Hua-Ching Ni for an excellent introduction.

The Ni family established the **Chi Health Institute** to promote the wider availability and more effective practice of useful forms of Chi Gong for personal and social improvement. The Institute serves as a custodian of the Ni Family Chi Movement Arts tradition, and actively works to sponsor training opportunities to develop additional training materials and to certify teachers.

We would be happy to assist you in selecting and learning a suitable form. We can provide a directory of certified teachers, information about available training workshops, ongoing classes, and self-study and distance learning options, as well as information about a variety of instructional materials. We would also be happy to assist you in becoming a certified teacher of the Ni Family Chi Movement Arts.

Please write to us at the address below for more information, and include your name, e-mail, telephone number, mailing address, and any special interests, or visit our website at www.chihealth.org. We look forward to helping you further your growth.

Chi Health Institute
P.O. Box 2035
Santa Monica, CA 90406
http://www.chihealth.org

HERBS USED BY ANCIENT MASTERS

The pursuit of health is an innate human desire. Long ago, Chinese esoteric Taoists went to the high mountains to contemplate nature, strengthen their bodies, empower their minds, and develop their spirit. From their studies and cultivation, they developed Chinese alchemy and chemistry, herbology, acupuncture, the *I Ching*, astrology, T'ai Chi Ch'uan, Chi Gong, and many other useful tools for health and self-improvement.

The ancient Taoists also passed down methods for attaining longevity and spiritual immortality, one of which was the development of herbal formulas that could be used to increase one's energy and heighten vitality. The Ni family has preserved this treasured collection of herbal formulas for centuries.

Now, through Traditions of Tao, the Ni family makes these ancient formulas available to assist you in building a strong foundation for health and spiritual self-cultivation. For further information about Traditions of Tao herbal products, please complete the following form or visit our website at: http://www.traditionsoftao.com or http://www.taoofwellness.com.

Traditions of Tao
13315 W. Washington Boulevard, Suite 200
Los Angeles, CA 90066
Phone: (310) 302-1206   Fax: (310) 302-1208

❑ Please send me a Traditions of Tao catalog.

Name: _____

Address: _____

City: _____ State: _____ Zip: _____

Phone: (daytime) _____ (evening) _____